# AAT

## Qualifications and Credit Framework (QCF)
## LEVEL 3 DIPLOMA IN ACCOUNTING

TEXT

Accounts Preparation I

2012 Edition

First edition July 2010

Third edition June 2012

ISBN 9781 4453 9459 6

(Previous edition 9780 7517 9729 9)

*British Library Cataloguing-in-Publication Data*
A catalogue record for this book is available from the British
Library

Published by

BPP Learning Media Ltd
BPP House
Aldine Place
London
W12 8AA

www.bpp.com/learningmedia

Printed in the United Kingdom

# CONTENTS

Introduction

BPP Learning Media's AAT materials     v

A note on terminology     vii

Assessment strategy     ix

AAT unit guide     xi

1    Accounting principles     1

2    Accounting concepts     35

3    Purchase of non-current assets     55

4    Depreciation of non-current assets     81

5    Disposal of non-current assets     101

6    Accruals and prepayments     121

7    Inventory     133

8    Irrecoverable debts and doubtful debts     147

9    Bank reconciliations     165

10    Control account reconciliations     179

11    The trial balance, errors and the suspense account     201

12    The extended trial balance     227

Answers to chapter tasks     251

Test your learning – answers     267

Index     293

# A NOTE ABOUT COPYRIGHT

Dear Customer

What does the little © mean and why does it matter?

Your market-leading BPP books, course materials and e-learning materials do not write and update themselves. People write them: on their own behalf or as employees of an organisation that invests in this activity. Copyright law protects their livelihoods. It does so by creating rights over the use of the content.

Breach of copyright is a form of theft – as well as being a criminal offence in some jurisdictions, it is potentially a serious breach of professional ethics.

With current technology, things might seem a bit hazy but, basically, without the express permission of BPP Learning Media:

- Photocopying our materials is a breach of copyright

- Scanning, ripcasting or conversion of our digital materials into different file formats, uploading them to Facebook or emailing them to your friends is a breach of copyright

You can, of course, sell your books, in the form in which you have bought them – once you have finished with them. (Is this fair to your fellow students? We update for a reason.)

And what about outside the UK? BPP Learning Media strives to make our materials available at prices students can afford by local printing arrangements, pricing policies and partnerships which are clearly listed on our website. A tiny minority ignore this and indulge in criminal activity by illegally photocopying our material or supporting organisations that do. If they act illegally and unethically in one area, can you really trust them?

# BPP LEARNING MEDIA'S AAT MATERIALS

Since July 2010 the AAT's assessments have fallen within the **Qualifications and Credit Framework** and most papers are now assessed by way of an on demand **computer based assessment**. BPP Learning Media has invested heavily to ensure our ground breaking materials are as relevant as possible for this method of assessment. In particular, our **suite of online resources** ensures that you are prepared for online testing by allowing you to practice numerous online tasks that are similar to the tasks you will encounter in the AAT's assessments.

The BPP range of resources comprises:

- **Texts**, covering all the knowledge and understanding needed by students, with numerous illustrations of 'how it works', practical examples and tasks for you to use to consolidate your learning. The majority of tasks within the texts have been written in an interactive style that reflects the style of the online tasks we anticipate the AAT will set. Texts are available in our traditional paper format and, in addition, as ebooks which can be downloaded to your PC or laptop.

- **Question Banks**, including additional learning questions plus the AAT's practice assessment and a number of other full practice assessments. Full answers to all questions and assessments, prepared by BPP Learning Media Ltd, are included. Our Question Banks are provided free of charge in an online environment containing tasks similar to those you will encounter in the AAT's testing environment. This means you can become familiar with being tested in an online environment prior to completing the real assessment.

- **Passcards**, which are handy pocket-sized revision tools designed to fit in a handbag or briefcase to enable you to revise anywhere at anytime. All major points are covered in the Passcards which have been designed to assist you in consolidating knowledge.

- **Workbooks**, which have been designed to cover the units that are assessed by way of project/case study. The workbooks contain many practical tasks to assist in the learning process and also a sample assessment or project to work through.

- **Lecturers' resources**, providing a further bank of tasks, answers and full practice assessments for classroom use, available separately only to lecturers whose colleges adopt BPP Learning Media material. The practice assessments within the lecturers' resources are available in both paper format and online in e format.

This Text for Accounts Preparation I has been written specifically to ensure comprehensive yet concise coverage of the AAT's new learning outcomes and assessment criteria. It is fully up to date as at June 2012 and reflects both the AAT's unit guide and the practice assessments provided by the AAT.

Each chapter contains:

- Clear, step by step explanation of the topic

- Logical progression and linking from one chapter to the next

- Numerous illustrations of 'how it works'

- Interactive tasks within the text of the chapter itself, with answers at the back of the book. In general, these tasks have been written in the interactive form that students can expect to see in their real assessments

- Test your learning questions of varying complexity, again with answers supplied at the back of the book. In general these test questions have been written in the interactive form that students can expect to see in their real assessments

The emphasis in all tasks and test questions is on the practical application of the skills acquired.

If you have any comments about this book, please e-mail paulsutcliffe@bpp.com or write to Paul Sutcliffe, Senior Publishing Manager, BPP Learning Media Ltd, BPP House, Aldine Place, London W12 8AA.

# A NOTE ON TERMINOLOGY

On 1 January 2012, the AAT moved from UK GAAP to IFRS terminology. Although you may be used to UK terminology, you need to now know the equivalent international terminology for your assessments.

The following information is taken from an article on the AAT's website and describes how the terminology changes impact on students studying for each level of the AAT QCF qualification.

**What is the impact of IFRS terms on AAT assessments?**

The list shown in the table that follows gives the 'translation' between UK GAAP and IFRS.

| UK GAAP | IFRS |
| --- | --- |
| Final accounts | Financial statements |
| **Trading and profit and loss account** | **Income statement or Statement of comprehensive income** |
| Turnover or Sales | Revenue or Sales Revenue |
| Sundry income | Other operating income |
| Interest payable | Finance costs |
| Sundry expenses | Other operating costs |
| Operating profit | Profit from operations |
| Net profit/loss | Profit/Loss for the year/period |
| **Balance sheet** | **Statement of financial position** |
| Fixed assets | Non-current assets |
| Net book value | Carrying amount |
| Tangible assets | Property, plant and equipment |
| Reducing balance depreciation | Diminishing balance depreciation |
| Depreciation/Depreciation expense(s) | Depreciation charge(s) |
| Stocks | Inventories |
| Trade debtors or Debtors | Trade receivables |
| Prepayments | Other receivables |
| Debtors and prepayments | Trade and other receivables |
| Cash at bank and in hand | Cash and cash equivalents |
| Trade creditors or Creditors | Trade payables |

| UK GAAP | IFRS |
|---|---|
| Accruals | Other payables |
| Creditors and accruals | Trade and other payables |
| Long-term liabilities | Non-current liabilities |
| Capital and reserves | Equity (limited companies) |
| Profit and loss balance | Retained earnings |
| Minority interest | Non-controlling interest |
| **Cash flow statement** | **Statement of cash flows** |

This is certainly not a comprehensive list, which would run to several pages, but it does cover the main terms that you will come across in your studies and assessments. However, you won't need to know all of these in the early stages of your studies – some of the terms will not be used until you reach Level 4. For each level of the AAT qualification, the points to bear in mind are as follows:

### Level 2 Certificate in Accounting

The IFRS terms do not impact greatly at this level. Make sure you are familiar with 'receivables' (also referred to as 'trade receivables'), 'payables' (also referred to as 'trade payables'), and 'inventories'. The terms sales ledger and purchases ledger – together with their control accounts – will continue to be used. Sometimes the control accounts might be called 'trade receivables control account' and 'trade payables control account'. The other term to be aware of is 'non-current asset' – this may be used in some assessments.

### Level 3 Diploma in Accounting

At this level you need to be familiar with the term 'financial statements'. The financial statements comprise an 'income statement' (profit and loss account), and a 'statement of financial position' (balance sheet). In the income statement the term 'revenue' or 'sales revenue' takes the place of 'sales', and 'profit for the year' replaces 'net profit'. Other terms may be used in the statement of financial position – eg 'non-current assets' and 'carrying amount'. However, specialist limited company terms are not required at this level.

### Level 4 Diploma in Accounting

At Level 4 a wider range of IFRS terms is needed, and in the case of Financial statements (FNST), are already in use – particularly those relating to limited companies. Note especially that an income statement becomes a 'statement of comprehensive income'.

**Note:** The information above was taken from an AAT article from the 'assessment news' area of the AAT website (www.aat.org.uk).

# ASSESSMENT STRATEGY

Accounts Preparation I (API) is the first of two financial accounting assessments at level 3. The AAT recommend that API is studied and taken before APII.

The assessment is normally a two hour computer based assessment.

The API assessment consists of eight tasks, two in Section 1 and six in Section 2.

**Section 1** is about accounting for non-current assets and will comprise two independent tasks. These will require managing a range of transactions involving non-current assets, including acquisitions, disposals and depreciation, by expecting the accurate completion of

- A non-current assets register
- A selection of relevant ledger accounts

There may also be short-answer parts testing the knowledge parts of the relevant units.

**Section 2** is about accounting adjustments and the extended trial balance and will comprise six independent tasks. These will include

- Understanding how to adjust income and/or expense ledger accounts for accruals and prepayments
- Preparing a trial balance
- Making journal entries for adjustments or recording adjustments in the extended trial balance
- Completing the extended trial balance by using the ledger balances and adjustments columns to correctly place figures in the income statement and statement of financial position columns, and calculating and entering the correct profit or loss figure
- Preparing reconciliations, for example between the sales ledger or purchases ledger and the corresponding control account, or between the cash book and the bank statement
- Short-answers to test the knowledge parts of the relevant units.

## Competency

Learners will normally be assessed by computer-based assessment and will be required to demonstrate competence in both sections of the assessment. For the purpose of assessment the competency level for AAT assessment is set at 70 per cent. The level descriptor in the table below describes the ability and skills students at this level must successfully demonstrate to achieve competence.

| QCF Level descriptor | **Summary** |
|---|---|
| | Achievement at level 3 reflects the ability to identify and use relevant understanding, methods and skills to complete tasks and address problems that, while well defined, have a measure of complexity. It includes taking responsibility for initiating and completing tasks and procedures as well as exercising autonomy and judgement within limited parameters. It also reflects awareness of different perspectives or approaches within an area of study or work. |

**Knowledge and understanding**

- Use factual, procedural and theoretical understanding to complete tasks and address problems that, while well defined, may be complex and non-routine

- Interpret and evaluate relevant information and ideas

- Be aware of the nature of the area of study or work

- Have awareness of different perspectives or approaches within the area of study or work

**Application and action**

- Address problems that, while well defined, may be complex and non routine

- Identify, select and use appropriate skills, methods and procedures

- Use appropriate investigation to inform actions

- Review how effective methods and actions have been

**Autonomy and accountability**

- Take responsibility for initiating and completing tasks and procedures, including, where relevant, responsibility for supervising or guiding others

- Exercise autonomy and judgement within limited parameters

# AAT UNIT GUIDE

## Accounts Preparation I (API)

### Introduction

Please read this document in conjunction with the standards for all relevant units.

The QCF units relating to Accounts Preparation I and Accounts Preparation II units overlap. Accounts Preparation I and II have been designed in order to avoid duplication of assessment and to match the appropriate parts of the knowledge unit (Principles of Accounts Preparation) with the corresponding skills.

Successful completion of this AAT unit alone will result in the award of two QCF units:

- Accounting for fixed assets (skills)
- Extending the trial balance using accounting adjustments (skills)

This unit also includes aspects of the QCF unit "Principles of accounts preparation", and some parts of the QCF unit "Prepare final accounts for sole traders". Accounts Preparation II completes these units.

Successful completion of the Accounts Preparation I unit together with Accounts Preparation II will result in the award of three further QCF units:

- Principles of accounts preparation (knowledge)
- Prepare final accounts for sole traders (skills)
- Preparing accounts for partnerships (knowledge and skills )

### The purpose of the unit

Accounts Preparation I is designed to develop basic double entry bookkeeping skills and knowledge, such as that acquired in the level 2 units Basic Accounting I and Basic Accounting II. The learner will deal with more advanced and complex situations such as those needed for preparing financial statements. It consolidates learning at level 2 and introduces new areas such as accounting for non-current assets and using the extended trial balance.

The logical progression from Accounts Preparation I is to Accounts Preparation II, which deals with financial statements, but the sequence in which the units are taken is not mandatory. After completion of both Accounts Preparation units, the learner will be ready to start developing skills and knowledge for the level 4 unit, Financial Statements.

### Terminology

Students should be familiar with IFRS terminology. Other terms are used in the AAT guidance document to match titles provided by the QCF. All AAT assessments will use IFRS terminology only from 1 January 2012.

### Learning objectives

The learner will be introduced to recording and accounting for non-current assets. The learner will be able to record both purchase and disposal of a non-current asset, identifying any gains or losses made on disposal and, will be able to calculate and apply depreciation charges by a given method.

The learner must already have an understanding of double entry bookkeeping including using ledger accounts and the journal. These skills will be developed into more advanced and complex areas, including adjustments for closing inventory, accrued and prepaid expenses and income, and how these are incorporated into an extended trial balance. Provisions for depreciation on non-current assets, irrecoverable debts and allowances for doubtful debts are also to be calculated and accounted for.

The learner will also need to demonstrate an appropriate understanding of the principles that lie behind these accounting procedures, including an awareness of the accounting systems that must be in place in order to produce meaningful information at the end of an accounting period. The learner should also develop an understanding of the environment and principles within which the business operates.

## Learning outcomes

There are three QCF units involved. Each is divided into component learning outcomes, which in turn comprise a number of assessment criteria.

| QCF Unit | Learning Outcome | Assessment Criteria | Covered in Chapter(s) |
|---|---|---|---|
| **Accounting for fixed assets (skills)** | Account for the purchase of fixed assets | Identify correctly all items of capital expenditure | 3 |
| | | Calculate total capital expenditure including all associated costs | |
| | | Record the prior authority for the capital expenditure | |
| | | Record in the appropriate accounts the acquisition of a non-current asset funded by cash purchase, part exchange or loan | |
| | | Accurately record the acquisition in a non-current asset register | |
| | | Close off or transfer the ledger account balances at the end of the financial period | |

| QCF Unit | Learning Outcome | Assessment Criteria | Covered in Chapter(s) |
|---|---|---|---|
| | Account accurately for depreciation | Calculate the depreciation charges for a non-current asset using the straight line and reducing balance methods | 4 |
| | | Record the depreciation charges in the non-current asset register | |
| | | Record depreciation charges in the appropriate ledger accounts | |
| | | Close off the ledger accounts at the end of the financial period, correctly identifying any transfers to the income statement account | |
| | Account for the disposal of fixed assets | Identify the correct asset and remove it from the non-current asset register | 5 |
| | | Correctly record in the appropriate accounts the disposal of the non-current asset | |
| | | Correctly calculate any gain or loss arising from the disposal and close off or transfer the account balance | |
| | Take appropriate action when dealing with issues arising from fixed asset records | Identify and resolve, or refer to an appropriate person any queries, unusual features or discrepancies relating to the accounting records for non-current assets | 5 |
| **Extending the trial balance using accounting adjustments (skills)** | Account for adjustments | Identify correctly items of expenses and income and accurately adjust each for accruals and prepayments | 6,7,8 |
| | | Record accurately the journal entries for closing inventory | |
| | | Record accurately the journal entries for accrued and prepaid | |

| QCF Unit | Learning Outcome | Assessment Criteria | Covered in Chapter(s) |
|---|---|---|---|
| | | expenses and income | |
| | | Record accurately the journal entries for provision for depreciation, irrecoverable debts and allowances for doubtful debts | |
| | | Make relevant journal entries to close off revenue accounts in preparation for the transfer of balances to the financial statements | |
| | Prepare a trial balance | Prepare and use ledger accounts and reconcile where appropriate, identifying any discrepancies and taking appropriate action to remedy these | **9,10,11** |
| | | Accurately account for a range of adjustments | |
| | | Accurately prepare a trial balance | |
| | Complete the trial balance | Prepare the trial balance after adjustments | **11,12** |
| | | Check for errors and/or inaccuracies in the trial balance and take appropriate action to remedy these | |
| Principles of accounts preparation (knowledge) | Understand generally accepted accounting principles and concepts | Explain the accounting principles of going concern, accruals, prudence and consistency | **1,2,4,6,7** |
| | | Explain the purpose and importance of maintaining financial records for internal and external use | |
| | | Describe the type of accounting records that a business should maintain and the main uses of each | |

| QCF Unit | Learning Outcome | Assessment Criteria | Covered in Chapter(s) |
|---|---|---|---|
| | | Describe the main requirements of accounting standards in relation to inventory and non-current asset valuations | |
| | Understand the principles of double entry bookkeeping | Explain the purpose and use of books of prime entry and ledger accounts | **1,9,10** |
| | | Explain the purpose of reconciliation of the sales and purchases ledgers, and the cash book | |
| | Understand the accounting methods used to record assets, liabilities, income, expenses and capital | Explain the differences between capital and revenue expenditure | **1,2,3,4,5, 6,8** |
| | | Describe how the acquisition of fixed assets can be funded (including part exchange) | |
| | | Explain the accounting treatment for recording the acquisition and disposal of non-current assets and the need for, and methods of, providing for depreciation on them | |
| | | Describe the contents and use of the non-current asset register | |
| | | Explain the accounting treatment of accruals and prepayments to expenses and revenue | |
| | | Explain the reasons for, and method of, accounting for irrecoverable debts and allowances for doubtful debts | |

1    "Extending the trial balance using accounting adjustments" covers aspects of QCF unit "Prepare final accounts for sole traders", which is awarded on completion of both Accounts Preparation I and Accounts Preparation II.

2    "Principles of accounts preparation" is covered across Accounts Preparation I and Accounts Preparation II, so is awarded on completion of both of these units.

## Delivery guidance: Accounting for fixed assets

### 1.   Account for the purchase of fixed assets

1.1  Identify correctly all items of capital expenditure

- Discriminate between capital expenditure and revenue expenditure in the context of the organisation in question by correctly applying any given capitalisation policy.

- Discriminate correctly between a range of different classes of non-current assets, eg, motor vehicles, furniture and fittings, machinery.

1.2  Calculate total capital expenditure including all associated costs

- Identify directly attributable costs that can be included in the cost of capital expenditure when non-current assets are acquired, in accordance with the relevant accounting standards (currently FRS15/IAS16).

- Identify revenue expenses that should not be included in the cost of capital expenditure when non-current assets are acquired.

1.3  Record the prior authority for the capital expenditure

- Identify why authorisation is necessary for an organisation

- Identify the appropriate person to provide authorisation within a given organisation

1.4  Record in the appropriate accounts the acquisition of a non-current asset funded by

Funding:

- Cash purchase (including standard commercial credit terms, eg, 30 days)

- Part exchange

- Loan

Accounts:

- Non-current asset at cost account – (eg, motor vehicles, machinery)

- Bank/cash account

1.5 Accurately record the acquisition in a non-current asset register

- Make the appropriate entries in accordance with the organisation's given policies and procedures

  Funding:

  - Cash purchase (including standard commercial credit terms eg. 30 days)
  - Part exchange
  - Loan
  - HP and finance leases – awareness only, no accounting entries or technical knowledge required

1.6 Close off or transfer the ledger account balances at the end of the financial period

## 2 Account accurately for depreciation

2.1 Calculate the depreciation charges for a non-current asset using

- **Straight line method**, using a percentage, fraction or over a period of time, including cases when there is expected to be a residual value. Pro-rata calculations for part of a year may be required.

- **Reducing balance method** using a percentage. Pro-rata calculations for part of a year will not be required.

2.2 Record the depreciation in the non-current asset register

- Make the appropriate entries in accordance with the organisation's given policies and procedures

2.3 Record depreciation charges in the appropriate ledger accounts

- Non-current asset accumulated depreciation account – (eg, motor vehicles, machinery)
- Depreciation charges account

2.4 Close off the ledger accounts at the end of the financial period, correctly identifying any transfers to the income statement account

## 3 Account for the disposal of fixed assets

3.1 Identify the correct asset and remove it from the non-current asset register

3.2 Correctly record in the appropriate accounts the disposal of the non-current asset

- No-current asset at cost account – (eg, motor vehicles, machinery)
- Non-current asset accumulated depreciation account – (eg, motor vehicles, machinery)
- Non-current asset disposals account (or just Disposals account)
- Bank/cash account

3.3 Correctly calculate any gain or loss arising from the disposal and close off or transfer the account balance

## 4 Take appropriate action when dealing with issues arising from fixed asset records

4.1 Identify and resolve, or refer to an appropriate person any queries, unusual features or discrepancies relating to the accounting records for non-current assets

- Non-current asset register, non-current asset accounts and/or physical check

## Delivery guidance: Extending the trial balance using accounting adjustments

### 1 Account for adjustments

1.1 Identify correctly items of expenses and income and accurately adjust each for accruals and prepayments

- To include accrued expenses, accrued income, prepaid expenses and prepaid income
- Calculate adjustments pro-rata using given information, including organisational policies
- Understand how opening and closing accruals and prepayments affect income and expense ledger accounts
- Identify the amount transferred to the income statement at the end of the period.

1.2 Record accurately the journal entries for closing inventory

- Calculate correct closing inventory figure in accordance with the relevant accounting standards (currently SSAP9/IAS2)
- Use closing inventory account– income statement
- Use closing inventory account– statement of financial position
- Journal narratives may be required

1.3 Record accurately the journal entries for accrued and prepaid expenses and income

- Calculate adjustments pro-rata using given information
- Prepare journal entries for these adjustments
- Journal narratives may be required
- Reversal journals will not be required

1.4 Record accurately the journal entries for provision for depreciation, irrecoverable debts and allowances for doubtful debts

Accurately calculate:

- Calculate a new allowance for doubtful debts according to a given policy
- Calculate the adjustment to an existing allowance (increase or decrease) according to a given policy

Correctly use the following accounts:

- Non-current asset accumulated depreciation account (SFP)
- Depreciation charges account (IS)
- Irrecoverable debts account (IS) / Sales ledger control account (SFP)
- Allowance for doubtful debts account (SFP)
- Allowance for doubtful debts adjustment account (IS)

1.5 Make relevant journal entries to close off revenue accounts in preparation for the transfer of balances to the final accounts

- Journal narratives may be required

## 2  Prepare a trial balance

2.1 Prepare and use ledger accounts and reconcile where appropriate, identifying any discrepancies and taking appropriate action to remedy these

- Sales ledger control account to sales ledger
- Adjustments may be required to either or both balances
- Purchases ledger control account to purchases ledger
- Adjustments may be required to either or both balances
- Bank account to bank statement; including an understanding that a debit entry or balance in the ledger will be a credit on the statement, and vice versa. Familiarity with terms such as BACS, direct debit etc will be expected.
- Correction to ledger accounts by journal

2.2 Accurately account for a range of adjustments

Account for the following adjustments by preparing journals or using the adjustment columns of the ETB:

- Closing inventory
- Accruals and prepayments to expenses and income
- Provisions for depreciation on non-current assets and depreciation charge
- Gain/loss on disposal of a non-current asset
- Purchase of non-current assets
- Irrecoverable debts (ignoring VAT)
- Allowance for doubtful debts
- Correction of errors

2.3 Accurately prepare a trial balance

- Transfer balances from ledger accounts, a list of balances or written task data into correct debit or credit column of trial balance

## 3 Complete the trial balance

3.1 Prepare the trial balance after adjustments

- Accurately extend figures in the ledger balances and adjustments columns into the income statement and statement of financial position columns of the extended trial balance

- Make appropriate entries for profit/loss for the year/period and total the columns

3.2 Check for errors and/or inaccuracies in the trial balance and take appropriate action to remedy these

- Correct errors creating imbalance and clear the suspense account:
  - One-sided entry
  - Entry duplicated on one side, nothing on the other.
  - Unequal entries
  - Account balance incorrectly transferred to trial balance

- Correct errors not revealed by trial balance
  - Errors of principle
  - Errors of original entry
  - Errors of omission
  - Errors of commission
  - Reversal of entries
  - Identification or explanation of the type of error will not need to be recalled.

### Delivery guidance: Principles of accounts preparation

## 1 Understand generally accepted accounting principles and concepts

1.1 Explain the accounting principles of going concern, accruals, prudence and consistency

- Including applying these principles (most notably accruals): eg provision for depreciation charges, allowance for doubtful debts, accruals and prepayments

- Recognise circumstances when a business is no longer a going concern and understand the effect this has on the value of its assets

1.2 Explain the purpose and importance of maintaining financial records for internal and external use

- Internal control
- Measuring business performance
- Obtaining credit/financing
- Statutory requirements

1.3 Describe the type of accounting records that a business should maintain and the main uses of each

- Non-current asset register
- Books of prime entry: day books, cash book and journal
- General ledger accounts
- Subsidiary ledger accounts: purchases and sales
- Inventory records

1.4 Describe the main requirements of accounting standards in relation to inventory and non-current asset valuations

- Currently SSAP9/IAS2
  - Lower of cost and net realisable value
  - How to calculate net realisable value
  - Recognition and acceptability of valuation methods (but no requirement to calculate) FIFO, LIFO, weighted average cost.
  - Basic recognition of what can be included in cost of inventory
- Currently FRS15/IAS16
  - Recognition of the need for depreciation charges and basic understanding of what depreciation is (including a link with the accruals concept)
  - Basic reasons for choices of depreciation method and rate
  - Basic recognition that depreciation methods should be reviewed (but not to include circumstances in which methods may or may not be changed)
  - Basic understanding of terms useful life, residual value, carrying amount
  - Not to cover impairments or revaluations

## 2 Understand the principles of double entry bookkeeping

2.1 Explain the purpose and use of books of prime entry and ledger accounts

- Day-books, cash book, journal, general (main, nominal) ledger accounts

2.2 Explain the purpose of reconciliation of the sales and purchases ledgers, and the cash book

- As external verification of correct bank balance

- To find errors including omissions

## 3 Understand the accounting methods used to record assets, liabilities, income, expenses and capital

3.1 Explain the differences between capital and revenue expenditure

- The importance of materiality in deciding whether to capitalise

- The relevance of the lifespan of the purchase in deciding to capitalise

- The relevance of the accruals concept; how the cost of the capital expenditure is charged to the income statement over time rather than at the time of purchase

3.2 Describe how the acquisition of non-current assets can be funded (including part exchange)

- Cash purchase (including standard commercial credit terms eg. 30 days)

- Part exchange

- Borrowing (loans, hire purchase, finance lease), but detailed knowledge of accounting treatment not required

- Recognition of the suitability of particular funding methods in the context of a given simple business situation

3.3 Explain the accounting treatment for recording the acquisition and disposal of non-current assets and the need for, and methods of, providing for depreciation on them

- Calculate depreciation charges for non-current assets acquired or disposed of during an accounting period in accordance with the policies of the organisation

3.4 Describe the contents and use of the non-current asset register

- To include verification of physical assets and/or general ledger accounts

3.5 Explain the accounting treatment of accruals and prepayments to expenses and revenue

3.6 Explain the reasons for, and method of, accounting for irrecoverable debts and allowances for doubtful debts

- Excluding VAT implications

- Recognise the recovery of a debt previously written off as irrecoverable

# chapter 1:
# ACCOUNTING PRINCIPLES

## chapter coverage 📖

In this introductory chapter we describe the types of accounting record that a business should maintain and the main uses of each. This will help to explain the purpose and importance of maintaining financial records for internal and external use. We also cover some accounting principles with which you should be familiar: double entry bookkeeping, the recording of assets, liabilities, income, expenses and capital, and the trial balance.

The topics covered are:

- ✐ The aim of an accounting system
- ✐ Transactions of a business
- ✐ Primary documents for transactions
- ✐ Primary records for transactions: books of prime entry
- ✐ The general ledger and memorandum ledgers
- ✐ Principles of double entry bookkeeping
- ✐ Balancing ledger accounts
- ✐ Preparing a trial balance

## AIM OF ACCOUNTING SYSTEM

The aim of any business's accounting system is to ensure that all transactions are correctly recorded and can be gathered together for a period in order to prepare a set of financial statements. There are a number of reasons why this is important:

- To ensure that the business can keep track of all its assets and activities, ie to maintain internal control over the business

- To facilitate measurement of the business's performance, ie to know how the business is doing, to spot whether things are going wrong and to take advantage of situations where things have gone right

- To help obtain financing or other forms of credit, ie to be able to show the outside world that the business is strong and is a good investment

- To meet statutory requirements, principally in relation to taxation (all businesses must maintain sufficient records to be able to calculate their taxable income) and company law (not relevant at Level 3)

The details of accounting systems vary across different businesses depending on the structure of each business, its administrative systems and the nature of its operations. However all accounting systems have the following general elements:

### THE ACCOUNTING SYSTEM

TRANSACTIONS

↓

PRIMARY DOCUMENTS

To ensure that all transactions are recorded in the financial records

↓

PRIMARY RECORDS:
BOOKS OF PRIME ENTRY

↓

LEDGER ACCOUNTS

↓

RECONCILIATIONS

To ensure transactions have been correctly recorded

↓

TRIAL BALANCE

↓

FINANCIAL STATEMENTS

To prepare a set of financial statements

# TRANSACTIONS

Typical transactions in a business are summarised below:

| | | |
|---|---|---|
| Cash sales | – | a sale whereby the customer pays at the time of the sale by cash, cheque, credit or debit card |
| Credit sales | – | a sale which is made but payment is not required from the customer for a specified period of time such as 30 days |
| | – | the customer then becomes a RECEIVABLE (also known as a DEBTOR) of the business as they now owe money to the business |
| Sales returns | – | where goods are returned by a customer as they are faulty or not what was ordered |
| Receipts from credit customer | – | these will be in the form of cheques received in the post or AUTOMATED PAYMENTS paid directly into the business's bank account using BACS (Bankers Automated Credit System) |
| Cash purchases | – | PURCHASES may be of goods for use in the manufacture of other goods that the business will sell (raw materials), or of goods that are due to be resold by the business (goods for resale) |
| | – | cash purchases are purchases that are paid for at the time of purchase, by cheque, cash, credit or debit card |
| Credit purchases | – | a purchase made from a supplier who gives a period of credit so payment is not due for say 30 days |
| | – | the supplier then becomes a PAYABLE (also known as a CREDITOR) being someone who is due to be paid by the business |
| | – | both cash and credit purchases may be of services such as phone charges or electricity, in which case they are called EXPENSES |
| Purchases returns | – | returns of goods to a credit supplier as the goods are faulty or not what was ordered |
| Payments to credit suppliers | – | these will normally be made by cheque or BACS but may also be made in cash (notes and coin) |
| Capital expenditure | – | purchase of NON-CURRENT ASSETS (also known as FIXED ASSETS) which are items that are to be used in the business for the long term (this will be considered in more detail in Chapter 3) |

| Revenue expenditure | – | general everyday purchases and expenses that a business incurs |
|---|---|---|
| Petty cash payments | – | most businesses need to make small cash payments, for example paying the window cleaner |
| Wages and salaries payments | – | nearly all businesses employ people other than the business's owner, so wages/salaries are an important type of payment. Payments also need to be made to HM Revenue and Customs (HMRC) in respect of payroll taxes (PAYE income tax and national insurance or NIC), and pension administrators in respect of pension contributions from employees and from the business as employer. |

## Task 1

K Jones owes your business £1,200. He is $\boxed{\text{a receivable/a payable}}$ of the business.

## PRIMARY DOCUMENTS

For each transaction considered above there will be some form of PRIMARY DOCUMENT to evidence it.

| Cash sales | – | either a receipt will be given for the monies received from the customer or the sale will be automatically recorded on a till roll |
|---|---|---|
| Credit sales | – | a SALES INVOICE will be issued to the customer showing the details of the goods or services sold, the amount due, the date the amount is due and any other terms such as discounts |
| Sales returns | – | a CREDIT NOTE is issued to the customer showing the details of the goods returned, the total amount of the goods and the reason for the credit note |
| Receipts from credit customers | – | the primary document may be the actual cheque received or a REMITTANCE ADVICE NOTE |
| Cash purchases | – | if a cheque is written for the goods then the primary document will be the CHEQUE BOOK STUB where the details of the amount and the payee will be recorded |

| Credit purchases | – | a PURCHASE INVOICE will be received from the supplier showing the details of the goods or services purchased, the amount due, the date that the amount is due and any other terms of payment |
| Purchases returns | – | a credit note will be received from the supplier showing the details of the goods returned, the amount of the credit and the reason for the return of the goods |
| Payments to credit suppliers | – | these will either be paid for by cheque, so the primary document will be the cheque book stub counterfoil, or by automated payment in which case there will be some form of authorisation to the bank to make the payment, plus remittance advice note |
| Cash payments | – | these will be made out of the PETTY CASH BOX, a small amount of cash kept on the premises for the purpose of making cash payments, and will only be paid if there is a valid PETTY CASH VOUCHER. Some businesses, such as retailers, may also pay for items out of cash collected from customers. In this case the receipt from the seller is the primary record |
| Wages and salaries payments | – | the primary record for wages and salaries payments is the PAYROLL, which sets out gross and net pay, statutory and voluntary deductions from pay, and additional expenses for the employer (NIC and pension contributions) |

## Task 2

When your business returns goods to a credit supplier you would expect to receive an invoice/a credit note/a receipt/a remittance advice note

# PRIMARY RECORDS FOR TRANSACTIONS: BOOKS OF PRIME ENTRY

Each of the different types of primary document will be recorded in its own PRIMARY RECORD or book of prime entry (also called a book of original entry or day book).

| | | |
|---|---|---|
| Receipts from cash sales | – | whether these are hand-written receipts or the till roll for the day they will be recorded in the Cash received column of the CASH RECEIPTS BOOK |
| Sales invoices | – | when sent out to customers these are all recorded in the SALES DAY BOOK |
| Credit notes issued to customers | – | these are recorded in the SALES RETURNS DAY BOOK |
| Cheques from credit sales | | The primary document for these in practice is the REMITTANCE ADVICE NOTE from the customer. These are recorded in the Cash received column of the CASH RECEIPTS BOOK |
| Purchases invoices | – | when received from suppliers these are all recorded in the PURCHASES DAY BOOK |
| Credit notes received | – | when credit notes are received from suppliers they are recorded in the PURCHASES RETURNS DAY BOOK |
| Cheque book stubs | – | the details of all cheque payments taken from the cheque book stubs will be recorded in the Bank payments column of the CASH PAYMENTS BOOK |
| Automated payments | – | the details of receipts by automated payment will be recorded from the customer's remittance advice note in the Bank receipts column of the CASH RECEIPTS BOOK. Automated payments to suppliers will be recorded in the Bank payments column of the CASH PAYMENTS BOOK |
| Petty cash payments | – | details of petty cash vouchers will be recorded in the PETTY CASH PAYMENTS BOOK. Receipts for cash payments out of cash that was collected in a till are recorded in the Cash payments column of the CASH PAYMENTS BOOK |
| Wages and salaries payments | - | details from the payroll as the primary document are recorded in the JOURNAL, which is the book of prime entry for payroll transactions and also for non-standard transactions such as writing off bad (irrecoverable) debts, posting opening entries and correcting errors |

## Task 3

The book of prime entry for invoices received from credit suppliers is the
sales day book/the purchases day book/the cash payments book .

# LEDGER ACCOUNTS

The totals and details from each of the books of prime entry are then transferred or posted to the general ledger accounts using the principles of double entry bookkeeping, and to the memorandum ledger accounts.

## General ledger

The GENERAL LEDGER (also known as the main ledger or nominal ledger) is where there is a separate ledger account for each type of income, expense, asset, liability and capital that the business has. For example there will be ledger accounts for sales, purchases, receivables, payables and non-current assets to name but a few.

In the general ledger the account for receivables is normally referred to as the SALES LEDGER CONTROL ACCOUNT and the account for payables is normally referred to as the PURCHASES LEDGER CONTROL ACCOUNT.

## Memorandum ledger – the sales ledger

In the SALES LEDGER there is a ledger account kept for each individual customer of the business showing precisely how much is owed by that customer and how that amount is made up.

## Memorandum ledger – the purchases ledger

In the PURCHASES LEDGER there is a ledger account kept for each individual supplier of the business showing precisely how much is owed to that supplier and how that amount is made up.

## Cash book (cash receipts and cash payments books)

In most accounting systems the cash book (made up of the cash receipts book and the cash payments book) is part of the general ledger as well as being a book of prime entry in its own right.

### Petty cash book

The petty cash book is used to record both the receipts of cash into the petty cash box and the payments of petty cash vouchers. In most accounting systems the petty cash book (made up of the petty cash receipts book and the petty cash payments book) is part of the general ledger as well as being a book of prime entry in its own right.

---

## Task 4

If you needed to find the details of how much your business owed to a particular supplier, you would consult the general ledger/the sales ledger/the purchases ledger .

---

## PRINCIPLES OF DOUBLE ENTRY BOOKKEEPING

There are three main principles that underlie the practice of recording transactions in a double entry bookkeeping system:

(a) The DUAL EFFECT of transactions – this means that each and every transaction that a business undertakes has two effects on the business

(b) The SEPARATE ENTITY CONCEPT – this means that the owner of a business is a completely separate entity to the business itself

(c) The ACCOUNTING EQUATION will always balance – the accounting equation is:

ASSETS minus LIABILITIES equals CAPITAL

- **Assets** are items that the business owns

- **Liabilities** are amounts that are owed to other parties

- The **capital** of the business is the amount that is owed by the business back to the owner – remember that under the separate entity concept the owner and the business are completely separate entities for accounting purposes

  - Income increases the business's capital

  - Expenses decrease the business's capital

Obviously it would not be possible in practice to draw up the accounting equation each time that a business makes a transaction. For that reason the dual effect of each transaction is recorded in ledger accounts using double entry accounting.

BPP
LEARNING MEDIA

## Rules for double entry

- If there is a payment made out of the bank/cash account then the entry in the bank/cash account is always a credit and therefore the debit must be to some other account

- If there is a receipt into the bank/cash account then the entry in the bank/cash account is always a debit and therefore the credit must be to some other account

- If a business incurs an expense then this is always a debit entry in the relevant expense account

- If a business earns income then this is always a credit entry in the relevant income account

- An increase in assets is always a debit entry

- An increase in liabilities is always a credit entry

- An increase in capital (the amount owed back to the business's owner) is always a credit entry

This can be summarised in the diagram below:

| DEBITS | CREDITS |
|---|---|
| Money into the business | Money out of the business |
| Increases in: | Increases in: |
|     Expenses |     Income |
|     Assets |     Liabilities |
| |     Capital |

## HOW IT WORKS

We will now complete some ledger accounts for a period of trading.

Jenny Fisher has just started trading and has the following transactions for the month of February recorded in her ledger accounts.

**1 Feb Paid £12,000 into a business bank account in order to start the business**

Debit      Bank/cash account (bank column) – money in
Credit      Capital account

### Bank/cash account

| Date | Details | Cash £ | Bank £ | Date | Details | Cash £ | Bank £ |
|---|---|---|---|---|---|---|---|
| 1 Feb | Capital | | 12,000 | | | | |

9

### Capital account

| Date | Details | £ | Date | Details | £ |
|------|---------|---|------|---------|---|
|      |         |   | 1 Feb | Bank/cash | 12,000 |

The 'details' recorded are the other side of the double entry as this helps to follow through the double entry accounting.

## 1 Feb Paid a cheque for £3,600 as six months' rent on the shop

Debit    Rent account – expense
Credit   Bank/cash account (bank column) – money out

### Bank/cash account

| Date | Details | Cash £ | Bank £ | Date | Details | Cash £ | Bank £ |
|------|---------|--------|--------|------|---------|--------|--------|
| 1 Feb | Capital |        | 12,000 | 1 Feb | Rent    |        | 3,600  |

### Rent account

| Date | Details | £ | Date | Details | £ |
|------|---------|---|------|---------|---|
| 1 Feb | Bank/cash | 3,600 |      |         |   |

## 1 Feb Buys goods for resale by cheque totalling £680

Debit    Purchases account – expense
Credit   Bank/cash account (bank column) – money out

### Purchases account

| Date | Details | £ | Date | Details | £ |
|------|---------|---|------|---------|---|
| 1 Feb | Bank/cash | 680 |      |         |   |

### Bank/cash account

| Date | Details | Cash £ | Bank £ | Date | Details | Cash £ | Bank £ |
|------|---------|--------|--------|------|---------|--------|--------|
| 1 Feb | Capital |        | 12,000 | 1 Feb | Rent    |        | 3,600  |
|       |         |        |        | 1 Feb | Purchases |      | 680    |

## 8 Feb Purchases a computer, to help with preparing the business accounts, for £900 by cheque

Debit    Non-current asset account – computer
Credit   Bank/cash account (bank column) – money out

### Non-current asset account – computer

| Date | Details | £ | Date | Details | £ |
|------|---------|---|------|---------|---|
| 8 Feb | Bank/cash | 900 |      |         |   |

### Bank/cash account

| Date | Details | Cash £ | Bank £ | Date | Details | Cash £ | Bank £ |
|------|---------|--------|--------|------|---------|--------|--------|
| 1 Feb | Capital | | 12,000 | 1 Feb | Rent | | 3,600 |
| | | | | 1 Feb | Purchases | | 680 |
| | | | | 8 Feb | Non-current asset | | 900 |

## 8 Feb Purchases more goods for resale from T Trainer on credit for £1,000

Debit      Purchases account – expense
Credit     Purchases ledger control account – liability

### Purchases account

| Date | Details | £ | Date | Details | £ |
|------|---------|---|------|---------|---|
| 1 Feb | Bank/cash | 680 | | | |
| 8 Feb | PL control | 1,000 | | | |

### Purchases ledger control account    ~~ToTAL cREDITORS~~

| Date | Details | £ | Date | Details | £ |
|------|---------|---|------|---------|---|
| | | | 8 Feb | Purchases | 1,000 |

## 12 Feb Cash takings of £1,380 for the first two weeks are banked (the cost of the goods was £840)

Debit          Bank/cash account (cash column) – money in
Credit         Sales account – income
Debit          Bank/cash account (bank column) – money in
Credit         Bank/cash account (cash column) – money banked

There is no need to know about the cost of the goods sold as in double entry bookkeeping only purchases and sales are recorded; any profit is dealt with at the end of the accounting period when we record purchases held as inventory into the next period (see Chapter 7).

### Bank/cash account

| Date | Details | Cash £ | Bank £ | Date | Details | Cash £ | Bank £ |
|------|---------|--------|--------|------|---------|--------|--------|
| 1 Feb | Capital | | 12,000 | 1 Feb | Rent | | 3,600 |
| 12 Feb | Sales | 1,380 | | 1 Feb | Purchases | | 680 |
| 12 Feb | Cash | | 1,380 | 8 Feb | Non-current asset | | 900 |
| | | | | 12 Feb | Bank | 1,380 | |

### Sales account

| Date | Details | £ | Date | Details | £ |
|------|---------|---|------|---------|---|
| | | | 12 Feb | Bank | 1,380 |

### 17 Feb Sells goods on credit to Jones Stores for £900 (the cost of these goods was £550)

Debit     Sales ledger control account – asset
Credit    Sales account – income

**Sales ledger control account**

| Date | Details | £ | Date | Details | £ |
|------|---------|-----|------|---------|-----|
| 17 Feb | Sales | 900 | | | |

**Sales account**

| Date | Details | £ | Date | Details | £ |
|------|---------|-----|--------|-----------|-------|
| | | | 12 Feb | Bank/cash | 1,380 |
| | | | 17 Feb | SL control | 900 |

### 22 Feb Paid £600 to T Trainer by cheque

Debit     Purchases ledger control account – reduction of a liability
Credit    Bank/cash account (bank column) – money out

**Purchases ledger control account**

| Date | Details | £ | Date | Details | £ |
|--------|-----------|-----|-------|-----------|-------|
| 22 Feb | Bank/cash | 600 | 8 Feb | Purchases | 1,000 |

**Bank/cash account**

| Date | Details | Cash £ | Bank £ | Date | Details | Cash £ | Bank £ |
|--------|---------|--------|--------|--------|-------------------|--------|--------|
| 1 Feb | Capital | | 12,000 | 1 Feb | Rent | | 3,600 |
| 12 Feb | Sales | 1,380 | | 1 Feb | Purchases | | 680 |
| 12 Feb | Cash | | 1,380 | 8 Feb | Non-current asset | | 900 |
| | | | | 12 Feb | Bank | 1,380 | |
| | | | | 22 Feb | PL control | | 600 |

## 25 Feb Received cheque for £700 from Jones Stores

Debit   Bank/cash account (bank column) – money in
Credit   Sales ledger control account – reduction of an asset

### Bank/cash account

| Date | Details | Cash £ | Bank £ | Date | Details | Cash £ | Bank £ |
|---|---|---|---|---|---|---|---|
| 1 Feb | Capital | | 12,000 | 1 Feb | Rent | | 3,600 |
| 12 Feb | Sales | 1,380 | | 1 Feb | Purchases | | 680 |
| 12 Feb | Cash | | 1,380 | 8 Feb | Non-current asset | | 900 |
| 25 Feb | SL control | | 700 | 12 Feb | Bank | 1,380 | |
| | | | | 22 Feb | PL control | | 600 |

### Sales ledger control account

| Date | Details | £ | Date | Details | £ |
|---|---|---|---|---|---|
| 17 Feb | Sales | 900 | 25 Feb | Bank/cash | 700 |

## 26 Feb Cash takings of £1,560 for the last two weeks are banked (the cost of the goods that were sold is estimated to be £950)

Debit   Bank/cash account (cash column) – money in
Credit   Sales account – income
Debit   Bank/cash account (bank column) – money in
Credit   Bank/cash account (cash column) – money banked

### Bank/cash account

| Date | Details | Cash £ | Bank £ | Date | Details | Cash £ | Bank £ |
|---|---|---|---|---|---|---|---|
| 1 Feb | Capital | | 12,000 | 1 Feb | Rent | | 3,600 |
| 12 Feb | Sales | 1,380 | | 1 Feb | Purchases | | 680 |
| 12 Feb | Cash | | 1,380 | 8 Feb | Non-current asset | | 900 |
| 25 Feb | SL control | | 700 | 12 Feb | Bank | 1,380 | |
| 26 Feb | Sales | 1,560 | | 22 Feb | PL control | | 600 |
| 26 Feb | Cash | | 1,560 | 26 Feb | Bank | 1,560 | |

### Sales account

| Date | Details | £ | Date | Details | £ |
|---|---|---|---|---|---|
| | | | 12 Feb | Bank/cash | 1,380 |
| | | | 17 Feb | SL control | 900 |
| | | | 26 Feb | Bank/cash | 1,560 |

**26 Feb Withdrew £1,200 for her own living expenses**

Debit        Drawings account – reduction in the liability of capital
Credit       Bank account – money out

Drawings are quite a tricky one to remember. Capital is the amount that is owed back to the owner and is therefore a credit balance. Drawings are effectively reducing the amount of capital owed to the owner so they must be a debit entry.

**Drawings account**

| Date | Details | £ | Date | Details | £ |
|------|---------|---|------|---------|---|
| 26 Feb | Bank/cash | 1,200 | | | |

**Bank/cash account**

| Date | Details | Cash £ | Bank £ | Date | Details | Cash £ | Bank £ |
|------|---------|--------|--------|------|---------|--------|--------|
| 1 Feb | Capital | | 12,000 | 1 Feb | Rent | | 3,600 |
| 12 Feb | Sales | 1,380 | | 1 Feb | Purchases | | 680 |
| 12 Feb | Cash | | 1,380 | 8 Feb | Non-current asset | | 900 |
| 25 Feb | SL control | | 700 | 12 Feb | Bank | 1,380 | |
| 26 Feb | Sales | 1,560 | | 22 Feb | PL control | | 600 |
| 26 Feb | Cash | | 1,560 | 26 Feb | Bank | 1,560 | |
| | | | | 26 Feb | Drawings | | 1,200 |

## Task 5

Enter the following transactions for a business in the blank ledger accounts given below. Today's date is 4 March.

(a)    Sale of goods on credit for £2,400
(b)    Purchase of goods on credit for £1,800
(c)    Payment of phone bill by cheque £140
(d)    Withdrawal of cash from the bank account by the owner £500

**Sales ledger control account**       TOTAL DEBTORS

| Date | Details | Amount £ | Date | Details | Amount £ |
|------|---------|----------|------|---------|----------|
| | | | | | |
| | | | | | |

## Sales

| Date | Details | Amount £ | Date | Details | Amount £ |
|------|---------|----------|------|---------|----------|
|      |         |          |      |         |          |
|      |         |          |      |         |          |

## Purchases

| Date | Details | Amount £ | Date | Details | Amount £ |
|------|---------|----------|------|---------|----------|
|      |         |          |      |         |          |
|      |         |          |      |         |          |

## Purchases ledger control account    TOTAL CREDITORS

| Date | Details | Amount £ | Date | Details | Amount £ |
|------|---------|----------|------|---------|----------|
|      |         |          |      |         |          |
|      |         |          |      |         |          |

## Phone

| Date | Details | Amount £ | Date | Details | Amount £ |
|------|---------|----------|------|---------|----------|
|      |         |          |      |         |          |
|      |         |          |      |         |          |

## Bank/cash

| Date | Details | Cash £ | Bank £ | Date | Details | Cash £ | Bank £ |
|------|---------|--------|--------|------|---------|--------|--------|
|      |         |        |        |      |         |        |        |
|      |         |        |        |      |         |        |        |

## Drawings

| Date | Details | Amount £ | Date | Details | Amount £ |
|------|---------|----------|------|---------|----------|
|      |         |          |      |         |          |
|      |         |          |      |         |          |

## BALANCING AND CLOSING OFF THE LEDGER ACCOUNTS

Now that we have entered all of the transactions for the month in Jenny Fisher's ledger accounts the next stage is to find the closing balance on each account.

## HOW IT WORKS

The steps to follow in finding the closing balance on a ledger account will be illustrated using Jenny Fisher's bank/cash account at the end of February.

Step 1   Total each column on both sides of the account making a working note of each total (£6,980 and £15,640 for the bank columns, £2,940 for each cash column). For the bank account, take the larger total and put this in as the total on both sides of the account leaving a spare line at the bottom of each side.

### Bank/cash account

| Date | Details | Cash £ | Bank £ | Date | Details | Cash £ | Bank £ |
|------|---------|--------|--------|------|---------|--------|--------|
| 1 Feb | Capital | | 12,000 | 1 Feb | Rent | | 3,600 |
| 12 Feb | Sales | 1,380 | | 1 Feb | Purchases | | 680 |
| 12 Feb | Cash | | 1,380 | 8 Feb | Non-current asset | | 900 |
| 25 Feb | SL control | | 700 | 12 Feb | Bank | 1,380 | |
| 26 Feb | Sales | 1,560 | | 22 Feb | PL control | | 600 |
| 26 Feb | Cash | | 1,560 | 26 Feb | Bank | 1,560 | |
| | | | | 26 Feb | Drawings | | 1,200 |
| | | | | | | | 6,980 |
| | | 2,940 | 15,640 | | | 2,940 | 15,640 |

Step 2   Make the smaller of the two sides of the account add up to this total by putting in the balancing figure and describing it as the balance carried down (bal c/d) at the end of the month, 28 February. Show the same figure below the total on the other side of the account described as the balance brought down (bal b/d) at 1 March (the start of the new accounting period).

### Bank/cash account

| Date | Details | Cash £ | Bank £ | Date | Details | Cash £ | Bank £ |
|---|---|---|---|---|---|---|---|
| 1 Feb | Capital | | 12,000 | 1 Feb | Rent | | 3,600 |
| 12 Feb | Sales | 1,380 | | 1 Feb | Purchases | | 680 |
| 12 Feb | Cash | | 1,380 | 8 Feb | Non-current asset | | 900 |
| 25 Feb | SL control | | 700 | 12 Feb | Bank | 1,380 | |
| 26 Feb | Sales | 1,560 | | 22 Feb | PL control | | 600 |
| 26 Feb | Cash | | 1,560 | 26 Feb | Bank | 1,560 | |
| | | | | 26 Feb | Drawings | | 1,200 |
| | | | | 28 Feb | Bal c/d | | 8,660 |
| | | 2,940 | 15,640 | | | 2,940 | 15,640 |
| 1 Mar | Bal b/d | | 8,660 | | | | |

This shows that Jenny has a balance of £8,660 in the bank account at the start of March. She had banked all her cash so she had no balance on the cash account.

## Task 6

As at the end of February calculate and write in a balance carried down and a balance brought down on the following ledger account, including dates.

### Sales ledger control account

| Date | Details | Amount £ | Date | Details | Amount £ |
|---|---|---|---|---|---|
| 17 Feb | Sales | 900 | 25 Feb | Bank/cash | 700 |
| | | | | | |
| | | | | | |
| | | | | | |

## TRIAL BALANCE

A TRIAL BALANCE is simply a list of all of the balances on the main ledger accounts split between the debit balances brought down and the credit balances brought down. One of the purposes of a trial balance is to serve as a check on the double entry bookkeeping. The total of the debit balances should be equal to the total of the credit balances and if there is an imbalance then this must be investigated and the cause of the imbalance corrected.

At this stage we are simply going to prepare the trial balance – dealing with imbalances and errors will be covered in Chapter 11.

## HOW IT WORKS

Given below are all of the balanced ledger accounts for Jenny Fisher's first month of trading.

### Bank/cash account

| Date | Details | Cash £ | Bank £ | Date | Details | Cash £ | Bank £ |
|------|---------|--------|--------|------|---------|--------|--------|
| 1 Feb | Capital | | 12,000 | 1 Feb | Rent | | 3,600 |
| 12 Feb | Sales | 1,380 | | 1 Feb | Purchases | | 680 |
| 12 Feb | Cash | | 1,380 | 8 Feb | Non-current asset | | 900 |
| 25 Feb | SL control | | 700 | 12 Feb | Bank | 1,380 | |
| 26 Feb | Sales | 1,560 | | 22 Feb | PL control | | 600 |
| 26 Feb | Cash | | 1,560 | 26 Feb | Bank | 1,560 | |
| | | | | 26 Feb | Drawings | | 1,200 |
| | | | | 28 Feb | Bal c/d | | 8,660 |
| | | 2,940 | 15,640 | | | 2,940 | 15,640 |
| 1 Mar | Bal b/d | | 8,660 | | | | |

### Capital account

| Date | Details | £ | Date | Details | £ |
|------|---------|---|------|---------|---|
| | | | 1 Feb | Bank/cash | 12,000 |

### Rent account

| Date | Details | £ | Date | Details | £ |
|------|---------|---|------|---------|---|
| 1 Feb | Bank/cash | 3,600 | | | |

### Non-current asset account – computer

| Date | Details | £ | Date | Details | £ |
|------|---------|---|------|---------|---|
| 8 Feb | Bank/cash | 900 | | | |

### Purchases account

| Date | Details | £ | Date | Details | £ |
|------|---------|---|------|---------|---|
| 1 Feb | Bank/cash | 680 | 28 Feb | Balance c/d | 1,680 |
| 8 Feb | PL control | 1,000 | | | |
| | | 1,680 | | | 1,680 |
| 1 Mar | Balance b/d | 1,680 | | | |

### Purchases ledger control account  *Tot creditors*

| Date | Details | £ | Date | Details | £ |
|------|---------|---|------|---------|---|
| 22 Feb | Bank/cash | 600 | 8 Feb | Purchases | 1,000 |
| 28 Feb | Balance c/d | 400 | | | |
| | | 1,000 | | | 1,000 |
| | | | 1 Mar | Balance b/d | 400 |

### Sales ledger control account  *Tot sale debtors*

| Date | Details | £ | Date | Details | £ |
|------|---------|---|------|---------|---|
| 17 Feb | Sales | 900 | 25 Feb | Bank/cash | 700 |
| | | | 28 Feb | Balance c/d | 200 |
| | | 900 | | | 900 |
| 1 Mar | Balance b/d | 200 | | | |

### Sales account

| Date | Details | £ | Date | Details | £ |
|------|---------|---|------|---------|---|
| 28 Feb | Balance c/d | 3,840 | 12 Feb | Bank/cash | 1,380 |
| | | | 17 Feb | SL control | 900 |
| | | | 26 Feb | Bank/cash | 1,560 |
| | | 3,840 | | | 3,840 |
| | | | 1 Mar | Balance b/d | 3,840 |

### Drawings account

| Date | Details | £ | Date | Details | £ |
|------|---------|---|------|---------|---|
| 26 Feb | Bank/cash | 1,200 | | | |

The trial balance as at 28 February is drawn up by listing all of the balances b/d as either debit or credit balances.

## Trial balance as at 28 February

| | Debits £ | Credits £ |
|---|---|---|
| Bank/cash | 8,660 | |
| Capital | | 12,000 |
| Rent | 3,600 | |
| Non-current asset – computer | 900 | |
| Purchases | 1,680 | |
| Payables | | 400 |
| Receivables | 200 | |
| Sales | | 3,840 |
| Drawings | 1,200 | |
| | 16,240 | 16,240 |

Note that the figure for payables is the balance on the purchases ledger control account and the figure for receivables is the balance on the sales ledger control account.

The total of the debit balances is equal to the total of the credit balances so the trial balance balances. This will not always be the case if errors have been made (see Chapter 12).

The closing balances at the end of February on these ledger accounts will still be the opening balances at the start of the next month's trading. Extracting a trial balance does not necessarily mean closing down a set of accounts.

## BOOKS OF PRIME ENTRY AND DOUBLE ENTRY BOOKKEEPING

Above we took each of Jenny's transactions as it occurred and entered it into the ledger accounts as a debit and a credit. In practice this would be too time-consuming and therefore all similar transactions are gathered together into the books of prime entry and it is the totals of these that are regularly posted to the ledger accounts.

## Task 7

What is a trial balance?

A   A list of ledger balances extracted from accounts which can act as a balance sheet for a business.

B   A list of ledger balances extracted from accounts which helps to ensure that the bookkeeping has been accurate.

C   An accounting document which a business must prepare.

D   A list of all transactions which have occurred in a period taken from ledger accounts.

# CHAPTER OVERVIEW

- The aim of any accounting system are to ensure that all transactions are accurately recorded in the financial records

- Each type of transaction that a business makes will be supported and evidenced by a primary record

- The main primary records for most businesses are receipts issued or till rolls, sales invoices and credit notes issued, cheques and remittance advice notes received from customers, purchase invoices and credit notes received, cheque book stubs for all types of payments, automated payment authorisations and petty cash vouchers

- Each type of primary record is recorded in its own book of prime entry

- Sales invoices are recorded in the sales day book and credit notes issued in the sales returns day book

- Purchase invoices are recorded in the purchases day book and credit notes received in the purchases returns day book

- Cheque and cash receipts, cheque payments and automated payments, and discounts received and allowed are all recorded in the three column cash book (often split into the cash receipts book and cash payments book)

- Petty cash payments are recorded in the petty cash book

- Non-standard transactions and payroll transactions are recorded in the journal

- The totals and details from the books of prime entry are recorded in the ledger accounts

- The principal ledgers are the general ledger and the memorandum ledgers, the sales ledger and the purchases ledger

- The cash book and the petty cash book usually operate as both books of prime entry and part of the general ledger

- The three principles of double entry bookkeeping are:

  - The dual effect of transactions
  - The separate entity concept
  - The accounting equation: assets minus liabilities equals capital

- The trial balance is a list of all of the balances in the general ledger – it is used in order to detect any errors in the ledger accounts and as a basis for preparing the financial statements

## Keywords

**Cash sales** – sales that are made for immediate payment by cash, cheque, credit or debit card

**Credit sales** – sales that are made now but payment is not required for a specified period of time

**Receivable** – someone who owes money to the business (the balance on the sales ledger control account is usually taken as the trade receivables figure)

**Sales returns** – returns of goods from customers

**Purchases** – purchase either of materials that are to made into goods for resale or purchase of goods that are to be resold to customers

**Cash purchases** – purchases made where payment is required immediately

**Credit purchases** – purchases made now where payment is not required until the end of a specified period of time

**Payable** – someone who is owed money by the business (the balance on the purchases ledger control account is usually taken as the trade payables figure)

**Purchases returns** – returns of goods to suppliers

**Capital expenditure** – payments made for non-current assets

**Non-current assets** – assets that are to be used for the long term within the business

**Revenue expenditure** – payments for everyday business expenses other than the purchase of non-current assets

**Primary document** – the document that supports and evidences a business transaction

**Primary record** – the book of prime entry for recording the details about business transactions shown in the primary document

**Sales invoice** – issued by the seller to the purchaser of goods on credit showing the details of the goods sold, the amount due and the due date of payment

**Credit note** – a document issued to a customer who returns goods showing the details of the goods returned and their value

**Remittance advice note** – a document sent with a payment setting out which amounts are being paid, and whether any settlement discount is being taken

**Cheque book stub** – the part of a cheque that remains in the cheque book when the cheque is removed and sent out, recording the details of the cheque

**Purchase invoice** – an invoice received from a credit supplier detailing the goods purchased, the amount due and the due date of payment

**Automated payments** – payments made directly from one bank account to the bank account of another party such as standing orders, direct debits, bank giro credits and BACS payments

**Petty cash box** – the locked box in which any amounts of cash are kept on the business premises in order to make small cash payments

**Petty cash voucher** – the voucher that must be completed and authorised before any petty cash will be paid out

**Book of prime entry** – the initial record of each type of transaction – a list of each type of primary record

**Sales day book** – a list of each of the sales invoices sent out by the business to credit customers

**Sales returns day book** – a list of each of the credit notes issued by the business to credit customers

**Purchases day book** – a list of the invoices received from credit suppliers

**Purchases returns day book** – a list of the credit notes received from suppliers

**Cash receipts book** – a record of all of the cash and cheques received by the business

**Cash payments book** – a record of all of the cheques and any automated payments made

**Petty cash book** – details of all of the petty cash payments made and the receipt of cash into the petty cash box

**Journal** – the book of prime entry for non-standard transactions

**General ledger** – the ledger in which is kept a ledger account for each type of income, expense, asset and liability

**Sales ledger control account** – the account in the general ledger for receivables representing the total of amounts owed by trade receivables

**Purchases ledger control account** – the account in the general ledger for payables representing the total of amounts owed by all trade payables

**Sales ledger** – the ledger in which is kept an account for each individual receivable (customer)

**Purchases ledger** – the ledger in which is kept an account for each individual payable (supplier)

**Accounting equation** – ASSETS minus LIABILITIES equals CAPITAL

**Trial balance** – a list of the balances on each of the ledger accounts in the general ledger

## TEST YOUR LEARNING

### Test 1

Given below are the transactions of a new business for its first month. The business is not registered for VAT.

1 Mar   Owner pays £20,000 into a business bank account

1 Mar   Furniture and fittings purchased by cheque for the office premises £3,200

4 Mar   Purchases of goods for resale made by cheque for £4,400

6 Mar   Rent paid by cheque £600

10 Mar  Sales for £1,800 cheque received

15 Mar  Sales on credit £4,900

20 Mar  Purchases on credit £2,700

24 Mar  Cheque received from credit customers £3,500

28 Mar  Owner withdraws £1,000 in cash

29 Mar  Sales on credit £1,600

30 Mar  Cheque for £1,800 sent to credit supplier

31 Mar  Wages paid by cheque of £900

Write up each of these transactions in the ledger accounts of the business, balance any accounts with more than one entry and then prepare a trial balance as at 31 March.

**Bank account**

| Date | Details | £ | Date | Details | £ |
|------|---------|---|------|---------|---|
|      |         |   |      |         |   |
|      |         |   |      |         |   |
|      |         |   |      |         |   |
|      |         |   |      |         |   |
|      |         |   |      |         |   |
|      |         |   |      |         |   |
|      |         |   |      |         |   |
|      |         |   |      |         |   |
|      |         |   |      |         |   |

## Capital account

| Date | Details | £ | Date | Details | £ |
|------|---------|---|------|---------|---|
|      |         |   |      |         |   |
|      |         |   |      |         |   |
|      |         |   |      |         |   |
|      |         |   |      |         |   |
|      |         |   |      |         |   |

## Furniture and fittings account

| Date | Details | £ | Date | Details | £ |
|------|---------|---|------|---------|---|
|      |         |   |      |         |   |
|      |         |   |      |         |   |
|      |         |   |      |         |   |
|      |         |   |      |         |   |
|      |         |   |      |         |   |

## Purchases account

| Date | Details | £ | Date | Details | £ |
|------|---------|---|------|---------|---|
|      |         |   |      |         |   |
|      |         |   |      |         |   |
|      |         |   |      |         |   |
|      |         |   |      |         |   |
|      |         |   |      |         |   |
|      |         |   |      |         |   |
|      |         |   |      |         |   |

## Rent account

| Date | Details | £ | Date | Details | £ |
|------|---------|---|------|---------|---|
|      |         |   |      |         |   |
|      |         |   |      |         |   |
|      |         |   |      |         |   |
|      |         |   |      |         |   |

## Sales account

| Date | Details | £ | Date | Details | £ |
|------|---------|---|------|---------|---|
|      |         |   |      |         |   |
|      |         |   |      |         |   |
|      |         |   |      |         |   |
|      |         |   |      |         |   |
|      |         |   |      |         |   |
|      |         |   |      |         |   |

BPP
LEARNING MEDIA

## Sales ledger control account

| Date | Details | £ | Date | Details | £ |
|------|---------|---|------|---------|---|
|      |         |   |      |         |   |
|      |         |   |      |         |   |
|      |         |   |      |         |   |
|      |         |   |      |         |   |
|      |         |   |      |         |   |

## Purchases ledger control account

| Date | Details | £ | Date | Details | £ |
|------|---------|---|------|---------|---|
|      |         |   |      |         |   |
|      |         |   |      |         |   |
|      |         |   |      |         |   |
|      |         |   |      |         |   |
|      |         |   |      |         |   |

## Drawings account

| Date | Details | £ | Date | Details | £ |
|------|---------|---|------|---------|---|
|      |         |   |      |         |   |
|      |         |   |      |         |   |
|      |         |   |      |         |   |
|      |         |   |      |         |   |
|      |         |   |      |         |   |

## Wages account

| Date | Details | £ | Date | Details | £ |
|------|---------|---|------|---------|---|
|      |         |   |      |         |   |
|      |         |   |      |         |   |
|      |         |   |      |         |   |
|      |         |   |      |         |   |
|      |         |   |      |         |   |

## Trial balance as at 31 March

| | Debits £ | Credits £ |
|---|---|---|
| Bank | | |
| Capital | | |
| Furniture and fittings | | |
| Purchases | | |
| Rent | | |
| Sales | | |
| Receivables | | |
| Payables | | |
| Drawings | | |
| Wages | | |

## Test 2

Given below are the books of prime entry of a small business for its first month of trading. The business is not registered for VAT.

### Sales day book

| Date | Customer | Invoice No. | Total £ |
|---|---|---|---|
| 4 Mar | J Simpson | 0001 | 420 |
| 12 Mar | F Barnet | 0002 | 350 |
| 18 Mar | H Jerry | 0003 | 180 |
| 28 Mar | D Dawson | 0004 | 440 |
| | | | 1,390 |

### Sales returns day book

| Date | Customer | Credit note No. | Total £ |
|---|---|---|---|
| 19 Mar | F Barnet | CN 001 | 40 |
| 25 Mar | H Jerry | CN 002 | 20 |
| | | | 60 |

### Purchases day book

| Date | Customer | Invoice No. | Total £ |
|---|---|---|---|
| 1 Mar | L Lilley | 89432 | 590 |
| 7 Mar | O Rools | 12332 | 400 |
| 24 Mar | R Terry | 0532 | 410 |
| | | | 1,400 |

### Purchases returns day book

| Date | Customer | Credit note No. | Total £ |
|---|---|---|---|
| 10 Mar | O Rools | C357 | 80 |

### Cash receipts book

| Date | Details | Total £ | Cash sales £ | Sales ledger £ | Other £ | Discounts allowed £ |
|---|---|---|---|---|---|---|
| 1 Mar | Capital | 15,000 | | | 15,000 | |
| 7 Mar | Cash sales | 930 | 930 | | | |
| 20 Mar | J Simpson | 420 | | 420 | | |
| 22 Mar | Cash sales | 740 | 740 | | | |
| 31 Mar | F Barnet | 300 | | 300 | | 10 |
| | | 17,390 | 1,670 | 720 | 15,000 | 10 |

### Cash payments book

| Date | Details | Cheque No. | Total £ | Cash purchases £ | Purchases ledger £ | Wages £ | Other £ | Discounts received £ |
|---|---|---|---|---|---|---|---|---|
| 2 Mar | Cash purchases | 0001 | 550 | 550 | | | | |
| 6 Mar | Shop fittings | 0002 | 1,100 | | | | 1,100 | |
| 12 Mar | L Lilley | 0003 | 560 | | 560 | | | 30 |
| 15 Mar | Cash purchases | 0004 | 780 | 780 | | | | |
| 18 Mar | Cash purchases | 0005 | 920 | 920 | | | | |
| 20 Mar | O Rools | 0006 | 310 | | 310 | | | 10 |
| 31 Mar | Wages | | 2,200 | | | 2,200 | | |
| | | | 6,420 | 2,250 | 870 | 2,200 | 1,100 | 40 |

### You are required to:

(a) Post all of the books of prime entry to the relevant accounts in the general ledger

(b) Post the individual entries to the subsidiary ledgers, the sales ledger and the purchases ledger

(c) Balance all of the main ledger accounts and subsidiary ledger accounts

(d) Prepare a trial balance as at 31 March

## General ledger

### Sales ledger control account

| Date | Details | £ | Date | Details | £ |
|------|---------|---|------|---------|---|
|      |         |   |      |         |   |
|      |         |   |      |         |   |
|      |         |   |      |         |   |
|      |         |   |      |         |   |
|      |         |   |      |         |   |
|      |         |   |      |         |   |
|      |         |   |      |         |   |
|      |         |   |      |         |   |

### Sales account

| Date | Details | £ | Date | Details | £ |
|------|---------|---|------|---------|---|
|      |         |   |      |         |   |
|      |         |   |      |         |   |
|      |         |   |      |         |   |
|      |         |   |      |         |   |
|      |         |   |      |         |   |
|      |         |   |      |         |   |

### Sales returns account

| Date | Details | £ | Date | Details | £ |
|------|---------|---|------|---------|---|
|      |         |   |      |         |   |
|      |         |   |      |         |   |
|      |         |   |      |         |   |
|      |         |   |      |         |   |
|      |         |   |      |         |   |
|      |         |   |      |         |   |

### Purchases ledger control account

| Date | Details | £ | Date | Details | £ |
|------|---------|---|------|---------|---|
|      |         |   |      |         |   |
|      |         |   |      |         |   |
|      |         |   |      |         |   |
|      |         |   |      |         |   |
|      |         |   |      |         |   |
|      |         |   |      |         |   |
|      |         |   |      |         |   |
|      |         |   |      |         |   |

## Purchases account

| Date | Details | £ | Date | Details | £ |
|------|---------|---|------|---------|---|
|  |  |  |  |  |  |
|  |  |  |  |  |  |
|  |  |  |  |  |  |
|  |  |  |  |  |  |
|  |  |  |  |  |  |
|  |  |  |  |  |  |

## Purchases returns account

| Date | Details | £ | Date | Details | £ |
|------|---------|---|------|---------|---|
|  |  |  |  |  |  |
|  |  |  |  |  |  |
|  |  |  |  |  |  |
|  |  |  |  |  |  |
|  |  |  |  |  |  |
|  |  |  |  |  |  |

## Capital account

| Date | Details | £ | Date | Details | £ |
|------|---------|---|------|---------|---|
|  |  |  |  |  |  |
|  |  |  |  |  |  |
|  |  |  |  |  |  |
|  |  |  |  |  |  |
|  |  |  |  |  |  |
|  |  |  |  |  |  |

## Discounts allowed account

| Date | Details | £ | Date | Details | £ |
|------|---------|---|------|---------|---|
|  |  |  |  |  |  |
|  |  |  |  |  |  |
|  |  |  |  |  |  |
|  |  |  |  |  |  |
|  |  |  |  |  |  |
|  |  |  |  |  |  |

## Wages account

| Date | Details | £ | Date | Details | £ |
|------|---------|---|------|---------|---|
|  |  |  |  |  |  |
|  |  |  |  |  |  |
|  |  |  |  |  |  |
|  |  |  |  |  |  |
|  |  |  |  |  |  |

## Shop fittings account

| Date | Details | £ | Date | Details | £ |
|------|---------|---|------|---------|---|
|      |         |   |      |         |   |
|      |         |   |      |         |   |
|      |         |   |      |         |   |
|      |         |   |      |         |   |
|      |         |   |      |         |   |
|      |         |   |      |         |   |

## Discounts received account

| Date | Details | £ | Date | Details | £ |
|------|---------|---|------|---------|---|
|      |         |   |      |         |   |
|      |         |   |      |         |   |
|      |         |   |      |         |   |
|      |         |   |      |         |   |
|      |         |   |      |         |   |

## Bank/cash

| Date | Details | £ | Date | Details | £ |
|------|---------|---|------|---------|---|
|      |         |   |      |         |   |
|      |         |   |      |         |   |
|      |         |   |      |         |   |
|      |         |   |      |         |   |
|      |         |   |      |         |   |

## Sales ledger

### J Simpson

| Date | Details | £ | Date | Details | £ |
|------|---------|---|------|---------|---|
|      |         |   |      |         |   |
|      |         |   |      |         |   |
|      |         |   |      |         |   |
|      |         |   |      |         |   |

### F Barnet

| Date | Details | £ | Date | Details | £ |
|------|---------|---|------|---------|---|
|      |         |   |      |         |   |
|      |         |   |      |         |   |
|      |         |   |      |         |   |
|      |         |   |      |         |   |
|      |         |   |      |         |   |
|      |         |   |      |         |   |

### H Jerry

| Date | Details | £ | Date | Details | £ |
|------|---------|---|------|---------|---|
|  |  |  |  |  |  |
|  |  |  |  |  |  |
|  |  |  |  |  |  |
|  |  |  |  |  |  |
|  |  |  |  |  |  |

### D Dawson

| Date | Details | £ | Date | Details | £ |
|------|---------|---|------|---------|---|
|  |  |  |  |  |  |
|  |  |  |  |  |  |
|  |  |  |  |  |  |
|  |  |  |  |  |  |
|  |  |  |  |  |  |
|  |  |  |  |  |  |

## Purchases ledger

### L Lilley

| Date | Details | £ | Date | Details | £ |
|------|---------|---|------|---------|---|
|  |  |  |  |  |  |
|  |  |  |  |  |  |
|  |  |  |  |  |  |
|  |  |  |  |  |  |
|  |  |  |  |  |  |
|  |  |  |  |  |  |

### O Rools

| Date | Details | £ | Date | Details | £ |
|------|---------|---|------|---------|---|
|  |  |  |  |  |  |
|  |  |  |  |  |  |
|  |  |  |  |  |  |
|  |  |  |  |  |  |
|  |  |  |  |  |  |
|  |  |  |  |  |  |
|  |  |  |  |  |  |
|  |  |  |  |  |  |

### R Terry

| Date | Details | £ | Date | Details | £ |
|------|---------|---|------|---------|---|
|  |  |  |  |  |  |
|  |  |  |  |  |  |
|  |  |  |  |  |  |
|  |  |  |  |  |  |
|  |  |  |  |  |  |
|  |  |  |  |  |  |

## Trial balance as at 31 March

|  | Debits £ | Credits £ |
|---|---|---|
| Receivables |  |  |
| Sales |  |  |
| Sales returns |  |  |
| Payables |  |  |
| Purchases |  |  |
| Purchases returns |  |  |
| Capital |  |  |
| Discounts allowed |  |  |
| Wages |  |  |
| Shop fittings |  |  |
| Discounts received |  |  |
| Bank/cash |  |  |

# chapter 2:
# ACCOUNTING CONCEPTS

## chapter coverage 📖

In this chapter we introduce the actual financial statements or final accounts that a business will eventually produce from the trial balance, namely the income statement (profit and loss account) and the statement of financial position (balance sheet). We also introduce some accounting concepts of which you need to be aware. The topics covered are:

✍ Recognising asset, liability, income, expense and capital balances in the trial balance

✍ The income statement

✍ The statement of financial position

✍ The relationship between the ledger accounts, the income statement and the statement of financial position

✍ Accounting standards

✍ Accounting concepts

## THE MEANING OF THE BALANCES IN A TRIAL BALANCE

Each balance in the trial balance will be one of the following:

- An asset
- A liability
- Income
- An expense
- Capital

You need to be able to distinguish between each of these types of balance.

## HOW IT WORKS

Given below is the trial balance for Hunter Traders, a small business that is not registered for VAT. For each figure we have stated whether it is an asset, liability, income, expense or capital, with an explanation wherever necessary.

|  | Debits £ | Credits £ | Category |
|---|---|---|---|
| Non-current assets | 10,200 |  | asset |
| Bank | 750 |  | asset |
| Cash | 50 |  | asset |
| Heat and light | 240 |  | expense |
| Loan |  | 2,000 | liability |
| Capital |  | 12,760 | capital |
| Marketing | 80 |  | expense |
| Discounts received |  | 280 | income |
| Sales |  | 44,000 | income |
| Opening inventory | 2,400 |  | (see note below) |
| Receivables | 3,800 |  | asset |
| Wages | 10,400 |  | expense |
| Discounts allowed | 440 |  | expense |
| Payables |  | 2,400 | liability |
| Rent | 600 |  | expense |
| Telephone | 320 |  | expense |
| Travel | 160 |  | expense |
| Drawings | 4,000 |  | (see note below) |
| Purchases | 28,000 |  | expense |
|  | 61,440 | 61,440 |  |

INVENTORY items are goods which have been accounted for as purchases in the period in which they were first bought, but which have not been sold in that period. Consequently they are being held by the business until the following period. This means that at the end of the first period, and the beginning of the next period, inventory is an **asset**.

The inventory figure in any trial balance is always the amount brought forward from the previous period. This will be explained and expanded upon in Chapter 7.

Drawings – although a debit balance these are neither an expense nor an asset. Drawings are instead a reduction in **capital**.

## Task 1

Given below is the trial balance of a small trader, N Lawson, who is not registered for VAT. In the space next to each balance you are required to state whether the balance is an asset, liability, income, expense or capital.

| | £ | |
|---|---|---|
| Rent | 480 | |
| Motor van | 7,400 | |
| Payables | 1,900 | |
| Heat and light | 210 | |
| Discounts received | 50 | |
| Motor expenses | 310 | |
| Sales | 40,800 | |
| Opening inventory | 2,100 | |
| Loan | 2,000 | |
| Stationery | 330 | |
| Capital | 7,980 | |
| Phone | 640 | |
| Discount allowed | 60 | |
| Purchases | 22,600 | |
| Receivables | 3,400 | |
| Wages | 9,700 | |

| Drawings | 4,000 | |
|----------|-------|--|
| Office cleaning | 220 | |
| Travel and accommodation | 660 | |
| Bank | 483 | |
| Cash | 137 | |

## THE FINANCIAL STATEMENTS

### The income statement (IS)

The INCOME STATEMENT (known in UK GAAP accounting terminology as the PROFIT AND LOSS ACCOUNT) is a summary of the activity of the organisation during the year. It is, in simple terms, a statement of the following:

INCOME minus EXPENSES equals PROFIT OR LOSS

- If the **income is greater than** the expenses then a **profit** is made.
- If the **expenses exceed the income** then a **loss** has been made.

However despite the simple concept of the income statement it is normally laid out in a particular manner.

## HOW IT WORKS

The trial balance for Hunter Traders and its income statement are set out below, together with an explanation of the important points. You will see that each item denoted as income or expense from the trial balance is used in the income statement. As you work through each figure in the income statement, tick it off on the trial balance to show that all of the income and expenses are included.

## Trial balance

| | Debits £ | Credits £ | Category |
|---|---|---|---|
| Non-current assets | 10,200 | | asset |
| Bank | 750 | | asset |
| Cash | 50 | | asset |
| Heat and light | 240 | | expense |
| Loan | | 2,000 | liability |
| Capital | | 12,760 | capital |
| Marketing | 80 | | expense |
| Discounts received | | 280 | income |
| Sales | | 44,000 | income |
| Opening inventory | 2,400 | | (see note below) |
| Receivables | 3,800 | | asset |
| Wages | 10,400 | | expense |
| Discounts allowed | 440 | | expense |
| Payables | | 2,400 | liability |
| Rent | 600 | | expense |
| Telephone | 320 | | expense |
| Travel | 160 | | expense |
| Drawings | 4,000 | | reduction in capital |
| Purchases | 28,000 | | expense |
| | 61,440 | 61,440 | |

In order to produce the income statement there is one further figure that is required. This is the value of the closing inventory at the date of the trial balance, which for Hunter Traders is £3,200. We need this figure so that we can calculate the cost of the goods actually sold in the period. This will not necessarily be the actual purchases in the period because, as we saw earlier, some of the purchases in the period may still be in stock at the end of the period. In addition, the opening inventory will have been sold during the current period. The income statement therefore needs to take into account both the 'using up' of the opening inventory balance and the retention of the closing inventory balance. Note where these figures are in the income statement below: this will be covered in detail in Chapter 7.

## Income statement

|  | £ | £ |
|---|---|---|
| Sales revenue |  | 44,000 |
| Less: cost of sales |  |  |
| Opening inventory | 2,400 |  |
| Purchases | 28,000 |  |
|  | 30,400 |  |
| Less: closing inventory | (3,200) |  |
| **Cost of sales** |  | (27,200) |
| **Gross profit** |  | 16,800 |
| Discounts received |  | 280 |
|  |  | 17,080 |
| **Less: expenses** |  |  |
| Heat and light | 240 |  |
| Marketing | 80 |  |
| Discounts allowed | 440 |  |
| Wages | 10,400 |  |
| Travel | 160 |  |
| Rent | 600 |  |
| Telephone | 320 |  |
|  |  | (12,240) |
| **Profit for the year** |  | 4,840 |

*Gross profit* – the first part ends in GROSS PROFIT: the profit earned by the business's trading activities. As you can see it is calculated as the sales value less the cost of those sales. This area will be considered in more detail in Chapter 7.

*Expenses* – the second part consists of a list of all of the business's expenses.

*Discounts* – discounts allowed to customers are an expense of the business and are therefore included in the list of expenses. Discounts received however are similar to income as they are a benefit to the business. Discounts received are normally shown as income just below the gross profit line. They may also be shown as a negative expense item (in brackets to indicate that the amount is to be deducted from the expenses).

*Profit for the year* – the PROFIT FOR THE YEAR is the final profit of the business after all expenses have been deducted.

---

## Task 2

A business has made sales of £136,700 and its purchases totalled £97,500. The opening inventory was £11,300 and the closing inventory was £10,600. What is the business's gross profit?

£

---

## The statement of financial position (SFP)

Whereas the income statement is a history of the transactions of the business during the accounting period the STATEMENT OF FINANCIAL POSITION (or SFP) in contrast is simply a 'snap shot' of the business on the final day of the accounting period. In UK GAAP accounting terminology the statement of financial position is called the BALANCE SHEET.

The statement of financial position (SFP) is a list of all of the assets, liabilities and capital of the business. It is also an expression of the accounting equation. Remember that the accounting equation is:

ASSETS minus LIABILITIES equals CAPITAL

The SFP is a vertical form of the accounting equation. It lists and totals the assets of the business and deducts the liabilities. This total is then shown to be equal to the capital of the business, which has been increased by the period's profit or decreased by its loss.

# HOW IT WORKS

When producing its income statement, in Hunter Traders' trial balance we ticked off all the expenses and income. This left a number of un-ticked items which will now all appear in the statement of financial position.

Like the income statement the statement of financial position is laid out in a particular format. The UK balance sheet format is illustrated below for Hunter Traders.

**Statement of financial position**

|  | £ | £ | £ |
|---|---|---|---|
| **Non-current assets** | | | 10,200 |
| **Current assets:** | | | |
| Inventory | 3,200 | | |
| Receivables | 3,800 | | |
| Bank/cash | 800 | | |
| | | 7,800 | |
| **Current liabilities:** | | | |
| Payables | | (2,400) | |
| **Net current assets** | | | 5,400 |
| | | | 5,600 |
| **Non-current liabilities:** | | | |
| Loan | | | (2,000) |
| **Net assets** | | | 13,600 |

*Financed by:*

|                                                            | £        |
|------------------------------------------------------------|----------|
| Capital (at the start of the period)                       | 12,760   |
| Add: profit for the period (from the income statement)     | 4,840    |
|                                                            | 17,600   |
| Less: drawings in the period                               | (4,000)  |
|                                                            | 13,600   |

*Accounting equation* – the statement of financial position falls naturally into two parts which are the two sides of the accounting equation – 'assets minus liabilities' (often known as NET ASSETS) and 'capital'.

*Non-current assets* – non-current assets are always shown as the first assets on the statement of financial position as they are the major long-term assets of the business.

*Current assets* – the CURRENT ASSETS of a business are the other, shorter term, assets: inventory followed by receivables and the money held in the bank account as cash in hand and as petty cash. Note that as the statement of financial position is prepared on the final day of the accounting period it is the closing inventory figure which is included in the statement of financial position.

*Current liabilities* – the CURRENT LIABILITIES of a business are the short term payables.

*Net current assets* – the NET CURRENT ASSETS figure is a sub-total of the current assets less the current liabilities. The net current asset total is then added in to the non-current asset total.

*Non-current liabilities* – the NON-CURRENT LIABILITIES are liabilities that are due to be paid after more than one year. In this case we have assumed that the loan is a long term loan, ie, is repayable after more than one year.

*Net assets* - the total for non-current liabilities is deducted from the total of non-current assets and net current assets to give the STATEMENT OF FINANCIAL POSITION TOTAL. In terms of the accounting equation this is the total of the assets minus liabilities, also known as NET ASSETS

*Capital* – the 'financed by' section of the statement of financial position shows the amounts that are owed back to the owner of the business, that is their total capital. This consists of the amount of the owner's capital at the start of the accounting period plus the profit that the business has earned (this figure of £4,840 is the net profit taken from the income statement less the drawings that the owner has taken out of the business during the accounting period. The total of the capital section is also the statement of financial position total ie it should equal the net assets total.

Note that drawings are part of the statement of financial position and are not included as expenses – they are a reduction of capital.

BPP LEARNING MEDIA

# Task 3

Given below is the trial balance of N Lawson. In the space next to each balance state whether the balance would appear in the income statement (P&L) or in the statement of financial position (BS).

| | Debit | Credit | Income Statement (✓) | Statement of Financial Position (✓) |
|---|---|---|---|---|
| | £ | £ | | |
| Rent | 480 | | ✓ | |
| Motor van | 7,400 | | | ✓ |
| Payables | | 1,900 | | ✓ |
| Heat and light | 210 | | ✓ | |
| Discounts received | | 50 | ✓ | |
| Motor expenses | 310 | | ✓ | |
| Sales | | 40,800 | ✓ | |
| Opening inventory | 2,100 | | ✓ | |
| Loan | | 2,000 | | ✓ |
| Stationery | 330 | | ✓ | |
| Capital | | 7,980 | | ✓ |
| Phone | 640 | | ✓ | |
| Discount allowed | 60 | | ✓ | |
| Purchases | 22,600 | | ✓ | |
| Receivables | 3,400 | | | ✓ |
| Wages | 9,700 | | ✓ | |
| Drawings | 4,000 | | | ✓ |
| Office cleaning | 220 | | ✓ | |
| Travel and accommodation | 660 | | ✓ | |
| Bank | 483 | | | ✓ |
| Cash | 137 | | | ✓ |
| | 52,730 | 52,730 | | |

## PREPARING THE FINANCIAL STATEMENTS FROM THE LEDGER ACCOUNTS

Before we leave the subject of the financial statements we must consider how the income statement and the statement of financial position are prepared from the general ledger accounts.

There is a distinct difference between the income statement ledger accounts and the statement of financial position ledger accounts.

- The INCOME STATEMENT is effectively a large ledger account in its own right. This means that each of the balances on **income** and **expense** accounts are transferred or 'cleared' to the profit and loss ledger account at the end of the accounting period. The effect of this is that there is no opening balance on the income and expense ledger accounts at the start of the following accounting period.

- In contrast the STATEMENT OF FINANCIAL POSITION is a list of all of the balances on the **asset**, **liability** and **capital** accounts (the drawings account is cleared to the capital account at the end of each period, along with the balance on the income statement itself). These assets, liabilities and capital will still exist at the start of the next accounting period and so the balances on these accounts are simply listed in the statement of financial position. They are carried down in the ledger accounts as the brought down or opening balances at the start of the next accounting period.

## ACCOUNTING STANDARDS

The way in which some entities, notably companies, prepare their annual financial statements is regulated both by the law and the accounting profession. The purpose of this regulation is to try to ensure that the financial statements of different companies and different types of business are as comparable as possible.

Many small businesses do not operate as companies and so the law in this area (the Companies Act 2006) does not affect them.

They are more affected by the accounting profession which aims to prepare financial statements for businesses in accordance with accounting standards that the profession issues. The aims of accounting standards are to:

- Reduce the variety of methods of dealing with accounting issues and

- Set out the best method to use in order to increase the comparability of the financial statements of different organisations.

UK accounting standards are either Statements of Standard Accounting Practice (SSAPs) or Financial Reporting Standards (FRSs). Together with UK company law, these rules are often referred to as 'UK GAAP' – or UK Generally Accepted Accounting Practice.

Accounting practice in the UK and elsewhere is increasingly influenced by International Accounting Standards (IASs) and International Financial Reporting Standards (IFRSs), issued by the International Accounting Standards Board (IASB). Many IASs and IFRSs take the same, or very similar, approaches to accounting as the UK SSAPs and FRSs.

There are some important differences in terminology between UK GAAP and IASs:

| IASs/IFRSs | UK GAAP |
|---|---|
| Non-current assets | Fixed assets |
| Inventory | Stock |
| Receivable | Debtor |
| Payable | Creditor |
| Irrecoverable debt | Bad debt |
| Income statement (IS) | Profit and loss account (P&L) |
| Statement of financial position (SFP) | Balance sheet (BS) |

In this Text we use the IFRS terms; AAT assessments from 1 January 2012 use IFRS terminology.

For the purposes of Accounts Preparation I the following accounting standards will be covered:

- Non-current assets – the international IAS 16 (Property, plant and equipment) and UK GAAP's FRS 15 (Tangible fixed assets) in Chapter 4

- Inventory – the international IAS 2 (Inventories) and UK GAAP's SSAP 9 (Stocks and long-term contracts) in Chapter 7

## ACCOUNTING CONCEPTS

A business's final ledger accounts and financial statements are prepared according to five well-known and well-understood ACCOUNTING CONCEPTS.

Two fundamental concepts – the GOING CONCERN CONCEPT and the ACCRUALS CONCEPT - play a very pervasive role in the preparation of financial statements.

## Going concern concept

The going concern concept is that a business will continue for the foreseeable future.

This concept affects in particular the values of non-current assets shown in the statement of financial position.

- If the business is a going concern then non-current assets will be shown in the statement of financial position at the amount that they cost less accumulated depreciation (we shall see what this means in Chapter 4).

- If the business is not a going concern and instead is due to close down in the near future then its non-current assets (such as specialised premises or machinery) have a very low value because they probably cannot easily be sold when the business closes. This value may be less than the amount that the assets cost in the first place, so the amount at which they are shown in the statement of financial position will be different than if the business was a going concern.

## Accruals concept

The accruals concept is that the effects of transactions are reflected in the financial statements for the period in which they occur rather than in the period in which any cash involved is received or paid.

This means that the amount of any income or expense appearing in the income statement should be the amount that was earned or incurred during the accounting period rather than the amount of cash that was received or paid.

We have already come across examples of this with credit sales and credit purchases. When a sale is made on credit, the sales account is credited immediately even though it may be a number of weeks before the cash is actually received from the customer.

We will come across further examples of applying the accruals concept when we deal with depreciation in Chapter 4 and accruals and prepayments in Chapter 6.

## Prudence

Where there are conditions of uncertainty, amounts in financial statements need to be treated with PRUDENCE. This means that a degree of caution is required so that assets or income are not overstated and liabilities or expenses are not understated.

Prudence must be exercised when preparing financial statements because of the uncertainty that surrounds many transactions, such as whether debts from credit customers will be paid, and how long plant and machinery will be usable in business.

Exercising prudence generally means that the **most cautious amount for assets is included in financial statements**. For example, in theory a business could choose to value its inventory at its selling price, but prudence tells us that this price may not be achieved, so the more cautious option of using its purchase price is chosen instead.

In addition, if a business **foresees a loss** but the exact amount of the loss is not known, an estimate should be made with a degree of caution, based on the best information available. For example, if a business purchases inventory for £1,200 but, because of a sudden slump in the market, only £900 is likely to be realised when the inventory is sold, the cautious valuation is that the inventory is valued at £900.

## Materiality — Business will set level of what is an expense / asset

The MATERIALITY CONCEPT concerns the accounting treatment of "small" or non-material items in the financial statements. What it means in practical terms is that although there are certain rules which underlie the preparation of financial statements these rules do not necessarily need to apply to non-material items.

For example we have seen that assets that are for long-term use in the business should be shown as non-current assets in the statement of financial position. However small items such as calculators and staplers for use in the office need not be treated as non-current assets if it is decided that they are not material – instead their cost would simply be an expense in the income statement. Similarly office stationery that is used in the business will be charged as an expense in the income statement.  This expense should strictly be adjusted to reflect any inventory of stationery left at the end of the year. However if these amounts are deemed to be immaterial then no adjustment is required.

What is a material amount? The answer to this will depend upon the size of the business itself. In some large businesses the materiality level may be set at something like £5,000. However in a small business it would be much lower, maybe with balances of £100 or less being considered immaterial.

## Consistency

To make financial statements more useful and comparable the CONSISTENCY CONCEPT is applied. This means that the presentation and classification of items in the financial statements should stay the same from one period to the next, unless there is a very good reason to change. Thus if a business treats capital expenditure of £500 or more as a non-current asset in its statement of financial position in one year, it should apply the same policy in the following year rather than deciding to treat capital expenditure on items of £100 or more as a non-current asset.

---

## Task 4

Credit sales and credit purchases are recorded in the books of account as they take place rather than when cash is received or paid. This demonstrates which accounting concept?

Going concern / accruals / prudence / materiality / consistency

---

# CHAPTER OVERVIEW

- The income statement shows the income of the business minus the expenses which will then give either a profit or a loss

- The income statement is a historical summary of the activities of the business during the accounting period

- The gross profit is the profit made from the trading activities of the business. Once all of the expenses have been deducted then there will be a profit or loss for the year

- Discounts allowed are expenses however discounts received can either be shown as income just below gross profit or as a negative expense, ie, as a reduction of the expenses total

- The statement of financial position is a 'snap-shot' of the business on the last day of the accounting period listing all of the assets and liabilities of the business (its net assets)

- The statement of financial position is a vertical form of the accounting equation showing that the net assets equal the capital balance

- The assets are listed in a particular order starting with non-current (fixed) assets and followed by current assets. The current assets are listed in a particular order starting with inventory and working down to bank and cash balances

- Current liabilities are the payables of the business that are due to be paid in less than 12 months' time – current liabilities are deducted from the total of the current assets to give a figure known as the net current assets

- Non-current liabilities payable after more than 12 months are deducted from the total of net current assets and non-current assets to give the final statement of financial position total for net assets

- Capital is made up of the opening balance of capital plus the profit/minus the loss for the year from the income statement minus the owner's drawings, coming to the same statement of financial position total as that for net assets

- The income statement is a large, summary ledger account to which income and expense ledger accounts are cleared at the end of the accounting period leaving no remaining balances on these accounts

- In contrast the statement of financial position is a list of the asset, liability and capital account balances on the last day of the accounting period – these balances remain in the ledger accounts to become the opening balances at the start of the next accounting period

## CHAPTER OVERVIEW CONT'D

- The format of a business's accounts is regulated by law (companies only) and accounting standards

- A business is a going concern, and the going concern concept should be applied to its accounts, if it will continue for the foreseeable future

- The accrual basis of preparing final accounts is that income and expenses should be included in the final accounts in the period in which they are earned or incurred rather than in the period in which the cash is received or paid

- The concept of prudence must be applied in preparing accounts so that assets and income are not overstated and liabilities and expenses are not understated

- The materiality concept allows immaterial items to be treated in a manner which would not be appropriate for material items – the level of materiality will depend upon the size of the business

- The consistency concept is applied to accounts to ensure they are useful and comparable

## Keywords

**Income statement (IS)** – one of the main financial statements showing the income of the business less the expenses of the business for the last accounting period

**Profit and loss account** – the UK GAAP accounting term for the income statement

**Gross profit** – the profit earned by the business from its trading activities (sales less cost of sales)

**Profit for the year** – the final profit of the business after all expenses have been deducted

**Statement of financial position (SFP)** – a list of all of the assets and liabilities of the business on the last day of the accounting period

**Balance sheet** – the UK GAAP accounting term for the statement of financial position

**Current assets** – the short term assets of the business – inventory, receivables and cash and bank balances

**Current liabilities** – liabilities that are due to be paid within one year of the statement of financial position (SFP) date

## Keywords cont'd

**Net current assets** – the total of the current assets minus the current liabilities

**Non-current liabilities** – liabilities that are due to be paid more than a year after the statement of financial position (SFP) date

**Net assets** – total assets less total liabilities as shown in the top half of the statement of financial position (SFP)

**SSAPs** – Statements of Standard Accounting Practice

**FRSs** – Financial Reporting Standards

**IASs** – International Accounting Standards

**IFRSs** – International Financial Reporting Standards

**Going concern concept** – financial statements are prepared on the basis that the organisation will continue in business for the foreseeable future

**Accruals concept** – income and expenses are recognised in the period in which they were earned or incurred rather than when the cash was received or paid

**Prudence** – caution is required in preparing accounts to ensure that assets and income are not overstated and liabilities and expenses are not understated

**Materiality** – the rules of accounting do not need to be applied to immaterial items

**Consistency concept** – a business should apply policies consistently when preparing accounts so the results are comparable across time and with those of other businesses

## TEST YOUR LEARNING

### Test 1

Given below is the trial balance for a small business that is not registered for VAT. You are required to state, in the space next to each balance, whether it is an asset, liability, income, expense or capital and whether the balance would appear in the income statement (IS) or the statement of financial position (SFP).

| | Debit £ | Credit £ | Type of balance | IS or SFP |
|---|---|---|---|---|
| Sales | | 41,200 | I | |
| Loan | | 1,500 | L | S |
| Wages | 7,000 | | E | |
| Non-current assets | 7,100 | | A | S |
| Opening inventory | 1,800 | | E | , |
| Receivables | 3,400 | | A | S |
| Discounts received | | 40 | I | |
| Postage | 100 | | E | |
| Bank | 300 | | A | S |
| Capital | | 9,530 | C | S |
| Rent | 500 | | E | |
| Purchases | 30,100 | | E | |
| Payables | | 2,500 | L | S |
| Discounts allowed | 70 | | E | |
| Drawings | 3,000 | | C | S |
| Electricity | 800 | | E | |
| Telephone | 600 | | E | |
| | 54,770 | 54,770 | | |

### Test 2

Complete the following sentences:

(a)  The gross profit of a business is the profit from [ trading activities ].

(b)  The total of the current assets minus the current liabilities is known as [ ].

Net current assets

**Test 3**

Each of the following statements is an example of which accounting concept?

(a) Sales on credit are recognised as sales at the date that the sales invoice is sent out to the customer. [                    ] *Accruals*

(b) Non-current assets are valued in the statement of financial position at an amount based on their original cost to the business. [            ] *Going concern* [          ]

(c) Staplers for the office have been charged as an expense to the income statement. [                    ] *Materally*

# chapter 3:
# PURCHASE OF NON-CURRENT ASSETS

## chapter coverage 📖

In this chapter we start to consider the first unit of Accounts Preparation I, 'Accounting for non-current assets'. We consider the distinction between capital expenditure and revenue expenditure and how to account for and control non-current assets. The topics we cover are:

✍ The distinction between capital and revenue expenditure

✍ The costs to be included as capital expenditure

✍ Revenue expenditure

✍ Accounting for non-current assets

✍ Journal entries for the acquisition of non-current assets

✍ Authorisation process for the acquisition of non-current assets

✍ Methods of funding the acquisition of non-current assets

✍ The non-current asset register

## CAPITAL EXPENDITURE AND REVENUE EXPENDITURE

Some of the items that a business spends its money on will be fairly major long-term assets of the business, some will be assets that are due to be sold shortly and some will be the business's everyday running expenses.

### Non-current assets

The assets that are purchased by a business for long-term use in the business are known as NON-CURRENT ASSETS. Non-current assets are necessary for the business to carry on its activities over more than one accounting period. Typical examples include:

- Buildings from which the business operates (classed as land and buildings)
- Machinery used in the manufacturing process (classed as machinery)
- Delivery vehicles to distribute goods (classed as motor vehicles)
- Cars for managers and sales representatives (classed as motor vehicles)
- Furniture and fittings for the office area (classed as furniture and fittings)
- Computers for the sales and administration departments (classed as computer equipment)

The cost of buying these non-current assets and getting them into operation is known as CAPITAL EXPENDITURE.

All other expenditure of the business, other than on the purchase of non-current assets, is known as REVENUE EXPENDITURE.

### The distinction between capital and revenue expenditure

The importance of the distinction between revenue and capital expenditure is due to their differing treatment in the financial statements.

Capital expenditure is classified as a non-current asset and as such is included as an asset in the statement of financial position. Revenue expenditure, in contrast, is charged as an expense to the income statement.

# HOW IT WORKS

A business spends £20,000 on a new machine to be used for making its products. If this were mistakenly classified as revenue expenditure then the income statement would have an extra large expense of £20,000 and the statement of financial position would not include this major asset of the business.

## What is included in capital expenditure? — *Something new*

Due to the differing treatment of capital and revenue expenditure we must ensure that the correct amounts are included in the statement of financial position as capital expenditure.

The cost of a non-current asset to be included in the statement of financial position, or CAPITALISED, is not just its purchase price. It is the directly attributable costs of getting the asset to its correct location and into full working order. Therefore the costs that might be included as capital expenditure include:

- The purchase price (acquisition cost) of the asset net of VAT (although on cars that have some private use the VAT is irrecoverable and must be included in the purchase price)
- Delivery/handling costs
- Site preparation, installation, assembly and set-up costs
- Testing costs to ensure the asset is functioning properly
- Any special alterations or equipment required in order to use the asset
- Professional fees such as legal fees

Both FRS 15 (Tangible fixed assets) and IAS 16 (Property, plant and equipment) make it clear that any major alteration or improvement of the asset is to be treated as capital expenditure.

## Revenue expenditure — *On something already there, running cost*

There will often be other expenses related to the non-current assets of a business and care must be taken to ensure that these are not capitalised in the balance sheet but are treated as revenue expenditure and charged as expenses in the profit and loss account.

Examples of revenue expenditure which might be confused with capital expenditure include:

- Costs of decorating a new building
- Repairs to a building or machinery
- General maintenance costs

- Costs of cleaning machinery
- Fuel costs
- Administrative and general overheads such as insurance costs
- Servicing and repairs to motor vehicles
- The road fund licence for a vehicle (often included in the invoice for a new vehicle, so take care)
- CDs and printer paper for a computer

## Capitalisation policy

Not all items that could be classified as capital expenditure have to be capitalised. A business may decide that non-material items purchased for long-term use in the business are too small in amount to be capitalised. For instance, the CAPITALISATION POLICY may be that a separate amount of expenditure on any item costing less than £100 – on a stapler for office use, say, or a toolbox for use in a workshop – should be treated as revenue rather than capital expenditure.

In addition, the business may decide to exclude from its capitalisation policy any assets that have a short expected LIFESPAN in use in the business. For instance, a PC could be used for many years in some businesses but may have only a short expected lifespan in a business where it would be used very heavily. Such a business's capitalisation policy would therefore state that assets with a restricted lifespan should be treated as revenue expenditure.

## Assets made by the business's employees

In some situations non-current assets may not be purchased but are instead made or constructed by the business's employees. For example a building firm may build a new set of offices for its own use.

Another situation might be that a business uses its own employees to install a new piece of machinery.

In each case the cost of the non-current asset will include the wages cost of the employees who worked on it together with the cost of any materials that they used. Therefore these wages and materials will be treated as capital expenditure.

## HOW IT WORKS

Harris Incorporated have just significantly enlarged the operations of their manufacturing business and as such have purchased a number of major assets.

Purchased a building to use as the factory at a cost of £80,000 plus £1,000 of legal fees

- The legal fees are part of the cost of purchasing the building and therefore are treated as capital expenditure – total capital expenditure £81,000

Carried out £10,000 of building work in order to make the building suitable for the manufacturing process

- Again this is part of the cost of the factory and would be treated as capital expenditure of £10,000

Purchased a TV1 machine for £4,000 which was installed by Harris's own employees using £200 of materials and incurring wages costs of £600

- The installation costs should be treated as capital expenditure as they are a cost of getting the asset into use – total capital expenditure £4,800

Redecorated a building that was already owned and is used for the sales and administration departments at a total cost of £1,400

- This is all revenue expenditure as these are running expenses of the business – total revenue expenditure £1,400

Purchased a computer to help in the administration department for £1,200 together with computer software costing £400 and a training course for the employees who will be using the computer at a cost of £200. The cost of the computer included £50 of CDs and £20 of printer paper that were delivered with it.

- The cost of the software could be treated as either capital or revenue expenditure – as the cost of this software is quite large it would probably be treated as capital expenditure. The cost of the training course would also be treated as capital expenditure as it is necessary in order to run the computer. The cost of the CDs and the paper is revenue expenditure as this is part of the cost of running the computer – total capital expenditure of £1,730, total revenue expenditure £70

Employed contract cleaners to clean the new TV1 machine after its first week of operation at a cost of £150

- This would be treated as revenue expenditure as it is part of the general running costs of the business – total revenue expenditure £150

Purchased a new delivery van at a cost of £16,400 which included £100 of delivery charges and £200 of road fund licence

- The delivery charges are part of the cost of the non-current (non-current) asset and are treated as capital expenditure but the road fund licence is a running cost of the vehicle and is treated as revenue expenditure – total capital expenditure £16,200, total revenue expenditure £200

Purchased some office furniture for £1,300 on credit

- Total capital expenditure £1,300

Purchased a car for £15,000, paying £10,000 cash and receiving a part exchange allowance of £5,000 on an old car which it traded in

- Irrespective of how the acquisition was funded, the total capital expenditure is £15,000

---

## Task 1

A business has two machines. Machine A has just undergone a major overhaul at a cost of £15,000 which has extended its life to the business by four years. Machine B has just been repaired due to the wearing out of a small working part at a cost of £4,000. Identify the capital and the revenue expenditure incurred.

Capital expenditure £    15000

Revenue expenditure £    4000

---

## ACCOUNTING FOR NON-CURRENT ASSETS

When non-current assets are purchased they are debited to separate asset ledger accounts for each type of non-current asset. The most common classifications of types of non-current asset are:

- Land and buildings
- Machinery
- Motor vehicles
- Furniture and fittings
- Computers

The assets may be purchased:

- For cash (ie by cheque), so the credit entry will be to the bank/cash account or

- On credit, so the credit entry will be to the purchases ledger control account for a purchase on credit or

- By means of a part exchange (or trade in) of an old asset. The value given in part exchange is debited to the non-current asset account, and the credit goes to the disposal account – we shall come back to the reasons for this in Chapter 5

- With a loan

- With a hire purchase or finance lease arrangement

When the business's own employees have made or installed non-current assets then the following double entry must be made:

| | |
|---|---|
| Materials | Debit Non-current asset account |
| | Credit Purchases account |
| Wages | Debit Non-current asset account |
| | Credit Wages account |

The effect of this is to remove the materials and wages that are capital expenditure from revenue expenditure accounts.

## HOW IT WORKS

We will now return to Harris Incorporated and show how each item of expenditure would be entered into the ledger accounts. All of the purchases were for cash other than the office furniture which was purchased on credit, and the car which was paid for partly in cash and partly by part exchanging an old vehicle.

**Purchased a building to use as the factory at a cost of £80,000 plus £1,000 of legal fees**

**Land and buildings account  GL001**

| | £ | | £ |
|---|---|---|---|
| Bank/cash | 81,000 | | |

**Bank/cash account GL002**

| | £ | | £ |
|---|---|---|---|
| | | Land and buildings | 81,000 |

**Carried out £10,000 of building work in order to make the building suitable for the manufacturing process**

### Land and buildings account GL001

| | £ | | £ |
|---|---|---|---|
| Bank/cash | 81,000 | | |
| Bank/cash | 10,000 | | |

### Bank/cash account GL002

| | £ | | £ |
|---|---|---|---|
| | | Land and buildings | 81,000 |
| | | Land and buildings | 10,000 |

**Purchased a TV1 machine for £4,000 which was installed by Harris's own employees using £200 of materials and incurring wages costs of £600**

### Machinery account GL003

| | £ | | £ |
|---|---|---|---|
| Bank/cash | 4,000 | | |
| Purchases | 200 | | |
| Wages | 600 | | |

### Bank/cash account GL002

| | £ | | £ |
|---|---|---|---|
| | | Land and buildings | 81,000 |
| | | Land and buildings | 10,000 |
| | | Machinery | 4,000 |

### Purchases account GL100

| | £ | | £ |
|---|---|---|---|
| | | Machinery | 200 |

### Wages account GL200

| | £ | | £ |
|---|---|---|---|
| | | Machinery | 600 |

**Redecorated a building that was already owned and is used for the sales and administration departments at a total cost of £1,400**

### Buildings maintenance account GL110

| | £ | | £ |
|---|---|---|---|
| Bank/cash | 1,400 | | |

This is an expense account not a non-current asset account as this is revenue expenditure.

### Bank/cash account GL002

| | £ | | £ |
|---|---|---|---|
| | | Land and buildings | 81,000 |
| | | Land and buildings | 10,000 |
| | | Machinery | 4,000 |
| | | Buildings maintenance | 1,400 |

**Purchased a computer to help in the administration department for £1,200 together with computer software costing £400. The cost of the computer included £50 of CDs and £20 of printer paper that were delivered with it**

### Computers account GL004

| | £ | | £ |
|---|---|---|---|
| Bank/cash | 1,530 | | |

### Stationery account GL120

| | £ | | £ |
|---|---|---|---|
| Bank/cash | 70 | | |

The CDs and the paper have been charged to an expense account as they are revenue expenditure not capital expenditure.

### Bank/cash account GL002

| | £ | | £ |
|---|---|---|---|
| | | Land and buildings | 81,000 |
| | | Land and buildings | 10,000 |
| | | Machinery | 4,000 |
| | | Buildings maintenance | 1,400 |
| | | Computers | 1,530 |
| | | Stationery | 70 |

**Employed contract cleaners to clean the new TV1 machine after its first week of operation at a cost of £150**

### Cleaning costs account GL130

| | £ | | £ |
|---|---|---|---|
| Bank/cash | 150 | | |

This is an expense account as this is revenue expenditure not capital expenditure.

**Bank/cash account  GL002**

| | £ | | £ |
|---|---|---|---|
| | | Land and buildings | 81,000 |
| | | Land and buildings | 10,000 |
| | | Machinery | 4,000 |
| | | Buildings maintenance | 1,400 |
| | | Computers | 1,530 |
| | | Stationery | 70 |
| | | Cleaning costs | 150 |

**Purchased a new delivery van at a cost of £16,400 which included £100 of delivery charges and £200 of road fund licence**

**Motor vehicles account GL005**

| | £ | | £ |
|---|---|---|---|
| Bank/cash | 16,200 | | |

**Motor expenses GL140**

| | £ | | £ |
|---|---|---|---|
| Bank/cash | 200 | | |

Again this is an expense account as the road fund licence is not capital expenditure.

**Bank/cash account GL002**

| | £ | | £ |
|---|---|---|---|
| | | Land and buildings | 81,000 |
| | | Land and buildings | 10,000 |
| | | Machinery | 4,000 |
| | | Buildings maintenance | 1,400 |
| | | Computers | 1,530 |
| | | Stationery | 70 |
| | | Cleaning costs | 150 |
| | | Motor vehicles | 16,200 |
| | | Motor expenses | 200 |

**Purchased some office furniture for £1,300 on credit**

**Furniture and fittings account GL006**

| | £ | | £ |
|---|---|---|---|
| Purchases ledger control | 1,300 | | |

**Purchases ledger control account GL007**

| | £ | | £ |
|---|---|---|---|
| | | Furniture and fittings | 1,300 |

**Purchased a car for £15,000, paying £10,000 cash and receiving a part exchange allowance of £5,000 on an old car which it traded in**

### Motor vehicles account GL005

| | £ | | £ |
|---|---|---|---|
| Bank/cash | 16,200 | | |
| Bank/cash | 10,000 | | |
| Disposal | 5,000 | | |

### Bank/cash account GL002

| | £ | | £ |
|---|---|---|---|
| | | Land and buildings | 81,000 |
| | | Land and buildings | 10,000 |
| | | Machinery | 4,000 |
| | | Buildings maintenance | 1,400 |
| | | Computers | 1,530 |
| | | Stationery | 70 |
| | | Cleaning costs | 150 |
| | | Motor vehicles | 16,200 |
| | | Motor expenses | 200 |
| | | Motor vehicles | 10,000 |

### Disposal GL008

| | £ | | £ |
|---|---|---|---|
| | | Motor vehicles | 5,000 |

At the end of each accounting period, the balance on each non-current asset account will be carried down as the opening balance in the new period's accounts. Each carried down balance will also appear on the statement of financial position at the end of the old accounting period.

## Task 2

A business has recently installed a new machine which cost £17,000 and was purchased on credit. The installation was carried out by its own employees and the wages costs of these employees for the time taken to install the machine are £1,400.

Write up the relevant ledger accounts to reflect the purchase and installation of this machine.

D                                                                                     C

### Machinery account

|  | £ |  | £ |
|---|---|---|---|
| Machine | 17000 |  |  |
| Wages | 1400 |  |  |
|  |  |  |  |

### Purchases ledger control account

|  | £ |  | £ |
|---|---|---|---|
|  |  | Payables | 17,000 |
|  |  |  |  |

### Wages account

|  | £ |  | £ |
|---|---|---|---|
| Wages | 1,400 | Wage | 1,400 |
|  |  |  |  |

### Journal entries

In practice the way in which the acquisition of a non-current asset is recorded in the ledger accounts is usually by way of a journal entry if it is acquired on credit or using part-exchange. If the asset is acquired for cash then the cash payments book is the book of prime entry for non-current assets.

In order to demonstrate clearly the double entry required in respect of non-current assets we shall produce journal entries for each of them.

## HOW IT WORKS

Returning to Harris Incorporated we will now prepare the journal entries for each of the purchases of non-current assets (in practice of course this would be done before the entries are made in the ledger accounts as the journal is the instruction to make the ledger account entries). Today's date is 5 February 20XX.

**Purchased a building to use as the factory at a cost of £80,000 plus £1,000 of legal fees, paid in cash**

| Date | Account | Ref | Debit £ | Credit £ |
|------|---------|-----|---------|----------|
| 20XX | | | | |
| 5 Feb | Land and buildings | GL001 | 81,000 | |
| | Bank/cash | GL002 | | 81,000 |
| | | | 81,000 | 81,000 |
| Being purchase of new factory building | | | | |

Note that the reference column would be used to enter the general ledger code for the accounts being debited and credited.

**Carried out £10,000 of building work in order to make the building suitable for the manufacturing process, paid in cash**

| Date | Account | Ref | Debit £ | Credit £ |
|------|---------|-----|---------|----------|
| 20XX | | | | |
| 5 Feb | Land and buildings | GL001 | 10,000 | |
| | Bank/cash | GL002 | | 10,000 |
| | | | 10,000 | 10,000 |
| Being alterations to new factory | | | | |

**Purchased a TV1 machine for £4,000 cash which was installed by Harris's own employees using £200 of materials and incurring wages costs of £600**

| Date | Account | Ref | Debit £ | Credit £ |
|------|---------|-----|---------|----------|
| 20XX | | | | |
| 5 Feb | Machinery | GL003 | 4,800 | |
| | Bank/cash | GL002 | | 4,000 |
| | Purchases | GL100 | | 200 |
| | Wages | GL200 | | 600 |
| | | | 4,800 | 4,800 |
| Being purchase and installation of TV1 machine | | | | |

**Redecorated a building that was already owned and is used for the sales and administration departments at a total cost of £1,400, paid in cash**

| Date | Account | Ref | Debit £ | Credit £ |
|------|---------|-----|---------|----------|
| 20XX | | | | |
| 5 Feb | Buildings maintenance | GL110 | 1,400 | |
| | Bank/cash | GL002 | | 1,400 |
| | | | 1,400 | 1,400 |
| Being redecoration of sales and administration department building | | | | |

**Purchased a computer to help in the administration department for £1,200 together with computer software costing £400. The cost of the computer included £50 of CDs and £20 of printer paper that were delivered with it. All transactions were paid in cash**

| Date | Account | Ref | Debit £ | Credit £ |
|------|---------|-----|---------|----------|
| 20XX | | | | |
| 5 Feb | Computers | GL004 | 1,530 | |
| | Stationery | GL120 | 70 | |
| | Bank/cash | GL002 | | 1,600 |
| | | | 1,600 | 1,600 |
| Being purchase of computer | | | | |

**Employed contract cleaners to clean the new TV1 machine after its first week of operation at a cost of £150, paid in cash**

| Date | Account | Ref | Debit £ | Credit £ |
|------|---------|-----|---------|----------|
| 20XX | | | | |
| 5 Feb | Cleaning costs | GL130 | 150 | |
| | Bank/cash | GL002 | | 150 |
| | | | 150 | 150 |
| Being cleaning of TV1 week 1 | | | | |

**Purchased a new delivery van at a cost of £16,400 which included £100 of delivery charges and £200 of road fund licence, all paid in cash**

| Date | Account | Ref | Debit £ | Credit £ |
|------|---------|-----|---------|----------|
| 20XX | | | | |
| 5 Feb | Motor vehicles | GL005 | 16,200 | |
| | Motor expenses | GL140 | 200 | |
| | Bank/cash | GL002 | | 16,400 |
| | | | 16,400 | 16,400 |
| Being purchase of new delivery van | | | | |

**Purchased some office furniture for £1,300 on credit**

| Date | Account | Ref | Debit £ | Credit £ |
|------|---------|-----|---------|----------|
| 20XX | | | | |
| 5 Feb | Furniture and fittings | GL006 | 1,300 | |
| | Purchases ledger control | GL007 | | 1,300 |
| | | | 1,300 | 1,300 |
| Being purchase of office furniture | | | | |

**Purchased a car for £15,000, paying £10,000 cash and receiving a part exchange allowance of £5,000 on an old car which it traded in**

| Date | Account | Ref | Debit £ | Credit £ |
|------|---------|-----|---------|----------|
| 20XX | | | | |
| 5 Feb | Motor vehicles | GL005 | 15,000 | |
| | Bank/cash | GL002 | | 10,000 |
| | Disposal | GL008 | | 5,000 |
| | | | 15,000 | 15,000 |
| Being purchase of new car for cash/part exchange | | | | |

## Task 3

A business has recently purchased four cars for use by its sales force at a total invoiced amount of £79,600. This total includes £400 of delivery charges and £800 of road fund licences. The amount due was paid by cheque upon delivery of the cars.

Draft the journal entry for the acquisition of these cars.

| Account name | Amount £ | Debit (✓) | Credit (✓) |
|--------------|----------|-----------|------------|
| | | | |
| | | | |
| | | | |

# AUTHORISATION FOR NON-CURRENT ASSET ACQUISITIONS

Clearly the acquisition of non-current assets is a major cost to a business and therefore it must be monitored and controlled. When a non-current asset is required by the business there is normally a strict procedure to follow:

- Acquisition application
- Price quotations
- Authorisation of application
- Monitoring of ongoing costs

## Acquisition application

If an area of a business needs a new non-current asset then this requirement will need to be justified to the owners/managers of the business. The procedure for applying to acquire a new non-current asset will depend upon the nature and the cost of the asset and the organisation and size of the business.

- The application to buy a desk and chair for a new employee in the accounts department may well be a simple memo to the accountant.

- The application to purchase a new piece of machinery costing £120,000 is likely to require a much more formal application with many details supporting the need for this acquisition. In larger businesses such applications will probably be dealt with by a capital expenditure committee or at the very least by a meeting of the senior management of the business.

## Price quotations

As with any purchase that a business makes, when purchasing a non-current asset it is important that the best possible combination of price, quality and service is found. This may well involve getting detailed quotations from a number of different suppliers. These quotations are likely to differ on price as well as the terms of after-sales service and the quality of the product. All of this will be relevant to the managers of the business who will make the decision as to whether to authorise this acquisition.

## Authorisation

When considering whether or not to authorise the acquisition the business's management will not only consider the cost of the asset and the terms that are being offered. Many other considerations also go into the authorisation process.

- Can we afford the asset? The question here is whether the business has enough money to buy the asset (different funding methods will be considered later in this chapter)

- What effect will the new asset have upon staffing levels? A major new production line could mean that new employees are required. A sophisticated computer system may mean that a specialist has to be employed

- New machinery or technology may mean that staff will need to be trained in order to be able to operate the machinery or understand the technology

- What effect will there be on productivity? If a new machine or production line is acquired will this increase production each hour or day?

- What will be the effect on profitability? Is the asset worthwhile? Its costs and benefits have to be considered over a number of years in order to determine whether it will add to the business or detract from it

## Monitoring of ongoing costs

Many capital acquisitions that a business makes will not be one-off purchases but rather an ongoing development over time. For example if a new factory is being built and stocked with machinery this may well take a number of months. When the initial purchase application was approved the business's management will have had a price quotation for the job but it is important that all aspects of the job are monitored over time to ensure that there are no unforeseen cost overruns.

# METHODS OF FUNDING

We have already seen that the acquisition of non-current assets is a major expense for any business. You need to know about the different methods of funding the acquisition, but you only need to know the detailed double entry for cash, credit and part exchange transactions, which we covered earlier in this chapter.

## Cash/Credit purchase

The most obvious choice is a CASH PURCHASE where the asset is paid for at the time of transaction or a CREDIT PURCHASE where payment is made at a later date (for example within 30 days of the invoice date). In both instances the business purchasing the asset will need to have the funds available, either immediately or within the credit period.

Many businesses will not have enough funds in their bank account to purchase such assets with cash or on normal commercial credit terms. Therefore alternative options have to be considered.

## Borrowing

Businesses may borrow the money to acquire new non-current assets either by a LOAN or a MORTGAGE. Loans are available from banks, building societies and many other providers of finance. A loan for the purchase of a non-current asset will normally be for a non-current amount for any period of time up to about ten years. Interest will be charged on the amount outstanding and the loan will normally be repaid by monthly or quarterly instalments.

A mortgage is a specific type of loan which might be a more suitable method of borrowing for the purchase of land and buildings. The mortgage loan can be for any amount up to 95% of the value of the property and can be repaid over a period of up to 25 years. The property serves as security for the loan in case the repayments are not made. Interest and capital will normally be paid in monthly instalments.

For any loan the interest charged will appear in the profit and loss account (income statement) as an expense each year and the outstanding amount of the loan will appear on the balance sheet as a long term liability.

## Hire purchase or finance lease

Many non-current assets such as motor vehicles, machinery, office equipment and computers can be purchased under a HIRE PURCHASE AGREEMENT or FINANCE LEASE.

Under these arrangements the business pays an initial deposit to the finance company and from that point onwards has full use of the asset although the asset remains, in legal terms, the property of the finance company. The business makes regular payments to the finance company, usually monthly or quarterly, which are designed to pay off the capital cost of the asset plus the interest charged by the finance company. At the end of a hire purchase period the asset legally becomes owned by the business. At the end of a finance lease period there is normally no option to purchase the asset.

The interest element of the repayments appears in the profit and loss account as an expense. Although the non-current asset is not legally owned by the business, best accounting practice is that it appears in the balance sheet as a non-current asset at its cost as if it had been purchased outright. There will also be a creditor for the amount still owed to the finance company.

## Part exchange

A part exchange deal to part-fund an acquisition is very common, particularly in the motor trade. If the business wishes to purchase a new asset it can offer an old asset in PART EXCHANGE. In the case of a car the car dealer will place a value on the old car and deduct this value from the cost of the new car so the business needs only to pay the difference.

## Task 4

A business purchases a new car costing £25,000, paying £15,000 in cash and receiving £10,000 as part exchange for an old car traded in.

Draft the journal entry for the this transaction (ignore VAT) and provide the narrative.

| Account name | Amount £ | Debit (✓) | Credit (✓) |
|---|---|---|---|
| mv | 25,000 | ✓ | |
| Cash | 15,000 | | ✓ |
| Disp | 10,000 | | ✓ |

M.Vehicle

Cash

Disposal

## RECORDING ACQUISITIONS IN THE NON-CURRENT ASSET REGISTER

As we have already seen it is important that a business has strict control over its non-current assets. In order to keep track of all of them most businesses will keep a NON-CURRENT ASSET REGISTER or FIXED ASSET REGISTER. For each non-current asset that the business acquires a detailed record will be kept in the register, typically showing the following:

- A description of the asset and possibly an asset number

- Its physical location within the business

- The supplier and the date of purchase

- The cost of the asset

- The estimated lifespan of the asset

- Any estimated scrap value of the asset at the end of its life

- The method of depreciation to be applied (see Chapter 4)

- The depreciation percentage

- The amount of depreciation charged each year

- The accumulated depreciation at the end of each year

- The carrying amount of the asset at the end of each year (see Chapter 4)

- Eventually the details of the disposal of the asset including sale proceeds and any profit or loss on disposal (see Chapter 5)

## HOW IT WORKS

Kendall Engineering has just purchased a new machine, the FD254, from Leyland Machinery for £120,000. Today's date is 1 March 20XX and the machine is allocated asset number 02635. The machine is located in the factory and is expected to be used for five years after which it will have an estimated scrap value of £20,000.

We will now enter these initial details in the non-current asset register. In Chapters 4 and 5 the remaining entries in the non-current asset register will be considered.

**Non-current asset number**
**Description** 02635
  Machine FD254
**Location** Factory
**Supplier** **Leyland Machinery**

| Acquisition date | Cost £ | Expected life (years) | Estimated residual value £ | Depreciation method | Depreciation rate | Depreciation charge for the year £ | Acc dep at end of the year £ | Carrying amount at end of year £ | Disposal proceeds £ | Profit or loss on disposal £ |
|---|---|---|---|---|---|---|---|---|---|---|
| **20X7** 1 Mar | 120,000 | 5 | 20,000 | | | | | | | |

## CHAPTER OVERVIEW

- Capital expenditure is the cost of acquiring non-current assets – assets for long-term use in the business rather than for sale

- Revenue expenditure is all other business expenditure

- The costs to be included as the cost of a non-current asset are the costs involved in purchasing the asset and getting it into working order – these are then included in the statement of financial position as non-current assets

- Revenue expenditure is charged to the income statement as an expense

- The double entry for acquiring a non-current asset is to debit the relevant non-current asset account and to credit either bank or the purchases ledger control account depending upon whether the asset was purchased for cash or on credit

- If a non-current asset has been made or installed by the business's own workforce then the materials and wages costs are debited to the non-current asset account and credited to purchases and wages respectively

- The entries to the ledger accounts are often initiated by a journal entry instructing the bookkeeper to account for the acquisition of the non-current assets where these are bought on credit or using part exchange

- Control and monitoring of non-current assets is extremely important and a non-current asset should only be acquired if its acquisition application is authorised

- Many non-current assets will not be acquired for cash but will be financed by a loan or purchased on a hire purchase agreement

- Old assets can often be given in part-exchange for a new asset in order to reduce the cost of the new asset

- The details of all non-current assets will be kept in a non-current asset register

## Keywords

**Non-current assets** – assets acquired for long-term use within the business

**Capital expenditure** – expenditure on acquiring non-current assets

**Revenue expenditure** – all other non-capital expenditure – therefore any expenditure that is not the acquisition or major improvement of non-current assets

**Capitalised** – when the cost of a non-current asset is included in the statement of financial position (SFP)

**Capitalisation policy** – the business's policy for determining when capital expenditure is capitalised

**Acquisition application** – an application by an area of the business to purchase a non-current asset

**Loan** – a fixed amount borrowed from a bank or building society etc which is to be repaid over a fixed period of time on which interest is paid on the outstanding amount

**Mortgage** – a specific type of loan for the purchase of buildings where the building itself acts as security for the loan

**Hire purchase agreement** – a method of financing the purchase of a non-current asset where an initial deposit is paid to the finance company followed by a fixed number of instalments after which the asset is owned by the business

**Finance lease** – a method of financing the purchase of a non-current asset which is very similar to a hire purchase agreement but where there is normally no option to purchase the asset at the end of the lease term

**Part exchange** – a method of reducing the cost of a new asset by offering an old asset in part exchange

**Non-current asset register** – a record of the details of all of the non-current assets of the business individually

## EST YOUR LEARNING

### Test 1

For each of the following transactions state the amounts that should be treated as capital expenditure and the amounts that should be treated as revenue expenditure.

(a) A machine is purchased on credit at a total cost of £15,800. This includes delivery costs of £350, installation costs of £550 and a supply of lubricating oil for the machine costing £100

Capital expenditure    £ 16,700

Revenue expenditure    £ 100

(b) A building plot is purchased for £60,000 plus surveyor's fees of £600 and legal fees of £500

Capital expenditure    £ 61,100

Revenue expenditure    £ 0

(c) A new computer system is installed at a cost of £65,000. The computer room has had to be re-wired for this system at a cost of £3,600 and, while the electricians were in the building, the sales department lighting system was repaired at a cost of £800

Capital expenditure    £ 68,600

Revenue expenditure    £ 800

### Test 2

Draft journal entries for each of the following non-current asset acquisitions.

(a) Desks and chairs for the head office at a cost of £4,200, paid for by cheque

| Account name | Amount £ | Debit (✓) | Credit (✓) |
|---|---|---|---|
| Furnishings | 4,200 | ✓ | |
| Bank | 4,200 | | ✓ |
| | | | |

(b) A new computer purchased on credit at a total cost of £2,400 including £100 of rewritable CDs

| Account name | Amount £ | Debit (✓) | Credit (✓) |
|---|---|---|---|
| EQUIPMENT PURCHASE | 2300 | ✓ | |
| PURCHASE CONTROL | 2,400 | | ✓ |
| PURCHASES | 100 | ✓ | |
| PURCHUSE Cℴ... | 100 | | |

(c) A new machine purchased at a cost of £9,600 by cheque and installed by the business's own employees using materials costing £200 and incurring wages costs of £800

| Account name | Amount £ | Debit (✓) | Credit (✓) |
|---|---|---|---|
| PURCHASES | | 10,600 | |
| Bank | | | 9000 9600 |
| WAGES | | | 800 |
| MATERIALS | | | 200 |
| | | | |

**Test 3**

If a machine is purchased under a hire purchase agreement when would it appear as a non-current asset in the business's statement of financial position?

|  | (✓) |
|---|---|
| On the date of payment of the deposit | ✓ |
| On the date of the final instalment | |
| Never | |

# chapter 4:
# DEPRECIATION OF NON-CURRENT ASSETS

## chapter coverage 📖

In this chapter we consider the detailed accounting treatment for non-current assets. They are recorded in the statement of financial position at their original cost but this cost must be charged over time to the income statement because the assets are being used to earn revenues for the business. This method of charging the cost of non-current assets to the income statement is known as depreciation. The topics covered are:

- 🖎 The purpose of depreciation
- 🖎 Methods of calculating depreciation
- 🖎 The straight line method of depreciation
- 🖎 Estimated residual values
- 🖎 The reducing balance method of depreciation
- 🖎 Comparison of the two methods of depreciation
- 🖎 Depreciation policies
- 🖎 Accounting for depreciation
- 🖎 Recording depreciation in the non-current asset register

# WHAT IS DEPRECIATION?

We will start with the technical definition of DEPRECIATION from the International Accounting Standard IAS 16 (Property, plant and equipment):

'Depreciation is the systematic allocation of the cost of an asset less its residual value over its useful life.'

UK GAAP's FRS 15 (Tangible fixed assets) defines it in rather more detail as follows:

'Depreciation is the measure of the cost ....... of the economic benefits of the tangible fixed asset that have been consumed during the period. Consumption includes the wearing out, using up or other reduction in the useful economic life of a tangible fixed asset whether arising from use, effluxion of time or obsolescence through either changes in technology or demand for goods and services produced by the asset.'

Now we will consider what these definitions actually mean.

The first element of the FRS 15 definition regards the accounting concept of **accruals**. When a fixed asset is purchased its entire cost is included in the relevant asset account and is then recorded as a fixed asset in the balance sheet. According to the accruals concept all of the costs involved in producing the income of the business during a period should be charged to the profit and loss account as an expense in the same period. Fixed assets that are used in the business are earning income for the business over several accounting periods, so a part of their cost should be charged to the profit and loss account in each accounting period in order to accord with the accruals concept – this is the depreciation charge.

The FRS 15 definition talks about the amount of the asset's cost that is 'consumed' or used up during the period as being the depreciation charge. This amount has to be estimated for each type of fixed asset. Different types of asset will be consumed or depreciated in different ways:

- Machinery, motor vehicles and furniture will tend to wear out through use

- Leases on buildings will be consumed by the passage of time as the lease term diminishes

- Computer equipment becomes obsolete as technology advances

The aim of depreciation therefore is to charge or allocate the asset's cost to the profit and loss account of each accounting period of its useful life as an expense in order to match with the income that the asset has earned in the period.

The only type of fixed asset that does not have to be depreciated is freehold land. Since it has an infinite life it is not consumed in the business.

If some of the asset's cost has been consumed then the asset is 'worth' less than its original cost. This is reflected in the balance sheet where fixed assets are shown at their cost less all of the depreciation charged to date.

This is known as the NET BOOK VALUE of the fixed asset. Under international standards net book value is called CARRYING AMOUNT.

| COST | − | DEPRECIATION TO DATE | = | NET BOOK VALUE/CARRYING AMOUNT |

## METHODS OF CALCULATING DEPRECIATION

The amount of depreciation on a non-current asset that is allocated to the income statement each year is just an estimate of how much of the asset's cost has been consumed during the year. In order to make such estimates businesses will have DEPRECIATION POLICIES that state the method to be used for depreciation of each type of non-current asset. This method should generally be used every year in order to be **consistent**.

The two methods of depreciation that are assessable in Accounts Preparation I are:

- The straight line method
- The reducing balance method

## STRAIGHT LINE METHOD

The aim of the STRAIGHT LINE METHOD of depreciation is to charge the same amount of depreciation on the non-current asset in each year of the asset's life.

To calculate the depreciation charge for a non-current asset under this method we need to know:

- The COST of the asset – see Chapter 3

- Its USEFUL LIFE – this is the time period over which it is estimated that the non-current asset will be used within the business

- Its RESIDUAL VALUE – this is the scrap value that it is expected the asset can be sold for when its useful life is over

Depreciation using the straight line method can be calculated using:

- A percentage of the asset's cost less residual value
- A fraction of the asset's cost less residual value
- A period of time

The calculated depreciation for one year is then added to any depreciation charged in previous years and deducted from the asset's acquisition cost to arrive at its carrying amount in the statement of financial position.

## HOW IT WORKS

Nick Waldron has recently set up a retail venture known as N W Traders. One of the non-current assets that has been purchased is an item of machinery that cost £8,000 and which Nick estimates will be used in the business for eight years. After this date it will need to be replaced due to technological changes, and it will have no resale (residual) value at that date. The machine is to be depreciated using the straight line method.

Using the **period of time method**, the annual depreciation charge is calculated as:

$$\frac{\text{Asset's acquisition cost}}{\text{Asset's estimated useful life}}$$

The depreciation charge for this asset will be:

$$\frac{£8,000}{8 \text{ years}} = £1,000 \text{ per year}$$

The same information allows us to calculate depreciation using the **percentage method**. If the asset is held for eight years then in each year $1/8 \times 100\% = 12.5\%$ of the cost is charged in each year. This comes out at $£8,000 \times 12.5\% = £1,000$ per year.

Again the same information is used to calculate depreciation using the **fraction method**. If the asset is held for eight years then in each year $1/8^{\text{th}}$ of the cost is charged, that is $£8,000 \times 1/8 = £1,000$ per year.

Whichever method of calculation is used, we can see that in each year:

- £1,000 will be charged to the income statement as an expense and

- £1,000 will be deducted from the cost of the non-current asset in the statement of financial position to arrive at its carrying amount.

At the end of the first year the carrying amount will be $£8,000 - £1,000 = £7,000$. At the end of the asset's estimated useful life its carrying amount will be:

Cost – depreciation to date

$£8,000 - (8 \times £1,000) = \text{nil}$

## Task 1

Using the non-current asset details given above what will be the carrying amount of the asset after it has been owned by N W Traders for three years?

£  5,000

### Residual value

In the previous example we were told that the asset would be worthless by the end of its useful life. However many non-current assets that a business purchases are likely to be sold on in the second-hand market at the end of their useful life to the business. This is probably especially the case with motor vehicles which may be kept for three or four years and then replaced. Such assets will have a resale value at the date of their sale.

With the straight line depreciation method, when the non-current asset is purchased we need to estimate:

- The asset's useful life and

- Its scrap value or resale value at the end of the useful life, known as the asset's RESIDUAL VALUE.

The amount that is to be depreciated over the asset's useful life is then:

| COST | – | RESIDUAL VALUE |
|------|---|----------------|

## HOW IT WORKS

N W Traders has also purchased a motor van for deliveries for £16,000. It is estimated that the van will be used for three years and then sold for £5,500.

The relevant figures for this non-current asset are therefore:

| | |
|---|---|
| Cost | £16,000 |
| Useful life | 3 years |
| Residual value | £5,500 |

Using the straight line period of time method of depreciation, the annual charge for depreciation will be:

$$\frac{\text{Cost - residual value}}{\text{Useful life}} = \frac{£1\,6,000 - £5,500}{3 \text{ years}}$$

$$= £3,500 \text{ per year}$$

BPP
LEARNING MEDIA

At the end of each year of the van's life this is how it will appear at its net book value in the statement of financial position (SFP):

| | | | |
|---|---|---|---|
| End of Year 1 | £16,000 – £3,500 | = | £12,500 |
| End of Year 2 | £16,000 – (2 × £3,500) | = | £9,000 |
| End of Year 3 | £16,000 – (3 × £3,500) | = | £5,500 |

---

## Task 2

A business has purchased a non-current asset for £22,000 which has a useful life of four years and a residual value at the end of this period of £9,000.

What is the annual depreciation charge using the straight line method?

£ [          ]

What is the carrying amount of the asset after two years?

£ [          ]

---

## REDUCING BALANCE METHOD

The aim of the REDUCING BALANCE METHOD of depreciation is to have a higher charge for depreciation in the early years of the non-current asset's life and a lower charge in later years. This reflects the pattern of consumption or loss of value to the business of certain assets, such as motor vehicles, that tend to lose more of their value in the early years of their life. Note that the value to the business may be quite different from any market value an asset may have.

To calculate the annual depreciation charge using the reducing balance method we use a fixed percentage rate.

- In the first year the percentage is applied to the **cost** of the asset
- In subsequent years the percentage is applied to the asset's **carrying amount** as at the beginning of the period

Determining the percentage rate is a complicated calculation which you do not need to carry out – you will be given the percentage rate to use.

This method is sometimes referred to as the DIMINISHING BALANCE method.

---

## HOW IT WORKS

N W Traders has purchased a motor van for deliveries for £16,000 which it will use for three years and then sell for £5,500.

This van is to be depreciated under the reducing balance method at a rate of 30% per annum.

|  | £ | Annual depreciation charge £ |
|---|---|---|
| Original cost | 16,000 | |
| Year 1 depreciation £16,000 × 30% | 4,800 | 4,800 |
| NBV at end of Year 1 | 11,200 | |
| Year 2 depreciation £11,200 × 30% | 3,360 | 3,360 |
| NBV at end of Year 2 | 7,840 | |
| Year 3 depreciation £7,840 × 30% | 2,352 | 2,352 |
| NBV at end of Year 3 | 5,488 | |

Note that:

- The depreciation charge is higher in year 1 and subsequently decreases

- The calculations have brought the carrying amount of the asset down to approximately its residual value, £5,500, at the end of its three year useful life

## Task 3

A business has purchased a non-current asset for £22,000 which has a useful life of four years and a residual value at the end of this period of £9,000. It is to be depreciated using the reducing balance method at a rate of 20%.

What is the depreciation charge for each year of the asset's life, and the asset's carrying amount at the end of each year?

| | Depreciation charge £ | Carrying amount £ |
|---|---|---|
| Year 1 | 4 400 | 17, 600 |
| Year 2 | 3 520 | 14, 080 |
| Year 3 | 2 816 | 11, 264 |
| Year 4 | 2 253 | 9 011 |

Nearest £

## CHOICE OF METHOD

Both FRS 15 and IAS 16 allow businesses to choose the method of depreciation that is most appropriate to their non-current assets. Most businesses will choose different depreciation methods and rates for different types of asset.

- The **straight line** method is often used for assets that are likely to be kept for their entire useful lives and to have low expected resale values, such as machinery and office furniture and fittings

- The **reducing balance** method is usually found to be more appropriate for assets such as motor vehicles that lose more of their value to the business in early years and are likely to be sold before the end of their possible lives.

## DEPRECIATION POLICIES

Once the depreciation method and rates have been set they should be kept under review but should only be changed for a good reason. This is in order to comply with the accounting concept of **consistency** which states that items in the accounting records should be dealt with in the same manner each year.

### Depreciation on classes of asset

In the examples so far we have seen how to calculate the depreciation for an individual non-current asset by looking at its cost, its useful life and its residual value. You also need to be able to calculate the depreciation charge for the year for an entire class of assets. In order to do this in an assessment you will be told the depreciation policy for that class of non-current asset.

## HOW IT WORKS

Harris Incorporated has a number of different classes of non-current asset, including buildings and motor vehicles. The depreciation policies for these two classes of asset are:

- Buildings – straight line method at 2% per year
- Motor vehicles – 25% using the reducing balance method

To determine the depreciation charge for each class of non-current asset for the year certain information is required.

- As the buildings are being depreciated using the straight line method we need to know the cost of the buildings at the end of the year. Let us suppose this is £100,000.

- For the motor vehicles the policy is to use the reducing balance method and therefore we need the figure for the carrying amount of the motor vehicles at the end of the year. In this case let us suppose this is £40,000.

The depreciation charge for the year for each class of non-current assets is therefore:

| | | | |
|---|---|---|---|
| Buildings | £100,000 × 2% | = | £2,000 |
| Motor vehicles | £ 40,000 × 25% | = | £10,000 |

## Assets purchased during the year

If non-current assets are purchased part of the way through the year then the business has a choice: it can depreciate the new asset for the whole year or it can depreciate it only for the period since it was purchased.

This choice will be set out in the depreciation policy. The two alternatives are normally expressed as follows:

**'A full year's depreciation charge is made in the year of acquisition and none in the year of disposal'** – this means that no matter when the new asset was purchased during the year, a full year's depreciation is charged in that year, but no charge is made in the year of disposal irrespective of when in that year the asset was disposed of.

**'Depreciation is charged at 10% per annum on cost'** – the words 'per annum' show that the depreciation charge must be based on the number of months in the year that the asset has actually been owned.

## HOW IT WORKS

Two businesses purchase a piece of machinery on 1 April 20XX for £20,000 and both businesses have an accounting period which runs from 1 January to 31 December.

Business A depreciates its machinery at 10% using the straight line method with a full year's charge in the year of acquisition.

Business B depreciates its machinery at 10% per annum on the straight line basis.

BPP
LEARNING MEDIA

The depreciation charges for each business in the year of acquisition for this machinery is:

A    £20,000 × 10%                    =    £2,000
B    £20,000 × 10% × 9/12         =    £1,500 (as the asset has only been
                                                            owned for 9 months of the year)

## ACCOUNTING FOR DEPRECIATION

Accounting entries for the annual depreciation charge reflect the treatment of depreciation that we have already discussed.

Each year the income statement is charged with the DEPRECIATION CHARGE for the year. This is a **debit in the depreciation charge account**.

ACCUMULATED DEPRECIATION that has been charged to date on the non-current assets is deducted from their cost to give the carrying amount – this accumulated depreciation is sometimes known as the PROVISION FOR DEPRECIATION. Therefore the depreciation for the year is entered as **a credit in the accumulated depreciation account**.

Debit   Depreciation charge account
Credit  Accumulated depreciation account

Note that there are no entries to the non-current asset at cost account. This contains the original cost and it is not changed.

## HOW IT WORKS

We shall now return to N W Traders who purchased a motor van for deliveries for £16,000 with a useful life of three years and a residual value of £5,500. The annual depreciation charge calculated using the straight line method is:

$$\frac{£16,000 - 5,500}{3 \text{ years}} = £3,500$$

We will record this in the ledger accounts for each of the three years (in practice the book of prime entry to record these entries is the journal).

### Year 1

The depreciation charge of £3,500 is debited to the depreciation charge account and credited to the accumulated depreciation account.

**Depreciation charge**

|                              | £     |     | £ |
|------------------------------|-------|-----|---|
| Accumulated depreciation     | 3,500 |     |   |

### Accumulated depreciation

| | £ | | £ |
|---|---|---|---|
| | | Depreciation charge | 3,500 |

At the end of Year 1 the depreciation charge account will be cleared to the income statement as it is an expense item, so there will be no remaining balance on the account.

### Depreciation charge

| | £ | | £ |
|---|---|---|---|
| Accumulated depreciation | 3,500 | Income statement | 3,500 |

The accumulated depreciation account however will appear in the statement of financial position and the balance will remain as the opening balance for Year 2.

### Accumulated depreciation

| | £ | | £ |
|---|---|---|---|
| Year 1 Balance c/d | 3,500 | Year 1 Depreciation charge | 3,500 |
| | | Year 2 Balance b/d | 3,500 |

In the financial statements at the end of Year 1 the depreciation is treated as follows:

**Income statement Year 1**

| | £ |
|---|---|
| Expenses: | |
| Depreciation charge | 3,500 |

**Statement of financial position Year 1**

| Non-current assets | Cost | Depreciation | Carrying amount |
|---|---|---|---|
| | £ | £ | £ |
| Motor vehicles | 16,000 | 3,500 | 12,500 |

### Year 2

Year 2's depreciation charge of £3,500 is debited to the depreciation charge account and credited to the accumulated depreciation account.

### Depreciation charge

| | £ | | £ |
|---|---|---|---|
| Accumulated depreciation | 3,500 | | |

### Accumulated depreciation

|  | £ |  | £ |
|---|---|---|---|
|  |  | Year 2 Balance b/d | 3,500 |
|  |  | Year 2 Depreciation charge | 3,500 |

At the end of Year 2 the depreciation charge account is once again cleared to the income statement so there is no remaining balance on it.

### Depreciation charge

|  | £ |  | £ |
|---|---|---|---|
| Accumulated depreciation | 3,500 | Income statement | 3,500 |

The accumulated depreciation account however will appear in the statement of financial position as the provision for depreciation, and its balance will remain as the opening balance for Year 3.

### Provision for depreciation

|  | £ |  | £ |
|---|---|---|---|
| Year 2 Balance c/d | 7,000 | Year 2 Balance b/d | 3,500 |
|  |  | Year 2 Depreciation charge | 3,500 |
|  | 7,000 |  | 7,000 |
|  |  | Year 3 Balance b/d | 7,000 |

In the financial statements at the end of Year 2 depreciation is treated as follows:

**Income statement Year 2**

| Expenses: | £ |
|---|---|
| Depreciation charge | 3,500 |

**Statement of financial position Year 2**

| Non-current assets | Cost | Depreciation | Carrying amount |
|---|---|---|---|
|  | £ | £ | £ |
| Motor vehicles | 16,000 | 7,000 | 9,000 |

### Year 3

The depreciation charge of £3,500 is debited to the depreciation charge account and credited to the accumulated depreciation account.

### Depreciation charge

|  | £ |  | £ |
|---|---|---|---|
| Accumulated depreciation | 3,500 |  |  |

**Accumulated depreciation**

| | £ | | £ |
|---|---|---|---|
| | | Year 3 Balance b/d | 7,000 |
| | | Depreciation charge | 3,500 |

At the end of the year the depreciation charge account is cleared to the income statement so there is no remaining balance on it.

**Depreciation charge**

| | £ | | £ |
|---|---|---|---|
| Accumulated depreciation | 3,500 | Income statement | 3,500 |

The accumulated depreciation account however will appear in the statement of financial position and the balance will remain.

**Accumulated depreciation**

| | £ | | £ |
|---|---|---|---|
| Year 3 Balance c/d | 10,500 | Year 3 Balance b/d | 7,000 |
| | _____ | Year 3 Depreciation charge | 3,500 |
| | 10,500 | | 10,500 |
| | | Year 4 Balance b/d | 10,500 |

In the financial statements at the end of Year 3 the depreciation is treated as follows:

**Income statement Year 3**

| | £ |
|---|---|
| Expenses: | |
| Depreciation charge | 3,500 |

**Statement of financial position 3**

| Non-current assets | Cost | Depreciation | Carrying amount |
|---|---|---|---|
| | £ | £ | £ |
| Motor vehicles | 16,000 | 10,500 | 5,500 |

## Task 4

A business which has just completed its first year trading has machinery costing £120,000. The depreciation policy is to depreciate machinery at the rate of 20% using the straight line method.

Show the ledger entries for the depreciation for the first year and the entries in the income statement and statement of financial position at the end of the year.

**Depreciation charge**

| | £ | | £ |
|---|---|---|---|
| A. Depn | 24 000 | = > | 24000 |

**Accumulated depreciation**

| | £ | | £ |
|---|---|---|---|
| | 24000 | charge | 24,000 |

**Income statement**

| Expenses: | £ |
|---|---|
| Depn | 24000 |

**Statement of financial position**

| Non-current assets | Cost | Depreciation | Carrying amount |
|---|---|---|---|
| | £ | £ | £ |
| Machinery | 120,000 | 24,000 | 96,000 |

## DEPRECIATION AND THE NON-CURRENT ASSET REGISTER

You will remember from Chapter 3 that all details for all non-current assets are kept in the non-current asset register. This includes entries for the annual depreciation charge and accumulated depreciation on each asset.

# HOW IT WORKS

Kendall Engineering purchased a new machine, the FD254, from Leyland Machinery for £120,000 on 1 March 20X7. The machine is to be depreciated using the reducing balance method at a rate of 30% per annum with a full year's charge in the year of purchase. The business's accounting year ends on 31 December.

It is now 31 December 20X7 and the entries relating to depreciation for the first year must be made. The charge is £120,000 x 30% = £36,000

| NON-CURRENT ASSET REGISTER | | | | | | |
|---|---|---|---|---|---|---|
| Non-current asset number | | | 02635 | | | |
| Description | | | Machine FD254 | | | |
| Location | | | Factory | | | |
| Supplier | | | Leyland Machinery | | | |
| Acquisition date 20X7 | Cost £ | Depreciation charge for the year £ | Accumulated depreciation at end of the year | Carrying amount at end of year £ | Disposal proceeds | Disposal date |
| 1 Mar | 120,000 | | | | | |
| 31 Dec | | 36,000 | 36,000 | 84,000 | | |

## Task 5

The reducing balance method of accounting for depreciation gives the same amount of depreciation charged each year.

True ☐

False ☑

# CHAPTER OVERVIEW

- Depreciation is a method of applying the accruals concept by charging some of the cost of non-current assets to the income statement each year that they are used by the business

- The amount to be charged is an estimate of the amount of the cost that has been 'consumed' in the accounting period – this is estimated by calculating the depreciation charge either under the straight line method or the reducing balance method

- The cost of the non-current asset minus the depreciation charged to date is known as the carrying amount (IAS) or net book value (UK GAAP)

- The straight line method of depreciation ensures that the same amount of depreciation is charged for each year of the asset's life

- Straight line depreciation is calculated as the cost of the asset less the residual value spread over the useful life of the asset

- The reducing balance method of depreciation charges a larger amount of depreciation in the early years of the asset's life and a lower amount in the later years of its life

- Reducing balance depreciation is calculated by applying a fixed percentage to the carrying amount of the non-current asset

- Care has to be taken over the precise depreciation policy of a business – some businesses charge a full year's depreciation on an asset no matter when it was purchased during the year, while other businesses charge depreciation only for the months that the asset has been owned in the first year

- When accounting for the depreciation charge it is debited to the depreciation charge account and credited to the accumulated depreciation account

- The depreciation charge account is cleared as an expense to the income statement at the end of each year but the balance on the accumulated depreciation account is carried down as the opening balance for the following period

- The depreciation charge is shown as an expense in the income statement

- The balance on the accumulated depreciation account is shown in the statement of financial position where it is deducted from the cost of the non-current asset to arrive at the carrying amount

- The depreciation method, rate, expense for the year, accumulated depreciation and carrying amount are all recorded in the non-current asset register

## Keywords

**Depreciation** – the annual charge to the income statement to reflect the use of the non-current asset during the period

**Carrying amount** – the cost of the non-current asset minus the depreciation charged to date over one or more years

**Depreciation policies** – the stated methods and rates of depreciation for a business

**Straight line method** – a method of calculating the depreciation charge to give the same amount of depreciation charge each year

**Useful life** – the period over which the business estimates that the non-current asset will be used

**Residual value** – the anticipated resale value of the non-current asset at the end of its useful life to the business

**Reducing balance method** – method of calculating depreciation so that a larger amount is charged in the earlier years and smaller amounts in subsequent years

**Depreciation charge** – the amount of depreciation charged to the income statement each year

**Accumulated depreciation** – the statement of financial position ledger account that records the accumulated depreciation to date on a non-current asset

**Provision for depreciation** – this is another name for the statement of financial position accumulated depreciation account

# TEST YOUR LEARNING

**Test 1**

The main accounting concept underlying the depreciation of non-current assets is the | materiality/consistency/accruals | concept.

**Test 2**

A business has a machine that was purchased on 1 January 20X7 costing £11,500 with a useful life of five years and a residual value of £2,500. The policy is to depreciate machinery using the straight line method.

What is the depreciation charge for the year ended 31 December 20X8?

£ [          ]

What is the carrying amount of the machine at 31 December 20X8?

£ [          ]

**Test 3**

A business owns a car that was purchased on 1 January 20X7 for £16,400. It has a useful life of three years and a residual value of £4,500 at that date. The car is to be depreciated at 35% each year using the reducing balance method.

What is the depreciation charge for the year ended 31 December 20X8?

£ [          ]

What is the carrying amount of the car at 31 December 20X8?

£ [          ]

**Test 4**

A business has machinery with a cost of £240,000 and depreciation to date at the start of the year of £135,000. The policy is to depreciate the machinery at the rate of 30% using the reducing balance method.

What is this year's depreciation charge?

£ [          ]

**Test 5**

A business purchased a delivery lorry for £24,000 on 1 June 20XX which is to be depreciated using the straight line method at a rate of 20% per annum.

What is the depreciation charge for the accounting year ending 31 December 20XX?

£ [          ]

# chapter 5:
# DISPOSAL OF NON-CURRENT ASSETS

## chapter coverage 📖

Having considered the acquisition of non-current assets and their accounting treatment during their useful lives we must now consider the process of selling a non-current asset when it is of no more use to the business. In this chapter we also consider the relationship between the non-current asset register and the actual non-current assets held. At regular intervals the details of assets in the non-current asset register should be physically checked to the actual assets held on the premises. The topics covered are:

- ✍ Accounting for disposals of non-current assets

- ✍ Profit and loss on disposal

- ✍ Part exchange deals

- ✍ Disposals and the non-current asset register

- ✍ Physical checks of assets to the non-current asset register

## ACCOUNTING FOR DISPOSALS

When a non-current asset is sold there are two effects on the accounts of the business:

- All accounting entries for the asset must be removed from the accounting records

- Any profit or loss on the disposal of the asset must be calculated and accounted for

With regard to the general ledger all of this can be done in one ledger account – the DISPOSALS ACCOUNT.

The first step is to use the journal to remove the cost of the asset and the accumulated depreciation for that asset from the ledger accounts – these amounts are taken out of the relevant accounts and put into the disposals account:

Debit    Disposals account
Credit   Non-current asset at cost account

- with the original cost of the asset

Debit    Accumulated depreciation account
Credit   Disposals account

- with the accumulated depreciation on the asset up to the date of disposal

This has removed all traces of the asset sold from the general ledger accounts – now we must deal with the sale proceeds:

Debit    Bank/cash or Sales ledger control account
Credit   Disposals account

- with the sale proceeds – if a cheque is received then the bank account will be debited, if cash is received the cash account will be debited, and if the sale is made on credit then the sales ledger control account will be debited

The final step is to calculate the balance on the disposals account. This will be either a PROFIT ON DISPOSAL if there is a credit balance or a LOSS ON DISPOSAL if there is a debit balance. This will be credited to the income statement as income if it is a profit, or debited as an expense if it is a loss.

# HOW IT WORKS

Harris Incorporated purchased a machine on 1 January 20X6 with a cheque for £15,000. This was to be depreciated using the straight line method at a rate of 20% per annum. The machine was sold for £5,000 on 31 December 20X8. The buyer paid by cheque.

Before we look at the accounting entries for this sale we will examine what has happened here. The machine was owned for the whole of 20X6, 20X7 and 20X8 and therefore had three years of depreciation charges at £3,000 (£15,000 × 20%) per annum.

|  | £ |
|---|---|
| Cost of machine | 15,000 |
| Accumulated depreciation | 9,000 |
| Carrying amount at 31 December 20X8 | 6,000 |
| Sale proceeds | 5,000 |
| Loss on sale | 1,000 |

At the date of the disposal the machine had a carrying amount of £6,000 but was sold for only £5,000. Therefore a loss was made on the disposal of £1,000.

Now we will consider the accounting entries:

Debit   Disposals account
Credit   Non-current asset at cost account

- **with the original cost of the asset**

**Machine at cost account**

|  |  | £ |  |  | £ |
|---|---|---|---|---|---|
| 20X6 |  |  | 20X8 |  |  |
| 1 Jan | Bank/cash | 15,000 | 31 Dec | Disposals | 15,000 |

**Disposals account**

|  |  | £ |  | £ |
|---|---|---|---|---|
| 20X8 |  |  |  |  |
| 31 Dec | Machine | 15,000 |  |  |

Debit   Accumulated depreciation account
Credit   Disposals account

- **with the accumulated depreciation on the asset up to the date of sale**

### Accumulated depreciation account

| | | £ | | | £ |
|---|---|---|---|---|---|
| **20X6** | | | **20X6** | | |
| 31 Dec | Balance c/d | 3,000 | 31 Dec | Depreciation | 3,000 |
| | | 3,000 | | | 3,000 |
| **20X7** | | | **20X7** | | |
| 31 Dec | Balance c/d | 6,000 | 1 Jan | Balance b/d | 3,000 |
| | | 6,000 | 31 Dec | Depreciation | 3,000 |
| | | | | | 6,000 |
| **20X8** | | | **20X8** | | |
| 31 Dec | Disposals | 9,000 | 1 Jan | Balance b/d | 6,000 |
| | | 9,000 | 31 Dec | Depreciation | 3,000 |
| | | | | | 9,000 |

### Disposals account

| | | £ | | | £ |
|---|---|---|---|---|---|
| **20X8** | | | **20X8** | | |
| 31 Dec | Machine | 15,000 | 31 Dec | Accumulated depreciation | 9,000 |

Debit   Bank/cash
Credit   Disposals account

- **with the sale proceeds**

### Disposals account

| | | £ | | | £ |
|---|---|---|---|---|---|
| **20X8** | | | **20X8** | | |
| 31 Dec | Machine | 15,000 | 31 Dec | Accumulated depreciation | 9,000 |
| | | | 31 Dec | Bank/cash – proceeds | 5,000 |

Finally, balance the disposals account to find the profit or the loss on disposal:

### Disposals account

| | | £ | | | £ |
|---|---|---|---|---|---|
| **20X8** | | | **20X8** | | |
| 31 Dec | Machine | 15,000 | 31 Dec | Accumulated depreciation | 9,000 |
| | | | 31 Dec | Bank/cash – proceeds | 5,000 |
| | | | 31 Dec | Loss | 1,000 |
| | | 15,000 | | | 15,000 |

To complete the double entry for this loss on disposal there is a credit in the disposals account and a debit (an expense) to the income statement.

# Task 1

*20o7, 2008 = 2 yrs*

A business purchased a motor car for £11,200 on 1 January 20X7 and this car was sold for £5,000 on 31 December 20X8. The depreciation policy for the motor car was 30% per annum on the reducing balance basis, with a full year's charge in the year of disposal.

(a) Calculate the carrying amount of the car on 31 December 20X8

£ [          ]

(b) Determine any profit or loss that has been made on the disposal

£ [          ]

(c) Write up the motor car at cost account, the accumulated depreciation on the motor car account and the disposals account

### Motor car at cost account

|  | £ |  | £ |
|---|---|---|---|
| Bank | 11,200 | Disposal | 11.200 |
|  |  |  |  |
|  |  |  |  |

### Accumulated depreciation on the motor car account

|  | £ |  | £ |  |
|---|---|---|---|---|
|  |  |  | 3360 | 7840 |
|  |  |  | 2352 | 5488 |
|  |  |  |  |  |
|  |  |  |  |  |

### Disposals account

|  | £ |  | £ |  |
|---|---|---|---|---|
| Machine | 11,200 | Depn | 5712 | 10712 |
|  |  | Bank Proceeds | 5,000 |  |
|  |  | Loss | 488 |  |
|  |  |  |  |  |

## Date of disposal

Some care must be taken with the depreciation policy details when an asset is disposed of part way through the year. Depreciation should be charged on the asset up to the date of disposal according to the depreciation policy of the organisation.

# HOW IT WORKS

Two businesses each purchase a machine on 1 August 20X6 for £3,600. Both businesses have an accounting period which runs from 1 January to 31 December. Both businesses sell their asset on 31 October 20X8 for £2,800.

Business A depreciates its machinery at 10% on the straight line basis with a full year's charge in the year of acquisition and none in the year of disposal.

Business B depreciates its machinery at 10% per annum on the straight line basis.

The profit or loss on disposal for each business is:

|  | Business A £ |  | Business B £ |
|---|---|---|---|
| Cost | 3,600 |  | 3,600 |
| Depreciation – |  |  |  |
| to 31 December 20X6 | (360) | × 5/12 | (150) |
| to 31 December 20X7 | (360) |  | (360) |
| to 31 October 20X8 | – | × 10/12 | (300) |
| Carrying amount | 2,880 |  | 2,790 |
| Sale proceeds | 2,800 |  | 2,800 |
| Loss on disposal | 80 | Profit | 10 |

# PROFIT AND LOSS ON DISPOSAL

A profit on disposal means that the proceeds received on the disposal of the asset are greater than the carrying amount of the asset at the date of disposal.

The aim of depreciation is to charge the cost of the asset (less its residual value if any) to the income statement over its useful life. Consequently, if depreciation had been correctly charged over the asset's useful life, the carrying amount of the asset at the date of disposal would be equal to the sales proceeds (ie its actual residual value). In practice, of course, the depreciation charged is only the business's best estimate and therefore it is usual for either a profit or loss to arise on the disposal.

In effect a profit on disposal means that the asset has been OVER-DEPRECIATED i.e. the asset's cost has been reduced by depreciation to a carrying amount that is less than its actual residual value.

Similarly a loss on disposal means that the proceeds received on the disposal of the asset are less than the carrying amount of the asset at the date of disposal. Accordingly, a loss on disposal means that the asset has been UNDER-DEPRECIATED i.e. the asset's cost has not been sufficiently reduced by depreciation, and its carrying amount at the date of disposal is more than its actual residual value.

## PART EXCHANGE OF AN ASSET

In many cases when a business is selling a non-current asset it will be in order to replace it with a new or newer model. This is often done by means of a PART EXCHANGE, most frequently in the case of motor vehicles.

This means that when the new asset is purchased the old asset is taken as part of the purchase price – a PART EXCHANGE ALLOWANCE is given on the old asset in order to reduce the cash price of the new asset. This part exchange allowance is therefore:

- Part of the cost of the new asset (as we saw in Chapter 3) as well as the cash that is also paid
- Effectively the disposal proceeds of the old asset

There are no cash proceeds for the sale of the old asset but the part exchange allowance is treated as the sale proceeds as follows:

Debit   Non-current asset at cost account for the new asset
Credit   Disposals account

- **with the part exchange allowance.**

The asset's cost and accumulated depreciation are removed from their respective accounts and entered into the disposals account as well, as in a normal disposal for cash.

The credit to the disposals account allows us to calculate a profit or loss on disposal by comparing the part exchange allowance with the carrying amount.

The debit to the non-current asset at cost account recognises that the part exchange allowance is part of the cost of the new asset together with the remainder of the cash cost, as we saw in Chapter 3.

## HOW IT WORKS

Harris Incorporated is buying a new car for an employee with a list price of £12,000. The car dealer has agreed to take the employee's old car in part exchange with a part exchange allowance of £3,800.

The old car cost £13,500 on 1 January 20X6. At the date of disposal, 30 June 20X8, there was accumulated depreciation charged to it of £9,250.

The profit or loss on disposal of the old car can first be calculated:

|  | £ |
|---|---|
| Cost | 13,500 |
| Accumulated depreciation | 9,250 |
| Carrying amount | 4,250 |
| Part exchange allowance | 3,800 |
| Loss on disposal | 450 |

The cash to be paid for the new car can also be calculated:

|  | £ |
|---|---|
| List price | 12,000 |
| Less: part exchange allowance | (3,800) |
| Cash payable | 8,200 |

Now we will deal with the entries in the ledger accounts:

### Motor car at cost account

|  |  | £ |  |  | £ |
|---|---|---|---|---|---|
| 20X6 |  |  | 20X8 |  |  |
| 1 Jan | Bank/cash | 13,500 | 30 Jun | Disposals | 13,500 |
| 20X8 |  |  | 20X8 |  |  |
| 30 Jun | Bank/cash | 8,200 | 30 Jun | Balance c/d | 12,000 |
| 30 Jun | Disposals | 3,800 |  |  |  |
|  |  | 12,000 |  |  | 12,000 |
| 1 Jul | Balance b/d | 12,000 |  |  |  |

Note that the cost of the old car has been removed and taken to the disposals account and the cost of the new car in full, £12,000, has been entered into the account by making two entries, one from the bank/cash account for the cash payable and one from the disposals account for the part exchange allowance.

## Motor car accumulated depreciation account

| | | £ | | | £ |
|---|---|---|---|---|---|
| 20X8 | | | 20X8 | | |
| 30 Jun | Disposals | 9,250 | 30 Jun | Balance b/d | 9,250 |

## Disposals account

| | | £ | | | £ |
|---|---|---|---|---|---|
| 20X8 | | | 20X8 | | |
| 30 Jun | Motor car at cost | 13,500 | 30 Jun | Motor car accumulated depreciation | 9,250 |
| | | | 30 Jun | Motor car at cost – allowance | 3,800 |
| | | | 30 Jun | Loss on disposal | 450 |
| | | 13,500 | | | 13,500 |

# Task 2

A business purchased a car on 1 March 20X6 for £10,000. This car was part exchanged for a new one with a total list price of £11,000 on 31 May 20X8. At that date the old car had had £5,500 of accumulated depreciation charged to it. The part exchange allowance given on the old car was £4,800.

Show the accounting entries necessary to record the sale of the old car and purchase of the new car.

### Car at cost account

| | £ | | £ |
|---|---|---|---|
| Bank car 1 | 10,000 | Disposal | 10,000 |
| Bank car 2 | 6,200 | | |
| Money from Disposal | 4,800 | | |
| | 21,000 | | 10,000 |
| Balance | 11,000 | | |

### Car accumulated depreciation account

| | £ | | £ |
|---|---|---|---|
| Disposal | 5500 | Balance | 5500 |
| | | | |
| | | | |

### Disposals account

| | £ | | £ |
|---|---|---|---|
| Cor 1 | 10,000 | Depn | 5500 |
| Poft | 300 | Allowance PE | 4800 |
| | 10,300 | | 10,300 |

## DISPOSALS AND THE NON-CURRENT ASSET REGISTER

We have already seen how entries should be made in the non-current asset register when an asset is purchased and in each year of its life to record the depreciation. When a non-current asset is sold the register is then completed with entries being made for the disposal proceeds and any profit or loss on disposal. Once the profit or loss on disposal has been recorded in the register the asset is effectively removed from the register.

## HOW IT WORKS

We saw in Chapter 4 that an FD254 machine was purchased by Kendall Engineering for £120,000 on 1 March 20X7. It is being depreciated at 30% reducing balance with a full year's charge in the year of acquisition but none in the year of disposal. Let us now complete the picture by supposing that this machine was sold on 1 February 20X9 for £50,000. Kendall Engineering has a 31 December year end.

In the register we need to record the disposal and remove the asset by entering:

- The date of disposal (1 Feb 20X9)
- The disposal proceeds (£50,000) and
- The profit or loss on disposal (£50,000 – £58,800 = £8,800 loss)

| Non-current asset register | | | | | | |
|---|---|---|---|---|---|---|
| Non-current asset number | | 02635 | | | | |
| Description | | Machine FD254 | | | | |
| Location | | Factory | | | | |
| Supplier | | Leyland Machinery | | | | |
| Date | Cost £ | Depreciation charge for the year £ | Accumulated depreciation at end of the year | Carrying amount at end of year £ | Disposal proceeds | Profit or loss on disposal £ |
| 20X7<br>1 Mar | 120,000 | | | | | |
| 31 Dec | | 36,000 | 36,000 | 84,000 | | |
| 31 Dec<br>20X8 | | 25,200 | 61,200 | 58,800 | 31 Dec<br>20X8 | 31 Dec<br>20X8 |
| 31 Dec<br>20X9 | | | | | 50,000 | (8,800) |

## Task 3

On 1 May 20X5 Kendall Engineering purchased from Leyland Machinery a fork lift truck type XC355 which is used in the warehouse for £34,000. The truck was given the asset number 24116 and was estimated to have a useful life of four years and a residual value of £6,250.

The truck is depreciated at 30% using the reducing balance method with a full year's charge in the year of acquisition and none in the year of disposal. The business's year end is 31 December. The truck was sold on 20 March 20X8 for £10,500.

Make all the entries required for this truck in the non-current asset register given below.

**NON-CURRENT ASSET REGISTER**
**Non-current asset number** 2 4116
**Description** FLT
**Location** Warehouse
**Supplier** Leyland Machiney

| Date | Cost £ | Expected life (years) | Estimated residual value | Depreciation method | Depreciation rate | Depreciation charge for the year £ | Acc dep at end of the year £ | Carrying amount at end of year £ | Disposal proceeds £ | Profit or loss on disposal £ |
|------|--------|----------------------|-------------------------|--------------------|-------------------|-----------------------------------|------------------------------|----------------------------------|--------------------|------------------------------|
| **20X7** 1 Mar | 120,000 | 5 | 20,000 | | | | | | | |

## CHECKING PHYSICAL ASSETS TO THE REGISTER

The main reason for keeping the non-current asset register is to help in the control of the non-current assets of a business. These are often very expensive items and in some cases, such as laptops, are also easily portable. Once a non-current asset has been purchased by the business it is important to check that it is still physically within the business on a fairly regular basis.

Physical checks can be made in two ways:

- Check that every non-current asset in the register still exists somewhere in the business

- Check that every non-current asset in the business is recorded in the register.

It is unlikely that all the business's non-current assets will be physically checked at the same time in this manner but most businesses will have a rolling policy of checking categories of asset regularly so that all assets are checked once a year.

This physical check of the assets may show that there are some unusual features or discrepancies:

- Some assets that exist in the business may not be in the register – this means that when the asset was purchased no entries were made for the asset in the register

- Some entries in the register may not be up to date – for instance, the depreciation charge each year may not have been entered

- There may be no physical asset when one is recorded in the register – this may mean that an asset has been sold or scrapped but the disposal has not been recorded in the register, or it may mean the asset has been destroyed or stolen.

Any unusual features or discrepancies found when carrying out this physical check must be reported to management to be dealt with appropriately.

---

### Task 4

Which of the following reasons explains why an asset that is in use by the business does not appear in the non-current asset register?

A   The asset has been stolen.

B   Depreciation has not been charged.

C   The asset's carrying amount is zero.

D   No entry was made in the register when the asset was purchased.   ✓

---

BPP
LEARNING MEDIA

# CHAPTER OVERVIEW

- It is as important to control and authorise the disposal of non-current assets as it is their acquisition

- Accounting for the disposal takes place in the disposals account by entering the original cost and accumulated depreciation on the asset being disposed of together with the disposal proceeds

- The final balance on the disposal account will be either a profit on disposal – to be credited to the income statement – or a loss on disposal, to be debited to the income statement

- A profit on disposal represents over–depreciation and a loss on disposal represents under-depreciation

- In some cases a non-current asset will be disposed of by it being part exchanged in the purchase of a replacement asset – the part exchange allowance is treated as the disposal proceeds of the old asset and as part of the cost of the new asset

- When a non-current asset is disposed of the date of disposal, proceeds and the profit or loss should be recorded in the non-current asset register

- On a regular basis the physical non-current assets that a business has should be checked to the entries in the non-current asset register – any discrepancies should be reported to the appropriate person in the organisation for any required action to be taken

## Keywords

**Disposals account** – the ledger account used to record all aspects of the disposal of the non-current asset

**Profit or loss on disposal** – the difference between the carrying amount of the asset at the date of disposal and the sale proceeds

**Over-depreciation** – results in a profit on disposal

**Under-depreciation** – results in a loss on disposal

**Part exchange** – a method of disposal whereby the old asset is given in part exchange for a new asset

**Part exchange allowance** – the value assigned to the old asset being part exchanged by the supplier of the new asset

## TEST YOUR LEARNING

### Test 1

A business purchases a computer on 1 April 20X5 for £2,200. This is then sold on 14 May 20X8 for £200. The depreciation policy is to depreciate computers on a reducing balance basis at a rate of 40% with a full year's charge in the year of acquisition and none in the year of disposal. The business's accounting year ends on 31 December.

(a) Calculate the profit or loss on the sale of this computer.

£ [            ]

(b) Show all of the accounting entries for this computer from the date of purchase through to the date of sale.

**Computer at cost account**

|  | £ |  | £ |
|---|---|---|---|
|  |  |  |  |
|  |  |  |  |
|  |  |  |  |

**Computer accumulated depreciation account**

|  | £ |  | £ |
|---|---|---|---|
|  |  |  |  |
|  |  |  |  |
|  |  |  |  |
|  |  |  |  |
|  |  |  |  |
|  |  |  |  |
|  |  |  |  |
|  |  |  |  |

**Disposals account**

|  | £ |  | £ |
|---|---|---|---|
|  |  |  |  |
|  |  |  |  |
|  |  |  |  |

## Test 2

A business purchases a machine on 1 October 20X6 for £7,200 and this machine is then sold on 31 July 20X8 for £3,800. The machine is depreciated at a rate of 25% per annum on the straight line basis. The business's year end is 30 November.

(a) Calculate the profit or loss on the sale of this machine.

£ [                    ]

(b) Show all of the accounting entries for this machine from the date of purchase through to the date of sale.

### Machine at cost account

| | £ | | £ |
|---|---|---|---|
| | | | |
| | | | |
| | | | |

### Machine accumulated depreciation account

| | £ | | £ |
|---|---|---|---|
| | | | |
| | | | |
| | | | |
| | | | |
| | | | |
| | | | |

### Disposals account

| | £ | | £ |
|---|---|---|---|
| | | | |
| | | | |
| | | | |
| | | | |

## Test 3

(a) A loss on disposal can also be described as

over-depreciation/under- depreciation.

(b) A profit on disposal can also be described as

over-depreciation/under- depreciation.

### Test 4

A business is purchasing a new motor van with a list price of £16,700 on 30 April 20X8. The car dealer has agreed to take an old motor van in part exchange requiring the business to pay only £12,200 for the new van. The old van had originally cost £13,600 on 1 July 20X5 and the accumulated depreciation on this van at 30 April 20X8 totalled £9,000.

Show the accounting entries required in the ledger accounts on 30 April 20X8 to deal with the purchase of this new van and the part exchange of the old van.

**Van at cost account**

|  | £ |  | £ |
|---|---|---|---|
|  |  |  |  |
|  |  |  |  |
|  |  |  |  |
|  |  |  |  |
|  |  |  |  |

**Van accumulated depreciation account**

|  | £ |  | £ |
|---|---|---|---|
|  |  |  |  |
|  |  |  |  |

**Disposals account**

|  | £ |  | £ |
|---|---|---|---|
|  |  |  |  |
|  |  |  |  |
|  |  |  |  |

### Test 5

A business purchases a computer with a serial number 1036525 for £4,800 from Timing Computers Ltd on 1 March 20X6. The computer is allocated an internal non-current asset number 10435 and is to be used in the sales department.

The computer is estimated to have a four year useful life and a residual value at the end of that period of just £600. It is to be depreciated using the reducing balance method at a rate of 40% with a full year's charge in the year of acquisition and none in the year of disposal. The business's year end is 31 July.

On 27 June 20X8 the computer was sold for £700.

Record all of these details on the non-current asset register given.

BPP
LEARNING MEDIA

**NON-CURRENT ASSET REGISTER**
**Non-current asset number**
**Description**
**Location**
**Supplier**

| Date | Cost £ | Expected life (years) | Estimated residual value | Depreciation method | Depreciation rate | Depreciation charge for the year £ | Acc dep at end of the year £ | Carrying amount at end of year £ | Disposal proceeds £ | Profit or loss on disposal £ |
|---|---|---|---|---|---|---|---|---|---|---|
| **20X7** 1 Mar | 120,000 | 5 | 20,000 | | | | | | | |

# chapter 6:
# ACCRUALS AND PREPAYMENTS

─── **chapter coverage** 📖 ───

In this chapter we consider the accounting treatment of expenses and income, in particular in the context of the accounting concept of accruals. The topics that we cover are:

✍ The accruals concept

✍ Accounting for accruals of expenses

✍ Accounting for prepayments of expenses

✍ Accounting for accruals of income

✍ Accounting for prepayments of income

## ACCRUALS CONCEPT

apter 2 we considered the accounting concept of accruals or matching. The basic principle of the ACCRUALS CONCEPT is that the amount of income and expense that is included in the financial statements for an accounting period should be the income earned and the expenses incurred during the period rather than the cash received or paid. In this chapter we shall start to look at the practical application of this concept to the maintenance of financial records and the preparation of financial statements.

### Sales and purchases

When sales are made then either the cash is received now or the sale is made on credit. Either way the sale is recorded as soon as it is made. If the sale is on credit then a receivable is set up and the sale is recorded in the sales account. Therefore even though the money has not yet been received the sale has been included in the ledger accounts.

In just the same way when an invoice is received from a credit supplier this is recorded as a purchase and a payable. Even though the money has not yet been paid to the supplier the purchase has been recorded.

Therefore our system for recording sales and purchases automatically applies the accruals concept.

### Expenses

The system for recording some expenses is different. Some expenses will only be recorded in the ledger accounts when the payment for the expense is made since they are first recorded in the cash book rather than the sales or purchases day book.

For example when the rent is due it is paid and the double entry is:

Debit   Rent account
Credit   Bank account

The phone bill may be paid by direct debit and the double entry is:

Debit   Phone account
Credit   Bank account

This system means that initially the only expenses that are recorded in the ledger accounts are those that have been paid rather than those that were incurred in the period.

Therefore at the end of each accounting period each expense must be considered to ensure that the full amount of that expense that has been incurred in the period is shown as the expense rather than just the amount that has been paid.

Debit - where money goes
Credit - where it comes from

BPP
LEARNING MEDIA

## ACCRUALS OF EXPENSES

An ACCRUAL is an amount of an expense that has been incurr
accounting period but the business has not yet received an invoice for it
not yet been paid for. As such it does not appear in an expense ledger account.

The accounting treatment for an accrual of expenses is as follows:

- It must be added to the balance in the expense account to ensure that all of the expense incurred in the period is included in the income statement

- It must be shown as a type of current liability, called an accrual, in the statement of financial position

---

### Task 1

A business has paid £1,110 of phone bills during the accounting year. In the new accounting period it receives a further bill for charges of £260 which relate to the old accounting year.

This will | increase/decrease | phone expenses in the old accounting year, and it will be

shown as | an asset/a liability | on the statement of financial position at

the year end.

---

All the double entry for accounting for accruals takes place within the relevant expense account.

## HOW IT WORKS

Dawn Fisher runs a business designing and selling T shirts. On 31 March 20X5 she completed her first year of trading. Her electricity account shows a debit balance of £780 but on 5 April 20X5 she receives an electricity bill for the three months to 31 March 20X5 for £410.

This must be included in her accounts for the year by increasing the electricity expense by £410 and showing a liability, an accrual, for £410 in the statement of financial position.

Step 1    We debit the electricity account with the accrual (shown as accrual carried down), adding to the expense balance

Step 2    We bring down a credit balance on the electricity account (shown as accrual brought down) which will be listed in the statement of financial position as an accrual.

BPP
LEARNING MEDIA

Step 3    We transfer the total expense for the period to the income statement

**Electricity account**

| Date | Details | £ | Date | Details | £ |
|------|---------|---|------|---------|---|
| 31 Mar | Balance b/d | 780 | 31 Mar | Income statement | 1,190 |
| 31 Mar | Accrual c/d | 410 | | | |
| | | 1,190 | | | 1,190 |
| | | | 1 Apr | Accrual b/d | 410 |

When the electricity bill is paid in the new accounting period it will be debited to the electricity account. This cancels out the accrual brought down, leaving the account with a zero balance in respect of the new accounting period. In other words: the expense has been accounted for in the old accounting period by setting up the accrual, so paying the bill has no impact on the profit or loss of the new accounting period.

**Electricity account**

| Date | Details | £ | Date | Details | £ |
|------|---------|---|------|---------|---|
| 20 Apr | Bank/cash | 410 | 1 Apr | Accrual b/d | 410 |

## Task 2    Accural

A business has a debit balance of £2,600 on its phone expense account for the year ended 31 December 20X4. On 12 January 20X5 it receives a phone bill which includes £480 of call charges for the three months ended 31 December 20X4.

Show the accounting entries necessary to deal with this bill.

Accurals    **Phone account**

| | £ | | | £ |
|---|---|---|---|---|
| | | | | |
| | | | | |
| | | | | |
| | | | | |

## PREPAYMENTS OF EXPENSES

A PREPAYMENT is the opposite of an accrual. It is an amount of an expense that has been paid in the old accounting period but that relates to the new accounting period, not the old one. As it has already been paid it will appear as part of the balance in the expense account but it does not relate to that accounting period and therefore must be removed.

The accounting treatment for a prepayment is as follows:

- It must be deducted from the balance in the expense account to ensure that only the expense incurred in the period is included in the income statement

- It must be shown as a type of current asset, called a prepayment, in the statement of financial position

As with accruals, all the double entry for accounting for prepayments takes place within the relevant expense account.

## HOW IT WORKS

Dawn paid her insurance premium of £1,200 on 30 June 20X4 in advance for the following year. The insurance account reflects this with a debit balance of £1,200 at 31 March 20X5. However only the payment for the period from 30 June 20X4 to 31 March 20X5 (9 months) actually relates to the current accounting period. The remaining three months of the premium are an expense of the new accounting period, so they must be removed from the insurance account balance at 31 March 20X5.

The amount relating to the new period – £1,200 × 3/12 = £300 – must be excluded from her accounts for the year to 31 March 20X5 by decreasing the insurance expense by £300 and showing an asset, a prepayment, for £300 in the statement of financial position.

Step 1  We credit the insurance account with the prepayment carried down, reducing the expense balance

Step 2  We bring down a debit balance on the insurance account (prepayment b/d), which will be listed in the statement of financial position as a prepayment.

Step 3  We transfer the total expense for the period to the income statement

### Insurance account

| Date | Details | £ | Date | Details | £ |
|------|---------|-----|------|---------|-----|
| 31 Mar | Balance b/d | 1,200 | 31 Mar | Income statement | 900 |
| | | | 31 Mar | Prepayment c/d | 300 |
| | | 1,200 | | | 1,200 |
| 1 Apr | Prepayment b/d | 300 | | | |

The insurance account now shows a debit balance that will be listed as a prepayment among the current assets in the statement of financial position. This balance is part of the new period's insurance expense and therefore no further adjustments are necessary.

BPP
LEARNING MEDIA

Prepayment

---

## Task 3

A business pays rent for its premises quarterly in advance. The last payment was on 1 November for the following three months for £900. The business's year end is 31 December. The balance on the rent account at 31 December is £3,200.

Make the relevant entries to account for this prepayment.

<table>
<tr><td colspan="2" align="center">**Rent account**</td><td colspan="2" align="center">Prepayment</td></tr>
<tr><td></td><td align="center">£</td><td></td><td align="right">£</td></tr>
<tr><td></td><td></td><td></td><td></td></tr>
<tr><td></td><td></td><td></td><td></td></tr>
<tr><td></td><td></td><td></td><td></td></tr>
<tr><td></td><td></td><td></td><td></td></tr>
</table>

---

## ACCRUALS OF INCOME

The main income of a business comprises its sales, and these are automatically accounted for on the accruals basis by recognising receivables for credit sales. However some businesses have other sources of miscellaneous income which must also be accounted for in accordance with the accruals concept.

An ACCRUAL OF INCOME is an amount of income that is due or receivable for the accounting period but that has not been received as at the end of the period.

The accounting treatment for an accrual of income is as follows:

- It must be added to the credit balance in the income account to ensure that all of the income due in the period is included in the income statement

- It must be shown as a type of current asset, called accrued income or income receivable, in the statement of financial position

All the double entry for accounting for accruals of income takes place within the relevant income account.

---

## HOW IT WORKS

Dawn Fisher sells some clothes made by another business and receives a commission for the amounts that she sells. The commission received for the year to 31 March 20X5 has been £2,300 but there is a further £400 due for March commissions.

The accounting methods and entries are the same as for accruals and prepayments of expenses but you do need to think quite carefully about the entries as we are now dealing with income and not expenses.

The £400 income due but not received must be included in Dawn's accounts for the year by increasing the commission income by £400 and showing an asset, accrued income, for £400 in the statement of financial position.

Step 1   We credit the commission income account with the accrual of income carried down, adding to the income balance

Step 2   We bring down a debit balance on the commission income account (accrued income b/d), which will be listed in the statement of financial position as accrued income.

Step 3   We transfer the total income for the period to the income statement

**Commission income account**

| Date | Details | £ | Date | Details | £ |
|------|---------|---|------|---------|---|
| 31 Mar | Income statement | 2,700 | 31 Mar | Balance b/d | 2,300 |
|  |  |  | 31 Mar | Accrued income c/d | 400 |
|  |  | 2,700 |  |  | 2,700 |
| 1 Apr | Accrued income b/d | 400 |  |  |  |

Again the correct amount is credited to the income statement and the debit balance on the account is listed in the statement of financial position as accrued income or commission receivable (a current asset).

## PREPAYMENTS OF INCOME

It is also possible for another party to prepay income to the business. A PREPAYMENT OF INCOME is miscellaneous income that has been received in the old period but which was due in the new accounting period.

The accounting treatment for a prepayment of income is as follows:

- It must be deducted from the balance in the income account to ensure that only the income due in the period is included in the income statement

- It must be shown as a type of current liability, called prepaid income or income received in advance, in the statement of financial position

## HOW IT WORKS

Dawn Fisher sublets some of her premises to a local artist for a quarterly rental payable in advance of £250. The rental income account at 31 March 20X5 shows a credit balance of £1,000 but this includes £250 paid on 28 March for the following quarter.

The £250 income received in advance must be excluded from Dawn's accounts for the year by decreasing rental income by £250 and showing a liability, income received in advance, for £250 in the statement of financial position.

Step 1    We debit the rental income account with the prepayment of income carried down, reducing the income balance

Step 2    We bring down a credit balance on the rental income account (prepaid income b/d), which will be listed in the statement of financial position as income received in advance

Step 3    We transfer the total income for the period to the income statement

**Rental income account**

| Date | Details | £ | Date | Details | £ |
|------|---------|---|------|---------|---|
| 31 Mar | Income statement | 750 | 31 Mar | Balance b/d | 1,000 |
| 31 Mar | Prepaid income c/d | 250 | | | |
| | | 1,000 | | | 1,000 |
| | | | 1 Apr | Prepaid income b/d | 250 |

Again the income appearing in the income statement is the correct amount of £750 and a credit balance of £250, income received in advance, is listed as a current liability in the statement of financial position.

## Task 4

How is accrued income accounted for in the statement of financial position?

| | ✓ |
|------|------|
| Asset | |
| Liability | |

# CHAPTER OVERVIEW

- Accounts should be prepared according to the accruals concept which means that the income and expenses that are recognised should be those that have been earned or incurred in the period, not just the amounts of cash that have been received or paid

- By setting up control accounts for sales and purchases on credit these sales and purchases are automatically recorded according to the accruals concept – the sale and purchase is recognised when it is made not when the cash is received or paid

- Expenses are however treated differently – some expenses will only be recorded in the expense ledger account when they are actually paid, therefore at the end of each accounting year each expense account must be considered carefully to ensure that the balance represents the full amount of that expense that has been incurred in the period

- An accrual is an amount of expense that has been incurred but has not yet been invoiced for or paid and is therefore not yet recorded in the expense ledger account – this accrual must be added to the expense balance and shown in the statement of financial position as a liability, an accrual

- A prepayment is the opposite of an accrual – it is an amount of expense that has been paid and therefore appears in the ledger account but it relates to the following accounting period. This must be removed from the ledger account balance and is shown in the statement of financial position as a form of asset, a prepayment

- Many businesses will have sources of miscellaneous income – these can also be either accrued or prepaid

- An accrual of income is an amount that is due for the period but has not been received – this must be added to the income account balance and included in the statement of financial position as a form of asset, called accrued income or income receivable

- A prepayment of income is where income has been received but it actually relates to the following accounting period – this must be deducted from the income account balance and shown in the statement of financial position as a liability, income received in advance

## Keywords

**Accruals concept** – fundamental accounting concept that states that income and expenses shown in the income statement should be those that were earned or incurred during the period rather than simply the cash received or paid

**Accrual** – an amount of expense that has been incurred during the period but that has not yet been invoiced for or paid

**Prepayment** – an amount of expense that has been paid for but that relates to the following accounting period

**Accrual of income** – an amount of income that is due for the period but that has not yet been received

**Prepayment of income** – an amount of income that has been received but that relates to the following accounting period

To April 20 1990

March 20xx   April 20x1 →

Accrued due but   Prepayment
not paid

# TEST YOUR LEARNING

## Test 1

(a) Rent paid in advance for the following accounting period would appear as an accrual/a prepayment in the statement of financial position.

(b) Motor expenses owing to the local garage would appear as an accrual /a prepayment in the statement of financial position.

## Test 2

State what effect each of the following would have in the income statement and the statement of financial position of a business with an accounting year end of 31 March 20XX:

*accrual*

(a) The balance on the heat and light expense account of £670 does not include the latest bill which shows £200 of heat and light expenses for the first three months of 20XX.

In the income statement the heat and light expense would be £ 670 . In the statement of financial position there would be an accrual/a repayment for £ 200 .

(b) The rental income account balance of £380 includes £40 of rent received for April 20XX.

In the income statement the rental income would be £ 340 . In the statement of financial position there would be an accrual of income/a prepayment of income for £ 40 .

*prepay*

(c) The insurance account balance of £1,400 includes £300 for insurance for April to June 20XX.

In the income statement the insurance expense would be £ 1,100 . 1,000
In the statement of financial position there would be an accrual of income/a prepayment of income for £ 300 .

(d) The commissions income account balance of £180 does not include £20 of commission due for March 20XX.

In the income statement commissions income would be £ 200 .
In the statement of financial position there would be an accrual of income/a prepayment of income for £ 20 .

## Test 3

A business has an accounting year end of 30 June 20XX. On that date the motor expenses account shows a balance of £845. This includes £150 of road fund licence for the year from 1 January 20XX.

Show the accounting entries required for this in the motor expenses account.

**Motor expenses account**

| | | £ | | | £ |
|---|---|---|---|---|---|
| | | | | | |
| | | | | | |
| | | | | | |
| | | | | | |

## Test 4

A business has an accounting year end of 31 March 20XX. At that date the balance on the electricity account is £470. On 7 April 20XX a further electricity bill is received for January to March 20XX totalling £180. This bill is then paid on 25 April 20XX.

Show the accounting entries in the electricity account that are required to show the correct picture at the year end.

**Electricity account**

| | | £ | | | £ |
|---|---|---|---|---|---|
| | | | | | |
| | | | | | |
| | | | | | |
| | | | | | |

June 20xx

# chapter 7:
# INVENTORY

## chapter coverage 📖

An important asset that many businesses have is inventory, also known as stock. IAS 2 (Inventories) and SSAP 9 (Stock and long-term contracts) give us detailed rules as to how inventory should be valued and these are considered in this chapter together with the accounting treatment of inventory. The topics covered are:

✍ The physical count of inventory

✍ The closing inventory reconciliation

✍ IAS 2 and SSAP 9 requirements for valuation

✍ Methods of valuation

✍ Accounting for inventory in the ledger accounts

## INTRODUCTION TO INVENTORY

Businesses make a great many purchases of items for resale or for use in manufacture and administration. There is nearly always a timing difference between when the items are purchased and when they are used, and during that time they are held 'in inventory' (IAS) or 'in stock' (UK GAAP).

At a period end therefore the holding of inventory presents the accountant with a problem connected yet again with the **accruals** concept. When items are purchased either for cash or on credit the debit entry is always made to the purchases account, never to an 'inventory' or 'stock' account. Unless an adjustment is made to the purchases account, because of the timing difference it will include the cost not only of items that have been bought and used in the period but also of items that the business still holds at the period end. The income connected with the items which are in inventory at the period end will be earned in the new period.

At the end of each accounting period the business's inventory is:

- Physically counted
- Valued, then
- Adjusted in the ledger accounts so there is a statement of financial position asset and a credit to cost of sales in the income statement

We shall follow each step through in turn.

## RECORDING AND COUNTING ITEMS OF INVENTORY

For each item purchased there will be a stores record which shows the quantity purchased each time a delivery arrives, the quantity issued to sell or to process further in the factory, and the quantity on hand at any point in time. By this means the business tries to control and look after its key asset.

## HOW IT WORKS

Dawn Fisher buys a variety of different coloured T shirts, in different sizes, to decorate. The stores record, in units, for March 20X5 for the extra small white T shirts is given below:

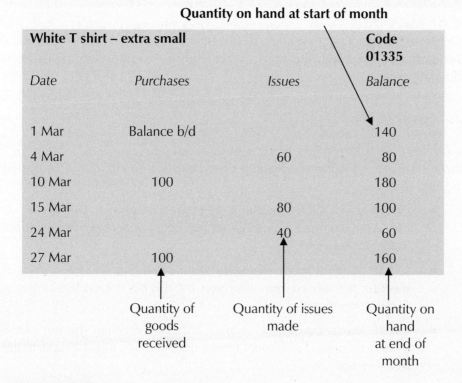

**Quantity on hand at start of month**

| White T shirt – extra small | | | Code 01335 |
|---|---|---|---|
| Date | Purchases | Issues | Balance |
| 1 Mar | Balance b/d | | 140 |
| 4 Mar | | 60 | 80 |
| 10 Mar | 100 | | 180 |
| 15 Mar | | 80 | 100 |
| 24 Mar | | 40 | 60 |
| 27 Mar | 100 | | 160 |

Quantity of goods received     Quantity of issues made     Quantity on hand at end of month

## Physical count

At the end of the accounting period each item of inventory is physically counted and listed. The quantity counted is then compared to the stores records. If there is a discrepancy between the actual quantity of inventory counted and the balance on the stores record then this must be investigated. The difference will normally be due to errors in the recording of purchases or issues of the item. However if there are fewer items than the records show then care should be taken to identify whether items have been stolen.

This process is known as the PHYSICAL INVENTORY COUNT and often takes place at other times of the year as well as at the year end in order to keep control over the business's inventory. However the year end inventory count is the most important as this is the one which will provide the figure for inventory that will appear in the financial statements.

# CLOSING INVENTORY RECONCILIATION

The physical quantity of each item must be checked to the stores record and any discrepancies investigated. This is done in the form of an INVENTORY RECONCILIATION.

## HOW IT WORKS

At 31 March 20X5 Dawn Fisher carried out a physical inventory count and compared the quantity of each line of goods to the stores records. In most cases the quantity agreed with the stores records but for two lines of goods Dawn found discrepancies.

|  | Green T – large | Blue T – medium |
|---|---|---|
| Quantity counted | 48 | 150 |
| Stores record quantity | 54 | 126 |

Dawn checked the stores records and documentation carefully and discovered the following:

- On 26 March six large green T shirts were returned to the supplier as they were damaged. The goods returns note has not yet been recorded in the stores record

- On 30 March a goods received note showed that 40 blue T shirts in medium size arrived from a supplier but this has not yet been entered in the stores record

- On 28 March Dawn took 16 blue T shirts in medium size out of the stores to process a rush order from a customer and forgot to update the stores record

Using these facts Dawn now prepares her inventory reconciliation.

### Inventory reconciliation – 31 March 20X5

| Green T – large | Quantity |
|---|---|
| Stores record | 54 |
| Less: returned to supplier 26 March | (6) |
| Counted 31 March | 48 |

| Blue T – medium | Quantity |
|---|---|
| Stores record | 126 |
| Add: Goods received note 30 March | 40 |
| Less: items issued for sale 28 March | (16) |
| Counted 31 March | 150 |

## VALUING INVENTORY

Dawn can now use her physical count quantities to prepare her closing inventory valuation for each line of goods.

Quantity of inventory × Value per item = Value of inventory

BPP
LEARNING MEDIA

## Lower of cost and NRV rule

The rules for valuing inventory come from IAS 2 and SSAP 9. The basic rule for valuation is:

**Inventory should be valued at the lower of COST and NET REALISABLE VALUE.**

Before we look at what is included in these two figures we will consider the purpose of this rule.

It is based upon the accounting concept of **prudence**, which we saw in Chapter 2. The normal situation is that an item will be purchased for say £30 and then resold for £40. In this case the inventory will be valued at cost of £30. However suppose the item could only be sold for £25. If we valued it at £30 we would be overstating its value as an asset. The prudence concept does not allow this so the item must be valued at its selling price of £25.

So what are cost and net realisable value?

- COST is defined by SSAP 9 as the cost of getting the stock into its current position – therefore this includes delivery charges. IAS 2 states that cost comprises 'all costs of purchase, costs of conversion and other costs incurred in bringing the items to their present location and condition'

- NET REALISABLE VALUE is the expected selling price of the inventory, less any further costs to be incurred such as selling or distribution costs. IAS 2 defines it as 'the estimated selling price in the ordinary course of business less the estimated costs of completion and the estimated costs necessary to make the sale'

## Task 1

A product that a business sells costs £13.80 to buy. Due to a fall in demand for this product it will only sell for £14.00 and in order to sell at this price it must be delivered to the customer at a cost of 50p per unit.

At what value should inventory of this product be included in the financial statements?

£ [          ]

## HOW IT WORKS

A small business has three lines of inventory A, B and C. The total cost and total net realisable value (NRV) of each line is given below:

|   | Cost | NRV |
|---|---|---|
|   | £ | £ |
| A | 1,250 | 2,000 |
| B | 1,400 | 1,200 |
| C | 1,100 | 1,900 |
|   | 3,750 | 5,100 |

Although the total cost of £3,750 is lower than the total net realisable value of £5,100 this is not the value of the business's closing inventory. The cost and net realisable value must be compared for each individual line of inventory as follows:

|   | Cost | NRV | Lower = Inventory value |
|---|---|---|---|
|   | £ | £ | £ |
| A | 1,250 | 2,000 | 1,250 |
| B | 1,400 | 1,200 | 1,200 |
| C | 1,100 | 1,900 | 1,100 |
|   | 3,750 | 5,100 | 3,550 |

The inventory should be valued at £3,550 which is the total of the lower of cost and net realisable value for each line.

## METHODS OF DETERMINING COST

Before they can apply the cost/NRV rule, businesses are often faced with the problem of determining the actual cost price of the items held. If there are deliveries and issues of an item on a regular basis then it will be difficult (if not impossible) to determine precisely which items have been sold and which remain as the closing inventory. If the prices at which each batch of the item was purchased differ then it becomes important that we know which purchases remain in inventory at the end of the accounting period.

The time and effort involved in determining exactly which item has been sold and exactly which remains in inventory will usually not be worthwhile for a business. Therefore the cost of inventory will be determined by using one of a number of assumptions as follows:

- **FIFO (FIRST IN FIRST OUT)** we assume that the items issued are the earliest purchases, so the inventory on hand comprise the most recent purchases.

- **LIFO (LAST IN FIRST OUT)** we assume that the items issued are the most recent purchases, so the items in inventory are the earliest purchases. SSAP 9 strongly discourages the use of LIFO and IAS 2 forbids it.

- **AVCO (WEIGHTED AVERAGE COST)** after each new purchase a weighted average cost for the items held is calculated – this is the total cost of the items held divided by the number of units held – the inventory is valued at this weighted average at the end of the period.

## HOW IT WORKS

Dawn Fisher's stores record for extra small white T shirts for March is shown below.

**White T shirt – extra small**         **Code 01335**

| Date | Purchases | Issues | Balance |
|---|---|---|---|
| 1 Mar | Balance b/d | | 140 |
| 15 Mar | | 80 | 60 |
| 27 Mar | 100 | | 160 |
| 28 Mar | | 40 | 120 |

The 140 items held on 1 March were all purchased at £7 per unit, and the purchase on 27 March was at £8 per unit.

The value of the 120 units remaining in inventory at the end of the month will be calculated on the FIFO, LIFO and AVCO basis.

### FIFO – First in first out

| Date | Purchases units | Cost/ unit £ | Issues units | Cost/ unit £ | Total units | Cost/ units £ | Total cost £ |
|---|---|---|---|---|---|---|---|
| 1 Mar (b/d) | | | | | 140 | 7.00 | 980.00 |
| 15 Mar | | | (80) | | (80) | 7.00 | (560.00) |
| 27 Mar | 100 | 8.00 | | | 100 | 8.00 | 800.00 |
| 28 Mar | | | (40) | | (40) | 7.00 | (280.00) |
| | | | | | 120 | | 940.00 |

## LIFO – Last in first out

| Date | Purchases units | Cost/ unit £ | Issues units | Cost/ unit £ | Total units | Cost/ Units £ | Total cost £ |
|---|---|---|---|---|---|---|---|
| 1 Mar (b/d) | | | | | 140 | 7.00 | 980.00 |
| 15 Mar | | | (80) | | (80) | 7.00 | (560.00) |
| 27 Mar | 100 | 8.00 | | | 100 | 8.00 | 800.00 |
| 28 Mar | | | (40) | 8.00 | (40) | 8.00 | (320.00) |
| | | | | | 120 | | 900.00 |

## AVCO – Weighted average cost

| Date | Purchases quantity | Cost per unit £ | Issues units | Cost per unit £ | Balance Units | Balance £ |
|---|---|---|---|---|---|---|
| 1 Mar Bal b/d | 140 | 7,00 | | 7.00 | 140 | 980.00 |
| 15 Mar | | | (80) | 7.00 | (80) | (560.00) |
| 27 Mar | 100 | 8.00 | | 8.00 | 100 | 800.00 |
| | Av. cost | 1,220/160 | | 7.625 | 160 | 1,220.00 |
| 28 Mar | | | (40) | 7.625 | (40) | (305.00) |
| | | | | | 120 | 915.00 |

As you can see the values of the inventory under the different methods vary:

|  | £ |
|---|---|
| FIFO | 940.00 |
| LIFO | 900.00 |
| AVCO | 915.00 |

---

## Task 2

A business buys 100 units of a product for £3.50 per unit on 1 May. A further 100 units are purchased on 20 May for £4.00 per unit. The sales for the month were 70 units on 12 May and 80 units on 30 May.

Determine the value of the closing inventory using the FIFO method.

£ [         ]

---

## LEDGER ACCOUNTING FOR INVENTORY

Whenever goods are purchased they must be debited to a purchases account, **never** to an inventory account. The inventory account is only used at the end of the accounting period in order to record the closing inventory of the business.

## HOW IT WORKS

Dawn Fisher has counted and valued all of her inventory at her year end 31 March 20X5 and it totals £6,450.

This figure is entered into the ledger accounts by a debit and a credit entry to two different inventory accounts:

Debit  Inventory account – statement of financial position
Credit  Inventory account – income statement

### Inventory account – statement of financial position

| | £ | | £ |
|---|---|---|---|
| 31 Mar 20X5 | 6,450 | | |

### Inventory account – income statement

| | £ | | £ |
|---|---|---|---|
| | | 31 Mar 20X5 | 6,450 |

The inventory - statement of financial position account balance, a debit balance, is the closing inventory asset that will be listed in the statement of financial position as a current asset.

The inventory - income statement balance is cleared out to the income statement at the end of the year, to be shown eventually as a deduction from purchases to give the cost of sales figure.

### Inventory account – income statement

| | £ | | £ |
|---|---|---|---|
| 31 Mar 20X5 Income statement | 6,450 | 31 Mar 20X5 | 6,450 |

Dawn's purchases account at the end of the year shows a debit balance of £76,850. This is also cleared to the income statement for the year. We deduct the inventory account – income statement balance to arrive at the figure for cost of sales:

| | £ |
|---|---|
| Cost of sales as at 31 March 20X5: | |
| Purchases | 76,850 |
| Less: closing inventory | (6,450) |
| | 70,400 |

The only inventory balance that remains in Dawn's books now is that on the inventory – statement of financial position account. This remains in her ledger accounts as the opening inventory balance without any further entries to it until the end of the following accounting period, 31 March 20X6. At this date the closing inventory is valued at £7,200 and the purchases for the year were £80,900.

As this is Dawn's second year we have both opening and closing inventory.

Step 1    At 31 March 20X6, clear the balance on the inventory account (which is the opening inventory ), to the income statement.

### Inventory account – statement of financial position

| | £ | | £ |
|---|---|---|---|
| 1 Apr 20X5 Bal b/d Opening inventory | 6,450 | 31 Mar 20X6 Income statement | 6,450 |

Step 2    Enter the closing inventory valuation at 31 March 20X6 into the two inventory accounts:

### Inventory account – statement of financial position

| | £ | | £ |
|---|---|---|---|
| | | 31 Mar 20X6 Income statement | 6,450 |
| 1 Apr 20X5 Bal b/d Opening inventory | 6,450 | | |
| 31 Mar 20X6 Closing inventory | 7,200 | | |

### Inventory account – income statement

| | £ | | £ |
|---|---|---|---|
| | | 31 Mar 20X6 Closing inventory | 7,200 |

Step 3    Clear the account for inventory – income statement to the income statement as the closing inventory:

### Inventory account – income statement

| | £ | | £ |
|---|---|---|---|
| 31 Mar 20X6 Income statement | 7,200 | 31 Mar 20X6 Closing inventory | 7,200 |

Step 4    Calculate the cost of sales in the income statement for the year ended 31 March 20X6:

| | £ |
|---|---|
| Cost of sales as at 31 March 20X6: | |
| Opening inventory | 6,450 |
| Purchases | 80,900 |
| | 87,350 |
| Less: closing inventory | (7,200) |
| | 80,150 |

## Journal entry for recording closing inventory

The journal entry with narrative for recording the closing inventory for Dawn Fisher would be as follows:

| Account name | Debit £ | Credit £ |
|---|---|---|
| Inventory account – statement of financial position | 7,200 | |
| Inventory account – income statement | | 7,200 |

*Being inventory held at 31 March 20X6*

To summarise:

---

Income statement

- Debit with opening inventory
- Credit with closing inventory

Statement of financial position

- Debit with closing inventory as a current asset

---

This may seem complicated now but when we start dealing with the extended trial balance it will become second nature!

---

## Task 3

When goods are purchased the cost should be debited to which ledger account:

| | ✓ |
|---|---|
| Inventory | |
| Purchases | |

---

## CHAPTER OVERVIEW

- When goods are purchased they are always debited to a purchases account and never to an inventory account

- At the end of the year, and often at other times during the year, the inventory must be counted and the quantity of each item listed – this is then compared to the stores record of the amount of that item that should exist – an inventory reconciliation will be carried out

- Once the quantity of each item of inventory is known then it must be valued – both SSAP 9 and IAS 2 state that each line of inventory should be valued at the lower of cost and net realisable value (NRV)

- In order to determine the cost of inventory a method has to be chosen – the most common methods are FIFO, LIFO (not permitted under IAS 2) and AVCO (weighted average cost)

- When the closing inventory has been valued it must be included in the final accounts as a current asset in the statement of financial position and as a deduction from purchases to give cost of sales in the income statement

- Opening inventory for a period is included as an expense in the income statement, being added to the purchases figure in the cost of sales calculation

## Keywords

**Inventory count** – the regular and year end process of counting each line of inventory and comparing the quantity to the quantity that should exist according to the stores records

**Closing inventory reconciliation** – comparison of inventory record quantity to quantity actually counted

**Cost** – the cost for inventory is the cost of getting the inventory to its current position which will include delivery costs

**Net realisable value (NRV)** – the expected selling price of the item less any further costs to be incurred such as selling or distribution expenses

**FIFO – first in first out** – method of inventory valuation that assumes that items issued are the earliest purchases so closing inventory contains the most recent purchases

**LIFO – last in first out** – method of inventory valuation that assumes that the items issued are the most recent purchases so closing inventory contains the earliest purchases

**AVCO – weighted average cost** – method of inventory valuation that operates by calculating a weighted average cost for the inventory after each new purchase

## TEST YOUR LEARNING

### Test 1

A business has 120 units of an item at the year end which cost £25.80 plus delivery charges of £1.00 per unit. This item can be sold for £28.00 per unit but must be delivered to the customer at a further cost of £1.10 per unit.

(a) The cost of each item is £ _____ and the net realisable value of each item is £ _____ .

(b) At what value would these 120 units appear in the statement of financial position?

£ _____

# chapter 8:
# IRRECOVERABLE DEBTS AND DOUBTFUL DEBTS

## — chapter coverage 📖 —

In this chapter we consider the receivables balance at the end of the accounting year and any adjustments that are required. The topics we cover are:

✍ Accounting treatment of irrecoverable debts

✍ Irrecoverable debts that are recovered

✍ Doubtful debts

✍ Accounting for doubtful debts

✍ Types of allowances for doubtful debts

✍ Adjusting the allowance for doubtful debts

## INTRODUCTION TO IRRECOVERABLE DEBTS

When a sale is made on credit it is recognised immediately in the accounting records by recording it as a sale and setting up a receivable for the amount due – this is in accordance with the **accruals** concept. We expect the debt to be honoured and the amount paid by the customer. However it is possible that some debts may never be paid so, in line with the **prudence** concept and to avoid any overstatement of assets, any debts that are unlikely to be paid should not be shown as an asset in the statement of financial position.

An IRRECOVERABLE DEBT is one that the business believes will never be paid (you may sometimes hear it being referred to as a 'bad debt').

## ACCOUNTING FOR IRRECOVERABLE DEBTS

If a debt is not going to be recovered then it should be removed from the business's accounts and it should not be shown as a receivable in the statement of financial position.

The double entry for this is:

Debit   Irrecoverable debts expense account
Credit   Sales ledger control account

This will remove the debt from the receivables balance and create an expense - irrecoverable debts expense – in the income statement.

The customer's individual account in the sales ledger must also have the debt removed from it by a credit entry here as well.

## HOW IT WORKS

The balance on Dawn Fisher's sales ledger control account at the year end date of 31 March 20X5 is £10,857. She is however very concerned about an amount of £337 owing from K Whistler. The last money received from this customer was in September 20X4 and Dawn's latest letter has been returned unopened with a scribbled comment on the envelope 'K Whistler not known at this address'. Dawn has now decided to accept that the debt will never be paid and is to write it off as irrecoverable.

**Irrecoverable debts expense account**

| Date | Details | £ | Date | Details | £ |
|------|---------|---|------|---------|---|
| 31 Mar | Sales ledger control | 337 | | | |

### Sales ledger control account

| Date | Details | £ | Date | Details | £ |
|------|---------|---|------|---------|---|
| 31 Mar | Balance b/d | 10,857 | 31 Mar | Irrecoverable debts expense | 337 |
| | | | 31 Mar | Balance c/d | 10,520 |
| | | 10,857 | | | 10,857 |
| 1 Apr | Balance b/d | 10,520 | | | |

The sales ledger control account now shows the amended balance of £10,520 after having removed K Whistler's debt. The irrecoverable debts expense account has a debit balance of £337 which is an expense of the business, one of the risks of making sales on credit, and as such will be charged in the income statement as an expense.

In the sales ledger K Whistler's account must also be credited with the amount of this irrecoverable debt to remove it from these records as well:

### K Whistler

| Date | Details | £ | Date | Details | £ |
|------|---------|---|------|---------|---|
| 31 Mar | Balance b/d | 337 | 31 Mar | Irrecoverable debt written off | 337 |

## Task 1

A business has receivables at the year end of £26,478. Of these it is felt that £976 should be written off as irrecoverable.

What is the journal entry, including narrative, for the write-off of these irrecoverable debts?

| Account name | Debit £ | Credit £ |
|--------------|---------|----------|
| | | |
| | | |
| | | |

## ACCOUNTING FOR IRRECOVERABLE DEBTS RECOVERED

Occasionally a debt will be settled by a customer after it has been written off by the business as irrecoverable.

The double entry for this requires the expense of the write-off to be removed from the irrecoverable debts account – as it has already been written off there is no adjustment to the sales ledger control account:

Debit   Bank/cash account
Credit  Irrecoverable debts expense account

---

## Task 2

A business has written off a debt for £1,000 from one of its customers and then three months later the amount is received.

Prepare the journal entry, including narrative, to record the recovery.

| Account name | Debit £ | Credit £ |
|---|---|---|
|  |  |  |
|  |  |  |
|  |  |  |

---

## INTRODUCTION TO DOUBTFUL DEBTS

We have seen that an irrecoverable debt is one that we are fairly sure will never be recovered. There may also be other debts that we are concerned about but that we are not yet ready to write off as irrecoverable. Our concern may arise from a customer querying an amount or not responding to initial requests for payment of an overdue debt.

These debts over which there is some concern are known as DOUBTFUL DEBTS.

There is also another scenario with customers owing money. A business may not necessarily be able to pinpoint specific debts that are doubtful but the sales ledger clerk may know from experience that, on average, a certain percentage of debts turn out to be doubtful. In this case the percentage can be applied to the total receivables figure to give an indication of the amount of doubtful debts.

## ACCOUNTING FOR DOUBTFUL DEBTS

According to the **prudence** concept if there is uncertainty as to the recoverability of debts then there is a possibility that an asset – receivables – will be overstated in the statement of financial position. While we need to include the most cautious figure for assets in the statement of financial position, we do not want to remove these debts from the sales ledger control account since they may well yet be recovered, unlike an irrecoverable debt. Consequently, we set up an ALLOWANCE FOR DOUBTFUL DEBTS.

An allowance is a ledger account with a credit balance which is deducted (or 'netted off') against an asset ledger account when the statement of financial position is prepared. The allowance for doubtful debts account is similar therefore to the accumulated depreciation account. On the statement of financial position this is presented as a depreciation balance that is deducted from the non-current assets at cost balance in order to arrive at their carrying amount.

In a similar way the allowance for doubtful debts is a credit balance which is deducted from the sales ledger control account balance to show the net figure for receivables that are recoverable in the statement of financial position. It is a less permanent way of achieving the prudent figure for receivables than writing the debt out of the sales ledger control account as an irrecoverable debt.

## Double entry to set up an allowance for doubtful debts

The double entry to set up an allowance for doubtful debts is:

    Debit    Allowance for doubtful debts adjustment account
    Credit   Allowance for doubtful debts account

The allowance for doubtful debts adjustment account is an expense account that will have a debit balance when an allowance is first set up.

# SPECIFIC AND GENERAL ALLOWANCES FOR DOUBTFUL DEBTS

We have seen that there are potentially two types of doubtful debt – the specific debts that can be pinpointed as doubtful and the more general percentage approach.

This means that a business could have a policy of having two elements to its allowance for doubtful debts:

- A Specific Allowance
- A General Allowance

# HOW IT WORKS

Dawn Fisher's balance on her sales ledger control account at 31 March 20X5 after writing off the irrecoverable debt from K Whistler is £10,520.

When Dawn considers these debts in detail she decides that she is concerned about the recoverability of one debt for £320. She has also been advised by friends in business that she is likely to have problems on average with about 2% of her receivables.

Therefore Dawn's policy is to set up an allowance for doubtful debts made up of two elements:

- A specific allowance for £320
- A general allowance of 2% of the remaining balance of receivables

Step 1   Calculate the total amount of the allowance. Before applying a percentage to the sales ledger control account total to calculate a general allowance you should always deduct:

- Any irrecoverable debts that are to be written off and
- Any debts against which a specific allowance is to be made.

|  | £ |
|---|---|
| Sales ledger control account balance after writing off irrecoverable debts | 10,520 |
| Specific allowance | (320) |
|  | 10,200 |
| General allowance 2% × £10,200 | 204 |
| Specific allowance | 320 |
| Amount of allowance to be set up | 524 |

Step 2   Enter the allowance into the ledger accounts

**Allowance for doubtful debts adjustment account**

| Date | Details | £ | Date | Details | £ |
|---|---|---|---|---|---|
| 31 Mar | Allowance for doubtful debts |  | 31 Mar | Income statement |  |
|  |  | 524 |  |  | 524 |
|  |  | 524 |  |  | 524 |

**Allowance for doubtful debts**

| Date | Details | £ | Date | Details | £ |
|---|---|---|---|---|---|
|  |  |  | 31 Mar | Allowance for doubtful debts adjustment | 524 |

Step 3   Close off the balance on the allowance for doubtful debts adjustment account of £524 to the income statement as an expense.

Step 4   When Dawn produces her statement of financial position the sales ledger control account balance will have the allowance deducted from it to show the figure for receivables that are truly recoverable:

|  | £ |
|---|---|
| Sales ledger control account | 10,520 |
| Less: allowance for doubtful debts account | (524) |
| Receivables figure in the statement of financial position | 9,996 |

## Task 3

A business has a sales ledger control account balance of £21,680. One debt of £680 is to be written off as irrecoverable and an allowance of 3% is to be made against the remainder.

Prepare the journal entries, including narrative, to record the irrecoverable debt and the allowance being set up.

| Account name | Debit £ | Credit £ |
|---|---|---|
| | | |
| | | |
| | | |
| | | |
| | | |

### Adjustments to the allowance for doubtful debts

In subsequent years the balance on the allowance for doubtful debts account will remain in the ledger accounts as it is a statement of financial position account, but it may require increasing or decreasing each year.

To increase the allowance for doubtful debts the double entry is:

Debit    Allowance for doubtful debts adjustment account
Credit   Allowance for doubtful debts account

- with the amount of the increase required

To decrease the allowance for doubtful debts the double entry is:

Debit    Allowance for doubtful debts account
Credit   Allowance for doubtful debts adjustment account

- with the amount of the decrease required

## HOW IT WORKS

A business has a policy of providing against 4% of its receivables at the year end. Its sales ledger control account balance at 31 December 20X6, the end of its first year of trading, was £24,000 after writing off irrecoverable debts of £200. At the end of 20X7 and 20X8 the balances were £30,000 and £26,000 again after writing off irrecoverable debts of £400 and £300 respectively.

Step 1   Calculate the allowances required at the end of each year:

20X6   £24,000 × 4%      = £960

20X7   £30,000 × 4%      = £1,200

20X8   £26,000 × 4%      = £1,040

Step 2   Set up the allowance for doubtful debts at 31 December 20X6

### Allowance for doubtful debts adjustment account

| Date 20X6 | Details | £ | Date 20X6 | Details | £ |
|---|---|---|---|---|---|
| 31 Dec | Allowance for doubtful debts | 960 <br> 960 | 31 Dec | Income statement | 960 <br> 960 |

### Allowance for doubtful debts account

| Date 20X6 | Details | £ | Date 20X6 | Details | £ |
|---|---|---|---|---|---|
| 31 Dec | | | 31 Dec | Allowance for doubtful debts adjustment | 960 |
| | Balance c/d | 960 | 20X7 | | |
| | | | 1 Jan | Balance b/d | 960 |

The allowance has been set up by charging the whole amount to the allowance for doubtful debts adjustment account. This is then taken to the income statement so no balance remains on that account. In contrast the allowance for doubtful debts is a statement of financial position account so it remains as the opening balance for 20X7.

Step 3   Increase allowance by (£1,200 − £960) = £240 to £1,200 at 31 December 20X7

### Allowance for doubtful debts adjustment account

| Date 20X7 | Details | £ | Date 20X7 | Details | £ |
|---|---|---|---|---|---|
| 31 Dec | Allowance for doubtful debts | 240 <br> 240 | 31 Dec | Income statement | 240 <br> 240 |

## Allowance for doubtful debts account

| Date 20X6 | Details | £ | Date 20X6 | Details | £ |
|---|---|---|---|---|---|
| 31 Dec | Balance c/d | 960 | 31 Dec | Allowance for doubtful debts adjustment | 960 |
| 20X7 | | | 20X7 | | |
| 31 Dec | Balance c/d | 1,200 | 1 Jan | Balance b/d | 960 |
| | | | 31 Dec | Allowance for doubtful debts adjustment | |
| | | | | | 240 |
| | | 1,200 | | | 1,200 |
| | | | 20X8 | | |
| | | | 1 Jan | Balance b/d | 1,200 |

The allowance for doubtful debts adjustment account has only been charged with the amount that is necessary to bring the balance on the allowance up to this year's required amount of £1,200 – in this case £240.

Step 4    Decrease allowance by (£1,200 – £1,040) = £160 to £1,040 as at 31 December 20X8

## Allowance for doubtful debts adjustment account

| Date 20X8 | Details | £ | Date 20X8 | Details | £ |
|---|---|---|---|---|---|
| 31 Dec | Income statement | 160 | 31 Dec | Allowance for doubtful debts | 160 |
| | | 160 | | | 300 |

## Allowance for doubtful debts account

| Date 20X6 | Details | £ | Date 20X6 | Details | £ |
|---|---|---|---|---|---|
| 31 Dec | Balance c/d | 960 | 31 Dec | Allowance for doubtful debts adjustment | 960 |
| 20X7 | | | 20X7 | | |
| 31 Dec | Balance c/d | 1,200 | 1 Jan | Balance b/d | 960 |
| | | | 31 Dec | Allowance for doubtful debts adjustment | 240 |
| | | 1,200 | | | 1,200 |
| 20X8 | | | 20X8 | | |
| 31 Dec | Allowance for doubtful debts adjustment | 160 | 1 Jan | Balance b/d | 1,200 |
| 31 Dec | Balance c/d | 1,040 | | | |
| | | 1,200 | | | 1,200 |
| | | | 20X9 | | |
| | | | 1 Jan | Balance b/d | 1,040 |

In this case the allowance had to be reduced by £160 so the allowance for doubtful debts adjustment account was credited and the allowance account debited in order to bring the allowance account balance down to the amount required.

At each year end in the statement of financial position the receivables would appear as follows:

|  | 20X6 £ | 20X7 £ | 20X8 £ |
|---|---|---|---|
| Sales ledger control account | 24,000 | 30,000 | 26,000 |
| Less: allowance for doubtful debts | 960 | 1,200 | 1,040 |
| Receivables | 23,040 | 28,800 | 24,960 |

## Task 4

On 31 December 20X7 a business had a balance on its allowance for doubtful debts account of £1,500. At the year end of 31 December 20X8 its sales ledger control account balance was £60,000. On consideration of these debts it was decided that £2,400 were to be written off as irrecoverable debts and that an allowance of 1% was to be made against the remainder.

Prepare the journal entries, including narrative, to record the irrecoverable debt and the adjustment to the allowance.

| Account name | Debit £ | Credit £ |
|---|---|---|
|  |  |  |
|  |  |  |
|  |  |  |
|  |  |  |
|  |  |  |

## Task 5

What is the double entry when the allowance for doubtful debts is to be **decreased**?

| Account name | Debit £ | Credit £ |
|---|---|---|
| Allowance for doubtful debts (SFP) | | |
| Allowance for doubtful debts adj (IS) | | |

## Task 6

Setting up an allowance for doubtful debts is an example of which accounting concept?

Going concern / accruals / prudence / materiality / consistency.

## CHAPTER OVERVIEW

- The accruals concept requires that sales on credit are recognised as soon as they are made rather than waiting until the cash is received from the customer – the prudence concept however requires that if money from a customer is unlikely to be received then it should not appear as an asset in the statement of financial position

- Any debts that are not going to be recovered should be written off as irrecoverable debts by debiting the irrecoverable debts expense account and crediting the sales ledger control account – the customer's individual account in the subsidiary sales ledger must also be credited with the amount of the irrecoverable debt

- If a customer eventually pays a debt that has already been written off as an irrecoverable debt then the bank/cash account is debited with the receipt and the irrecoverable debts expense account is credited

- A doubtful debt is one where there is concern about its recoverability – these are dealt with in the accounting records by setting up an allowance for doubtful debts

- In some cases the allowance will be against specific debts and in other cases a general allowance will be required at a percentage of the sales ledger control account balance less the specific allowance

- Once the allowance for doubtful debts has initially been set up then each year the balance must be increased or decreased to the amount that is required – this is done by debiting or crediting the allowance for doubtful debts adjustment account by the amount of the increase or decrease required

## Keywords

**Irrecoverable debt** – a debt that it is believed will not be paid

**Irrecoverable debts expense account** – the expense account used to record the irrecoverable debts that are written off – the balance appears as an expense in the income statement

**Doubtful debts** – amounts over which there is some doubt as to their recoverability

**Allowance for doubtful debts** – an amount that will be deducted from the sales ledger control account balance in the statement of financial position to reduce the balance for receivables to the prudent amount

**Allowance for doubtful debts adjustment account** – the account used to record the setting up and then adjustment of the allowance for doubtful debts – the balance appears initially as an expense in the income statement), though in subsequent periods it may appear as income (when the allowance is reduced)

**Specific allowance** – an allowance against particular debts that are recognised as doubtful

**General allowance** – an allowance set up as a percentage of the receivables balance to reflect the fact that on average a certain percentage of debts will be doubtful

## TEST YOUR LEARNING

### Test 1

A business has receivables at 30 April 20XX of £25,673. Of these it was decided that two debts were never going to be recovered, £157 from H Taylor and £288 from C Phelps. These are to be written off as irrecoverable.

Write up the general ledger and sales ledger accounts necessary to record these irrecoverable debts.

### General ledger

**Sales ledger control account**

|  | £ |  | £ |
|---|---|---|---|
|  |  |  |  |
|  |  |  |  |
|  |  |  |  |
|  |  |  |  |

**Irrecoverable debts expense account**

|  | £ |  | £ |
|---|---|---|---|
|  |  |  |  |
|  |  |  |  |
|  |  |  |  |

### Sales ledger

**H Taylor**

|  | £ |  | £ |
|---|---|---|---|
|  |  |  |  |
|  |  |  |  |
|  |  |  |  |

**C Phelps**

|  | £ |  | £ |
|---|---|---|---|
|  |  |  |  |
|  |  |  |  |
|  |  |  |  |

### Test 2

In 20X7 a business had written off an irrecoverable debt from a customer of £250. During 20X8 this amount was unexpectedly received from the customer.

Write up the general ledger accounts in full to reflect this receipt.

### Bank account

| | £ | | £ |
|---|---|---|---|
| | | | |
| | | | |
| | | | |

### Irrecoverable debts expense account

| | £ | | £ |
|---|---|---|---|
| | | | |
| | | | |
| | | | |

## Test 3

At the end of the first year of trading a business has a sales ledger control account balance of £11,650. Of these it is decided that one debt of £350 is to be written off as irrecoverable. An allowance for doubtful debts is to be made against a further debt of £200 and a general allowance is required of 2% of the remainder.

(a) Calculate the amount of the allowance for doubtful debts that is required at the year end

£ [          ]

(b) Write up the irrecoverable debts expense account, sales ledger control account, allowance for doubtful debts adjustment account and allowance for doubtful debts account at the year end to reflect the position.

### Irrecoverable debts expense account

| | £ | | £ |
|---|---|---|---|
| | | | |
| | | | |
| | | | |

### Sales ledger control account

| | £ | | £ |
|---|---|---|---|
| | | | |
| | | | |
| | | | |

### Allowance for doubtful debts adjustment account

| | £ | | £ |
|---|---|---|---|
| | | | |
| | | | |
| | | | |

### Allowance for doubtful debts account

| | £ | | £ |
|---|---|---|---|
| | | | |
| | | | |
| | | | |

## Test 4

On 1 January 20X7 there is a balance on a business's allowance for doubtful debts account of £1,460. At 31 December 20X7 the balance on the sales ledger control account is £42,570. Of this it is decided that £370 should be written off as an irrecoverable debt and an allowance for doubtful debts of 4% is required against the remainder.

At 31 December 20X8 the sales ledger control account total was £38,400 of which £400 is to be written off as an irrecoverable debt. An allowance for doubtful debts of 4% of the remainder is required.

Write up the irrecoverable debts expense account, the allowance for doubtful debts adjustment account and the allowance for doubtful debts account for 20X7 and 20X8.

### Irrecoverable debts expense account

| | £ | | £ |
|---|---|---|---|
| | | | |
| | | | |
| | | | |

### Allowance for doubtful debts adjustment account

| | £ | | £ |
|---|---|---|---|
| | | | |
| | | | |
| | | | |
| | | | |
| | | | |

## Allowance for doubtful debts account

| | £ | | £ |
|---|---|---|---|
| | | | |
| | | | |
| | | | |
| | | | |
| | | | |
| | | | |
| | | | |
| | | | |
| | | | |
| | | | |
| | | | |

# chapter 9:
# BANK RECONCILIATIONS

## chapter coverage 📖

The cash book is one of the main books of prime entry and it is vital for any business to ensure control over its cash in hand and held at the bank. A key means of control is through the bank reconciliation process. The topics covered are:

✍ The procedure for comparing the cash book to the bank statement

✍ Types of discrepancies between the cash book and the bank statement

✍ Preparing the bank reconciliation statement

✍ Correcting ledger accounts by journal

## PURPOSE OF BANK RECONCILIATIONS

The bank reconciliation process, which is covered in detail for Level 2 in Basic Accounting II, involves checking transactions recorded in the bank account columns in the business's cash book to the bank statement issued by the business's bank.

In theory the balance on the cash book and on the bank statement should be the same, but in practice timing differences mean that they very rarely are.

Carrying out the bank reconciliation process has three purposes:

- To help **identify errors**:
  - made by the business in writing up its cash book
  - made by the bank in maintaining the business's bank account

- To help **identify omissions**:
  - from the cash book, such as bank charges and dishonoured cheques processed by the bank

  - from the bank statement, such as cheques that have been sent out to suppliers but have not yet been presented for payment

- To **verify the accuracy** of the balance for cash at bank as presented in financial statements at the end of the accounting period. Since the bank is a separate entity from the business, identifying and explaining the differences between the bank statement balance and the cash book balance means that a form of external verification has taken place.

## CHECKING THE BANK STATEMENT TO THE CASH BOOK

When checking the bank statement to the cash book it should always be borne in mind that the bank statement and the cash book are mirror images of each other:

- A **debit entry in the cash book** – a receipt of money – will appear as a **credit on the bank statement**

- A **credit entry in the cash book** – a payment of money – will appear as a **debit on the bank statement**.

A bank account which is 'in credit' according to the bank will have a debit balance on its cash book. A bank account which is 'overdrawn' according to the bank has a credit balance on the cash book – it is a liability, known as an overdraft, not an asset.

A bank statement for Anna Murphy is set out below as an example:

| GREEN BANK | | | | |
|---|---|---|---|---|
| 19 Market Square, Hentage, FR9 9PO | | | | |
| STATEMENT | | | | |
| Account Name: | | | | |
| Anna Murphy | | | | |
| Account No: 73-23-23  75487325 | | | | |
| Date | Details | DEBITS (Payments) | CREDITS (Receipts) | Balance |
| | | £ | £ | £ |
| 21/09 | Balance b/d | | | 10,000.00 CR |
| 22/09 | BGC | | 2,400.00 | |
| | Bank charges | 15.00 | | |
| | BACS – salaries | 1,200.00 | | |
| | Cheque 134257 | 45.00 | | |
| | Standing order | 50.00 | | |
| | Cheque returned unpaid | 200.00 | | 10,890.00 CR |

When the bank statement for the period is received the following steps should be followed for comparison with the cash book:

Step 1    Work through all of the receipts shown on the bank statement comparing each one to entries in the Bank receipts column in the cash book. When each receipt has been agreed to the Bank receipts column the entry on the bank statement and in the cash book should be ticked.

Step 2    Work through all of the receipts shown on the bank statement comparing each one to entries in the Bank receipts column in the cash book. When each receipt has been agreed to the Bank receipts column the entry on the bank statement and in the cash book should be ticked.

Step 3    Any un-ticked items on the bank statement must be checked to ensure that the bank has not made a mistake

Step 4    The un-ticked items on the bank statement can then be used to identify adjustments that are needed in the general ledger.

## HOW IT WORKS

Anna Murphy has completed the process of checking her cash book to her bank statement. She is satisfied that the opening credit balance on the bank statement of £10,000 is correct but she has identified the following items that appear on the bank statement but do not appear in the cash book:

- A bank giro credit receipt from a customer with a customer code of SL876 for £2,400. She has discovered a remittance advice note from the customer which shows that £40 settlement discount was taken

- Bank charges of £15

- A BACS payment of net salaries of £1,200

- A cheque number 134257 paid for cash purchases (no VAT) of £45. In the bank payments column of the cash book a cheque with the same number appears with an amount of £54

- A standing order payment of £50. On checking with the bank Anna discovered that this was paid in error by the bank

- A cheque paid in for £200 from a customer with a customer code of SL452 has been dishonoured by the bank

It is possible that each of these points will require a journal entry to correct the general ledger accounts, and possibly also the memorandum sales and purchases ledgers.

Let us take each item in turn.

- **A bank giro credit receipt from a customer with a customer code of SL876 for £2,400. She has discovered a remittance advice note from the customer which shows that £40 settlement discount was taken**

Because a receipt by automated payment from a customer is not physically received as cash or a cheque by the business, it is very common for such items to appear on the bank statement before being entered in the cash book. Since this receipt and the discount taken have been validated by reference to the customer's remittance advice note, a journal to amend the cash book and other general ledger accounts can be prepared as follows:

| Account name | Amount £ | Debit (✓) | Credit (✓) |
|---|---|---|---|
| Bank | 2,400 | ✓ | |
| Sales ledger control | 2,400 | | ✓ |
| Discounts allowed | 40 | ✓ | |
| Sales ledger control | 40 | | ✓ |

The sales ledger account SL876 also needs to be credited with £2,440 in total.

- **Bank charges of £15**

Bank charges are a cost to Anna's business so the journal entry needs to reflect this:

| Account name | Amount £ | Debit (✓) | Credit (✓) |
|---|---|---|---|
| Bank charges expense | 15 | ✓ | |
| Bank | 15 | | ✓ |

- **A BACS payment of net salaries of £1,200**

Payroll transactions are normally entered into the ledger accounts via the journal, so Anna needs to establish from the payroll exactly what entries should be made to record this payment in the general ledger. There is no doubt however that a payment by BACS (Bankers Automated Credit Service) should be credited to the bank payments column in the cash book.

- **A cheque number 134257 paid for £45. In the bank payments column of the cash book a cheque with the same number appears with an amount of £54**

Clearly the cheque should have been written in the cash book as £45 since this is the amount that the bank has paid out, so a journal entry needs to be made to correct the cash book and the purchases account. In the cash book £9 (£54 – £45) too much has been entered on the payments side, so the correcting journal is as follows:

| Account name | Amount £ | Debit (✓) | Credit (✓) |
|---|---|---|---|
| Bank | 9 | ✓ | |
| Purchases | 9 | | ✓ |

- **A standing order payment of £50. On checking with the bank Anna discovered that this was paid in error by the bank**

Although this payment has been made from Anna's bank account, reducing her balance by £50, it should not have been paid so it is up to the bank to process a correction. No correcting journal is needed for the ledger accounts.

- **A cheque paid in for £200 from a customer with a customer code of SL452 has been dishonoured by the bank**

When the cheque was entered in the cash book it would have been debited to bank and credited to sales ledger control. Now that the cheque has been dishonoured we must process a journal entry to remove the cash received and reinstate the debt:

| Account name | Amount £ | Debit (✓) | Credit (✓) |
|---|---|---|---|
| Sales ledger control | 200 | ✓ | |
| Bank | 200 | | ✓ |

The sales ledger account SL452 also needs to be debited with £200.

## Task 1

The bank balance in D Ltd's cash book shows a debit balance of £12,450. The bank statement has the following items that do not appear in the cash book:

| | |
|---|---|
| Standing order for rent of premises | 400 |
| BGC receipt from customer | 230 |
| Bank charges | 25 |

Calculate the adjusted balance in D Ltd's cash book.

£ [        ]

## Task 2

What is the journal entry for a cheque for £500 received from a customer and deposited with the bank but subsequently dishonoured?

| Account name | Amount £ | Debit (✓) | Credit (✓) |
|---|---|---|---|
| | | | |
| | | | |
| | | | |

## BANK RECONCILIATION STATEMENT

After correcting the cash book for all the legitimate items that appear on the bank statement we can calculate the correct balance for the bank account in the cash book. This does not mean however that the cash book balance will agree to that on the bank statement because we have not yet taken account of TIMING

BPP
LEARNING MEDIA

DIFFERENCES, the inevitable time lag between recording receipts and payments in the cash book and their appearance on the bank statement.

- Cash and cheques paid in by the business are recorded in the cash book but the clearing system means there is a delay before they appear on the bank statement. Such amounts are known as OUTSTANDING LODGEMENTS.

- When cheques are written to suppliers they are entered in the cash book immediately. The cheques are then sent to the supplier, the supplier must take them to the bank and then there will be a clearing period before they appear on the bank statement. Those cheque payments that are in the cash book but not on the bank statement yet are known as UNPRESENTED CHEQUES.

## HOW IT WORKS

Anna Murphy has processed all the journals prepared above and her three column cash book as at 22 September is as follows (we are ignoring the analysis columns):

| Details | Cash receipts | Bank receipts | Disc allowed | Details | Cheque number | Cash payments | Bank payments | Disc received |
|---------|---------------|---------------|--------------|---------|---------------|---------------|---------------|---------------|
| | £ | £ | £ | | | £ | £ | £ |
| Bal b/d | 320.00 | 10,000.00 | | Supplier X | 134255 | | 700.00 | |
| Customer A | 400.00 | | | Supplier Y | 134256 | | 480.00 | |
| BGC | | 2,400.00 | 40.00 | Bank charges | | | 15.00 | |
| Cash | | 720.00 | | BACS – salaries | | | 1,200.00 | |
| | | | | Cash purchases | 134257 | | 45.00 | |
| | | | | Dishonoured cheque | | | 200.00 | |
| | | | | Banking | | 720.00 | | |
| | | | | Bal c/d | | | 10,480.00 | |
| | 720.00 | 13,120.00 | 40.00 | | | 720.00 | 13,120.00 | |
| Bal b/d | | 10,480.00 | | | | | | |

We can now produce a BANK RECONCILIATION STATEMENT for Anna which will reconcile the corrected cash book balance for the bank account with the bank statement balance.

Firstly, we must remember to add back the standing order payment of £50 mistakenly made by the bank.

Next, by examining the Bank receipts column in the cash book we can see that there is an outstanding lodgement of cash and cheques for £720.00. This will increase the balance on the bank statement once they are recorded by the bank.

We can also see that there are two cheques which have not yet been paid out by the bank (cheque numbers 134255 and 134256). These are unpresented cheques which will make the bank statement figure smaller once they are paid. Therefore we deduct these in the bank reconciliation statement in order to come back to the cash book balance for the bank account of £10,480.00.

### Bank reconciliation statement

|  | £ | £ |
|---|---|---|
| Balance per bank statement |  | 10,890.00 |
| Add back: standing order payment made in error |  | 50.00 |
| Add: outstanding lodgement |  |  |
| Cash and cheques |  | 720.00 |
| Less: Unpresented cheques |  |  |
| 134255 | 700.00 |  |
| 134256 | 480.00 |  |
| Total to subtract |  | (1,180.00) |
| Balance as per corrected cash book |  | 10,480.00 |

---

## Task 3

Which of the following will **not** appear in a bank reconciliation statement?

A    Unpresented cheques

B    Outstanding lodgements

C    Journal entries

D    Bank errors

BPP
LEARNING MEDIA

# CHAPTER OVERVIEW

- In order to check the accuracy of the bank columns in the cash book, it must be checked at regular intervals to the bank statements received

- The debit and credit entries and balances on the bank statement are the opposite to the entries in the ledger accounts as the bank is considering the accounting from its own perspective

- When checking the bank statement to the cash book, check each of the receipts and payments from the bank statement to the bank receipts and payments columns in the cash book and tick each agreed item in both the cash book and the bank statement

- Any un-ticked but valid items on the bank statement should be adjusted for in the general ledger (and the memorandum ledgers if necessary) by processing journal entries

- Once the relevant corrections have been made to the cash book it must be cast and balanced

- Any errors made by the bank which are highlighted must be adjusted by the bank and will also appear on the reconciliation

- The un-ticked items in the cash book are used to prepare the bank reconciliation statement

- The closing balance on the bank statement is reconciled to the corrected cash book balance in the bank reconciliation statement. The reconciling items will be bank errors, outstanding lodgements and unpresented cheques

## Keywords

**Outstanding lodgements** – cheques that have been received and recorded in the cash receipts book but do not yet appear on the bank statement

**Dishonoured cheque** – cheque that is paid into a business's bank account and then is returned by the drawer's bank unpaid

**Timing differences** – the reason for the fact that the bank statement balance will rarely agree with the balance on the cash books, as receipts and payments recorded in the cash books will appear later in the bank statement due to the operation of the clearing system

**Unpresented cheques** – cheque payments that have been recorded in the cash payments book but do not yet appear on the bank statement

**Bank reconciliation statement** – a statement reconciling the bank statement balance to the corrected cash book balance

BPP
LEARNING MEDIA

# TEST YOUR LEARNING

### Test 1

While comparing the cash book to the bank statement the following differences have appeared. Prepare journal entries for the general ledger accounts as appropriate for each of these items.

(a) A receipt from a credit customer has been recorded in the cash receipts book as £310.50 but appears correctly on the bank statement as £301.50

| Account name | Amount £ | Debit (✓) | Credit (✓) |
|---|---|---|---|
| | | | |
| | | | |

(b) Bank charges on the bank statement are £15.80

| Account name | Amount £ | Debit (✓) | Credit (✓) |
|---|---|---|---|
| | | | |
| | | | |

(c) A direct debit payment is in the bank statement to English Gas Co for £300.00 but has not been recorded in the cash payments book

| Account name | Amount £ | Debit (✓) | Credit (✓) |
|---|---|---|---|
| | | | |
| | | | |

### Test 2

Given below is a business's cash receipts and payments book for the week ending 8 March, the bank statement for that week and the bank reconciliation statement for the week ended 1 March.

You are required to prepare the bank reconciliation statement for the week ending 8 March.

## Bank reconciliation as at 8 March

|  | £ |
|---|---|
| Balance per bank statement |  |
| Add: |  |
|  |  |
|  |  |
|  |  |
| Total to add: |  |
| Less: |  |
|  |  |
|  |  |
|  |  |
| Total to subtract: |  |
| Balance as per cash book |  |

## Cash Receipts Book

| Date | Details | £ |
|---|---|---|
| 4 March | J Killick | 365.37 |
|  | D Francis | 105.48 |
| 5 March | I Oliver | 216.57 |
| 6 March | L Canter | 104.78 |
| 7 March | R Trent | 268.59 |
| 8 March | P Otter | 441.78 |
|  |  | 1,502.57 |

## Cash Payments Book

| Date | Details | Cheque number | £ |
|---|---|---|---|
| 4 March | L L Partners | 002536 | 186.90 |
|  | P J Parler | 002537 | 210.55 |
| 5 March | J K Properties | 002538 | 500.00 |
|  | Harmer & Co | 002539 | 104.78 |
|  | Plenith Ltd | 002540 | 60.80 |
| 7 March | Wessex & Co | 002541 | 389.40 |
| 8 March | Filmer Partners | 002542 | 104.67 |
|  |  |  | 1,557.10 |

## Bank reconciliation statement at 1 March

|  | £ | £ |
|---|---|---|
| Balance per bank statement |  | 835.68 |
| Less: unpresented cheques |  |  |
| 002530 | 110.46 |  |
| 002534 | 230.56 |  |
| 002535 | 88.90 |  |
|  |  | (429.92) |
|  |  | 405.76 |
| Add: outstanding lodgement |  | 102.45 |
| Amended cash book balance |  | 508.21 |

# STATEMENT

### first national
30 High Street
Benham
DR4 8TT

**SOUTHFIELD ELECTRICAL LTD**

**Account number:** 20-26-33 3126897

CHEQUE ACCOUNT

**Sheet 023**

| Date | | Paid out | Paid in | Balance |
|------|--|----------|---------|---------|
| 1 Mar | Balance b/f | | | 835.68 |
| 4 Mar | Cheque no 002534 | 230.56 | | |
| | Credit | | 102.45 | 707.57 |
| 5 Mar | DD - National Telephones | 145.00 | | |
| | Bank charges | 7.80 | | 554.77 |
| 6 Mar | Cheque No 002530 | 110.46 | | |
| | BACS - J T Turner | | 486.20 | 930.51 |
| 7 Mar | Credit | | 470.85 | |
| | Cheque No 002537 | 210.55 | | |
| | Cheque No 002536 | 186.90 | | |
| | Cheque No 002538 | 500.00 | | 503.91 |
| 8 Mar | Cheque No 002535 | 88.90 | | |
| | Credit | | 216.57 | |
| | Cheque No 002539 | 104.78 | | 526.80 |
| 8 Mar | Balance c/f | | | 526.80 |

# chapter 10:
# CONTROL ACCOUNT RECONCILIATIONS

## ─── chapter coverage 📖 ───

In this chapter we consider the reconciliations that are prepared for the sales ledger and purchases ledger control accounts with the sales and purchases ledgers, and the adjustments that may arise from the process. The topics covered are:

✍  Sales ledger control account

✍  Purchases ledger control account

✍  Control accounts and contra entries

✍  Errors in control accounts and the memorandum ledgers

✍  Sales ledger control account reconciliation

✍  Purchases ledger control account reconciliation

# SALES LEDGER CONTROL ACCOUNT AND THE SALES LEDGER

Before we look at the control account procedures and reconciliations we will firstly run through how the accounting system works for sales on credit.

## Accounting system for sales on credit

The process of accounting for sales on credit is as follows:

- The sales invoices sent to customers are recorded in the sales day book

- The total of the sales day book is regularly posted to the sales ledger control account

- The individual invoices in the sales day book are posted to the individual customers' accounts in the memorandum sales ledger

- Receipts from credit customers are recorded in the cash receipts book

- The total of the cash receipts book is regularly posted to the sales ledger control account

- The individual receipts are posted to the individual customer's account in the sales ledger

# HOW IT WORKS

Fred Simpson has recently set up in business and is not registered for VAT. He currently has just three credit customers Bill, John and Karen. His sales day book, sales ledger control account and memorandum sales ledger accounts for the month of June are given below.

## Sales day book

| Date | Customer | Invoice no. | Ref | £ |
|------|----------|-------------|------|--------|
| 3/06 | Bill | 0045 | SL01 | 235.00 |
| 5/06 | Karen | 0046 | SL03 | 141.00 |
| 8/06 | John | 0047 | SL02 | 176.25 |
| 15/06 | Karen | 0048 | SL03 | 258.50 |
| 20/06 | John | 0049 | SL02 | 117.50 |
| 28/06 | Bill | 0050 | SL01 | 211.50 |
| | | | | 1,139.75 |

These figures must be posted to the sales ledger control account and the individual customers' accounts in the sales ledger:

## General ledger

### Sales ledger control account

| | £ | | £ |
|---|---|---|---|
| Balance b/d | 587.50 | | |
| SDB | 1,139.75 | | |

## Sales ledger

### Bill | | | | | SL01

| Date | Details | £ | Date | Details | £ |
|---|---|---|---|---|---|
| 1/06 | Balance b/d | 235.00 | | | |
| 3/06 | SDB 0045 | 235.00 | | | |
| 28/06 | SDB 0050 | 211.50 | | | |

### John | | | | | SL02

| Date | Details | £ | Date | Details | £ |
|---|---|---|---|---|---|
| 1/06 | Balance b/d | 117.50 | | | |
| 8/06 | SDB 0047 | 176.25 | | | |
| 20/06 | SDB 0049 | 117.50 | | | |

### Karen | | | | | SL03

| Date | Details | £ | Date | Details | £ |
|---|---|---|---|---|---|
| 1/06 | Balance b/d | 235.00 | | | |
| 5/06 | SDB 0046 | 141.00 | | | |
| 15/06 | SDB 0048 | 258.50 | | | |

The totals of the opening balances on each individual account in the memorandum ledger add up to the opening balance on the sales ledger control account.

**Opening balances**

| | £ |
|---|---|
| Bill | 235.00 |
| John | 117.50 |
| Karen | 235.00 |
| Sales ledger control account | 587.50 |

This should always be the case if the accounting has been correctly carried out – the totals of the balances at any point in time on the individual accounts in the sales ledger should be equal to the balance on the sales ledger control account.

Now we will deal with the receipts from these customers in the month of June:

**Cash receipts book**

| Date | Details | Ref | Bank £ | Discounts allowed £ | Sales ledger £ |
|------|---------|-----|--------|---------------------|----------------|
| 6/06 | John | SL02 | 117.50 | | 117.50 |
| 10/06 | Bill | SL01 | 225.60 | 9.40 | 225.60 |
| 13/06 | Karen | SL03 | 200.00 | | 200.00 |
| 20/06 | Bill | SL01 | 225.60 | 9.40 | 225.60 |
| 28/06 | Karen | SL03 | 100.00 | | 100.00 |
| 30/06 | John | SL02 | 176.25 | | 176.25 |
| | | | 1,044.95 | 18.80 | 1,044.95 |

These figures must also be posted to the general ledger and the sales ledger, and the accounts must be balanced.

**General ledger**

**Sales ledger control account**

| | £ | | £ |
|---|---|---|---|
| Balance b/d | 587.50 | CRB | 1,044.95 |
| SDB | 1,139.75 | CRB – discounts | 18.80 |
| | 1,727.25 | Balance c/d | 663.50 |
| | | | 1,727.25 |
| Balance b/d | 663.50 | | |

**Sales ledger**

**Bill**                 **SL01**

| Date | Details | £ | Date | Details | £ |
|------|---------|---|------|---------|---|
| 1/06 | Balance b/d | 235.00 | 10/06 | CRB | 225.60 |
| 3/06 | SDB 0045 | 235.00 | 10/06 | CRB – discount | 9.40 |
| 28/06 | SDB 0050 | 211.50 | 20/06 | CRB | 225.60 |
| | | | 20/06 | CRB – discount | 9.40 |
| | | | | Balance c/d | 211.50 |
| | | 681.50 | | | 681.50 |
| Balance b/d | | 211.50 | | | |

|  |  | **John** |  |  | **SL02** |
|---|---|---|---|---|---|
| Date | Details | £ | Date | Details | £ |
| 1/06 | Balance b/d | 117.50 | 6/06 | CRB | 117.50 |
| 8/06 | SDB 0047 | 176.25 | 30/06 | CRB | 176.25 |
| 20/06 | SDB 0049 | 117.50 | Balance c/d | | 117.50 |
|  |  | 411.25 |  |  | 411.25 |
| Balance b/d | | 117.50 |  |  |  |

|  |  | **Karen** |  |  | **SL03** |
|---|---|---|---|---|---|
| Date | Details | £ | Date | Details | £ |
| 1/06 | Balance b/d | 235.00 | 13/06 | CRB | 200.00 |
| 5/06 | SDB 0046 | 141.00 | 28/06 | CRB | 100.00 |
| 15/06 | SDB 0048 | 258.50 | Balance c/d | | 334.50 |
|  |  | 634.50 |  |  | 634.50 |
| Balance b/d | | 334.50 |  |  |  |

## Closing balances

The total of each of the individual customer balances equals the balance on the sales ledger control account at the end of June:

|  | £ |
|---|---|
| Bill | 211.50 |
| John | 117.50 |
| Karen | 334.50 |
| Sales ledger control balance | 663.50 |

If the double entry has all been correctly carried out then the total of the list of sales ledger balances will always equal the balance on the sales ledger control account.

# PURCHASES LEDGER CONTROL ACCOUNT AND THE PURCHASES LEDGER

## Accounting for credit purchases

The accounting process for credit purchases and suppliers is precisely the same as for credit customers except that the entries in the accounts are the other way around.

- The purchase invoices received are recorded in the purchases day book

- The total of the purchases day book is regularly posted to the purchases ledger control account

- Individual invoices in the purchases day book are posted to the individual suppliers' accounts in the memorandum purchases ledger

- Payments to credit suppliers are recorded in the cash payments book

- The total of the cash payments book is regularly posted to the purchases ledger control account

- Individual payments are posted to the individual suppliers' accounts in the purchases ledger

### Closing balances

In just the same way as with the accounting system for credit customers, if the double entry has been correctly performed then the closing balances on the individual supplier accounts in the purchases ledger should total back to the balance on the purchases ledger control account.

# CONTROL ACCOUNTS

We will now look in more detail at the figures that are likely to appear in the sales ledger and purchases ledger control accounts as so far we have only considered the basic entries for invoices and cash.

### Sales ledger control account

A typical sales ledger control account might have the following entries:

**Sales ledger control account**

|  | £ |  | £ |
|---|---|---|---|
| Balance b/d | X | Sales returns | X |
| Credit sales | X | Receipts from credit customers | X |
| Dishonoured cheques | X | Discounts allowed | X |
|  |  | Irrecoverable debts written off | X |
|  |  | Contra entry | X |
|  |  |  |  |
|  |  | Balance c/d | X |
|  | X |  | X |
| Balance b/d | X |  |  |

**Balance b/d** There is a debit opening balance on the account as the customers owe the business money. In some circumstances an individual customer may have a credit balance on their account in the sales ledger if they have overpaid, or are awaiting a credit note from the business for goods returned, but these would not show up separately on the control account.

**Credit sales** This is the figure that is posted from the sales day book.

**Dishonoured cheques** If a customer has paid for goods then there is a credit entry in the sales ledger control account, but if the bank then returns the cheque as unpaid ie, the cheque has been 'dishonoured', the entry must be reversed by debiting the control account and crediting the bank account.

**Sales returns** This is the posting from the sales returns day book.

**Receipts from credit customers** This is the posting of the sales ledger column total from the cash receipts book.

**Discounts allowed** This is the posting from the memorandum discounts allowed column in the cash receipts book.

**Irrecoverable debts written off** This entry was covered in detail in Chapter 8.

**Contra entry** A CONTRA ENTRY, sometimes known as a set off, comes about where a customer of the business is also its supplier ie, we both sell to them and buy from them on credit. The contra entry is an amount owing by the customer which is set off against the amount we owe to them as a supplier. This will be dealt with in more detail later in the chapter.

**Balance c/d and b/d** A debit balance is carried down on the credit side and brought down on the debit side.

## Purchases ledger control account

A typical purchases ledger control account might look like this:

**Purchases ledger control account**

| | £ | | £ |
|---|---|---|---|
| | | Balance b/d | X |
| Purchases returns | X | Credit purchases | X |
| Payments made to credit suppliers | X | | |
| Discounts received | X | | |
| Contra entry | X | | |
| Balance c/d | X | | |
| | X | | X |
| | | Balance b/d | X |

**Balance b/d** The balance brought down will be on the credit side of the account as we owe the suppliers money.

**Purchases returns** This is the posting from the purchases returns day book.

**Payments made to credit suppliers** This is the posting from the cash payments book.

**Discounts received** This is the posting from the memorandum discounts received column total from the cash payments book.

**Contra entry** This is the other side of the posting from the sales ledger control account – see below for more detail.

**Credit purchases** This is the posting from the purchases day book.

**Balance c/d and b/d** A credit balance is carried down on the debit side and brought down on the credit side.

## Contra entries

It is entirely possible that a person or business can be both a receivables (debtor) and a payable (creditor) of your business at the same time. This would come about if your business makes credit sales to this person and buys goods on credit from the same person. If the business is owed money by this person and also owes money to them then it would make sense to net the two amounts off against each other and only pay or receive the difference. This is what a CONTRA ENTRY reflects.

# HOW IT WORKS

Dawn Fisher sells goods on credit to Emma Jones and currently Emma owes Dawn £210. Dawn also sometimes buys goods on credit from Emma and currently Dawn owes Emma £100. The accounts for Emma in Dawn's sales ledger and purchases ledger appear as follows:

**Sales ledger**

| Emma Jones | | |
|---|---|---|
| | £ | £ |
| Balance b/d | 210 | |

**Purchases ledger**

| Emma Jones | | |
|---|---|---|
| | £ | £ |
| | | Balance b/d 100 |

Dawn and Emma have discussed this situation and have agreed that rather than Emma paying Dawn £210 and then Dawn paying Emma £100 it would be easier to net the two amounts off and for Emma simply to pay Dawn the remaining £110 that she owes.

This £100 will be debited to Emma's account in the purchases ledger and credited to her account in the sales ledger.

**Sales ledger**

| Emma Jones | | | |
|---|---|---|---|
| | £ | | £ |
| Balance b/d | 210 | Contra | 100 |
| | | Balance c/d | 110 |
| | 210 | | 210 |
| Balance b/d | 110 | | |

BPP
LEARNING MEDIA

## Purchases ledger

**Emma Jones**

| | £ | | | £ |
|---|---|---|---|---|
| Contra | 100 | Balance b/d | | 100 |

This leaves Dawn with a balance of £110 on Emma's account in the sales ledger reflecting the agreed situation.

However if entries are made in the memorandum ledgers then they must also be reflected in the general ledger by a journal entry:

| Account name | Amount £ | Debit (✓) | Credit (✓) |
|---|---|---|---|
| Purchases ledger control | 100 | ✓ | |
| Sales ledger control | 100 | | ✓ |

### General ledger

**Sales ledger control account**

| | £ | | £ |
|---|---|---|---|
| | | Contra | 100 |

**Purchases ledger control account**

| | £ | | £ |
|---|---|---|---|
| Contra | 100 | | |

## Task 1

A business owes £500 to a supplier and that supplier also owes the business £800. They agree to net these amounts off.

Prepare the journal entry to reflect this agreement in the general ledger.

| Account name | Debit £ | Credit £ |
|---|---|---|
| | | |
| | | |
| | | |

# CONTROL ACCOUNT RECONCILIATIONS

We have seen that if all of the double entry in the general ledger and entries in the memorandum ledger are correctly carried out then the totals of the balances on the memorandum ledger should be equal to the balance on the control account.

## Control account balances

The balances on the sales ledger and purchases ledger control accounts are the figures that will appear in the trial balance for receivables and payables and eventually in the financial statements. Therefore it is important to ensure that these figures are correct. This is done by carrying out a SALES LEDGER CONTROL ACCOUNT RECONCILIATION and a PURCHASES LEDGER CONTROL ACCOUNT RECONCILIATION.

The process involves comparing the balance on the control account to the total of the balances of the individual accounts in the memorandum ledger. If the two totals do not agree then there have been errors made in either the control account or the memorandum ledger or both. These errors must be investigated, discovered and corrected.

Some of the errors might have been made in the double entry in the general ledger so they affect the control account. Other errors might have been made when posting entries to the individual accounts in the memorandum ledger or in listing the balances in the memorandum ledger.

To summarise, the purpose of these reconciliations is to help:

- **Identify errors**
- **Identify omissions**

## Errors affecting the control account

Typical types of errors that may have been made in the double entry in the general ledger, therefore affecting the control account balance may include the following:

- The books of prime entry may have been undercast or overcast so the incorrect total is posted to the control account (this would not affect the individual balances since these are posted with individual transactions from the books of prime entry)

- Postings from the books of prime entry may have been made to the wrong side of the control account

- The discounts recorded in the cash book may be incorrectly treated in the control account

BPP
LEARNING MEDIA

- An irrecoverable debt may not have been entered into the general ledger although it was written off in the sales ledger

- A contra entry may have been made in the memorandum ledgers but not entered into the general ledger accounts

## Errors affecting the list of balances

Some errors will not affect the double entry in the general ledger but will mean that the individual balances in the memorandum ledger are not correct or that these balances are listed and totalled incorrectly. Typical errors include the following:

- A transaction from the books of prime entry might be posted to the wrong account in the memorandum ledger

- Entries from the books of prime entry may be posted to the wrong side of the memorandum ledger account

- An entry from the books of prime entry may be posted as the wrong amount to the memorandum ledger account

- A balance on an account in the memorandum ledger may be included in the list of balances as the wrong amount or as the wrong type of balance, eg a debit rather than a credit

## Task 2

If the sales day book total for a week is overcast by £1,000 this would affect the sales ledger control account/the individual accounts in the sales ledger.

## SALES LEDGER CONTROL ACCOUNT RECONCILIATION

A sales ledger control account reconciliation is a comparison of the balance on the sales ledger control account to the total of the list of balances from the sales ledger to check for errors and omissions. This is carried out on a regular basis, usually monthly.

## HOW IT WORKS

Dawn Fisher is carrying out her sales ledger control account reconciliation at the end of December 20X4. The balance on the sales ledger control account is £11,578. The total of the list of account balances from the sales ledger is £11,104.

**Step 1**   Check whether the control account total agrees to the total of the memorandum ledger balances.

|  | £ |
|---|---|
| Control account total | 11,578 |
| List of balances | 11,104 |
| Difference | 474 |

The reasons for this difference must be investigated.

**Step 2**   The control account and the individual accounts and balances must be checked and any errors or omissions noted.

In Dawn's case the following errors were noted:

(a)   A page of the cash receipts book had been undercast by £100

(b)   The total from the sales day book for a week had been posted as £2,340 instead of £2,430

(c)   An irrecoverable debt of £80 had been written off in the individual customer's account but not in the general ledger

(d)   An invoice to G Harper for £250 had been entered into the account of G Draper instead

(e)   A cash receipt from David Carr had been entered into his account as £175 instead of the correct figure from the cash receipts book of £157

(f)   A debit balance of £406 on one customer's account had been omitted from the list of balances

(g)   A credit balance of £20 on a customer's account had been included in the list of balances as a debit balance

**Step 3**   The accounts must be adjusted for any errors that affect them. We shall take each one in turn and identify the adjustment needed:

(a)   **A page of the cash receipts book had been undercast by £100**

The total from the cash receipts book would have been credited to the sales ledger control account so if it was undercast by £100 the account must be credited with a further £100

| Adjustment | Amount | Debit (✓) | Credit (✓) |
|---|---|---|---|
|  | £ |  |  |
| Sales ledger control | 100 |  | ✓ |

(b) **The total from the sales day book for a week had been posted as £2,340 instead of £2,430**

The total from the sales day book is debited to the sales ledger control account and as the entry was for £90 too little an extra debit entry of £90 is required

| Adjustment | Amount £ | Debit (✓) | Credit (✓) |
|---|---|---|---|
| Sales ledger control | 90 | ✓ | |

(c) **An irrecoverable debt of £80 had been written off in the individual customer's account but not in the general ledger**

To write off an irrecoverable debt the sales ledger control account must be credited

| Adjustment | Amount £ | Debit (✓) | Credit (✓) |
|---|---|---|---|
| Sales ledger control | 80 | | ✓ |

(d) **An invoice to G Harper for £250 had been entered into the account of G Draper instead**

This does not affect the sales ledger control account at all and also does not affect the total of the sales ledger balances – the correct amount was entered on the correct side, but in the wrong account

(e) **A cash receipt from David Carr had been entered into his account as £175 instead of the correct figure from the cash receipts book of £157**

The receipt was recorded at a figure of £18 too much therefore the balance on this customer's account should be £18 higher

| Adjustment | Amount £ | Debit (✓) | Credit (✓) |
|---|---|---|---|
| Sales ledger balances | 18 | ✓ | |

(f) **A debit balance of £406 on one customer's account had been omitted from the list of balances**

The balance omitted must be added in to the total of the list of balances.

| Adjustment | Amount £ | Debit (✓) | Credit (✓) |
|---|---|---|---|
| Sales ledger balances | 406 | ✓ | |

(g) **A credit balance of £20 on a customer's account had been included in the list of balances as a debit balance**

The error must be removed by removing the £20 debit balance, and then the correct credit balance of £20 must be entered, so in the end the correction is a £40 credit in the list of balances

| Adjustment | Amount £ | Debit (✓) | Credit (✓) |
|---|---|---|---|
| Sales ledger balances | 40 | | ✓ |

Step 4   Process the adjustments to the sales ledger control account.

**Sales ledger control account**

| | | £ | | | £ |
|---|---|---|---|---|---|
| Balance b/d | | 11,578 | (a) | Cash receipts books | 100 |
| (b) | Sales day book | 90 | (c) | Irrecoverable debt | 80 |
| | | | | Balance c/d | 11,488 |
| | | 11,668 | | | 11,668 |
| Balance b/d | | 11,488 | | | |

Step 5   Adjust the total of the list of balances by adding or deducting the errors that affect this total.

| | £ |
|---|---|
| Original total | 11,104 |
| Add: (e) cash receipt adjustment (175 – 157) | 18 |
| Add: (f) balance omitted | 406 |
| Less:(g) credit balance included as debit balance | (40) |
| Amended total of the list of balances | 11,488 |

The amended total of the list of balances now agrees to the amended sales ledger control account balance, and the general ledger and sales ledger are reconciled. The balance on the sales ledger control account can now be used as the receivables figure in the trial balance.

---

## Task 3

The total of the discounts allowed column from the cash receipts book of £120 was not posted for a period. Set out the adjustment necessary in the sales ledger control account.

| Adjustment | Amount £ | Debit (✓) | Credit (✓) |
|---|---|---|---|
| | | | |

## PURCHASES LEDGER CONTROL ACCOUNT RECONCILIATION

A purchases ledger control account reconciliation works in exactly the same manner as a sales ledger control account reconciliation with the entries on the opposite sides, and no entry possible for irrecoverable debts.

## HOW IT WORKS

Dawn Fisher is currently preparing her purchases ledger control account reconciliation at the end of October 20X4. The balance on the purchases ledger control account was £9,240 and the total of the list of balances from the purchases ledger was £9,040.

The following errors and omissions were noted:

(a) One page of the purchases day book has been undercast by £100

(b) An invoice has been posted to an individual account in the purchases ledger as £863 instead of the correct figure from the purchases day book of £683

(c) The total of discounts received of £160 was credited to the purchases ledger control account

(d) One of the balances in the purchases ledger was included in the total at a figure of £235 instead of £325

(e) A contra entry for £70 had been made in the purchases ledger but not in the general ledger

Step 1   The accounts must be adjusted for any errors that affect them. We shall take each one in turn and identify the adjustment needed:

(a)   **One page of the purchases day book has been undercast by £100**

The total from the purchases day book is credited to the purchases ledger control account and therefore if it was undercast by £100 then the account must be credited with £100

| Adjustment | Amount | Debit (✓) | Credit (✓) |
|---|---|---|---|
| | £ | | |
| Purchases ledger control | 100 | | ✓ |

(b) **An invoice has been posted to an individual account in the purchases ledger as £863 instead of the correct figure from the purchases day book of £683**

An invoice would be posted to the credit side of the supplier's account – in this case it was posted at a figure £180 too high and therefore the balances would be reduced when the account was amended

| Adjustment | Amount | Debit | Credit |
|---|---|---|---|
| | £ | (✓) | (✓) |
| Purchases ledger balances | 180 | ✓ | |

(c) **The total of discounts received of £160 was credited to the purchases ledger control account**

The discounts received should have been debited to the purchases ledger control account – instead they were credited and therefore not only should there be one debit of £160 but two, one to cancel out the credit and one to put the debit entry in, therefore a debit of £320

| Adjustment | Amount | Debit | Credit |
|---|---|---|---|
| | £ | (✓) | (✓) |
| Purchases ledger control | 320 | ✓ | |

(d) **One of the balances in the purchases ledger was included in the total at a figure of £235 instead of £325**

The balance that was misstated was shown as £90 too small – therefore the balances need to be increased by £90

| Adjustment | Amount | Debit | Credit |
|---|---|---|---|
| | £ | (✓) | (✓) |
| Purchases ledger balances | 90 | | ✓ |

(e) **A contra entry for £70 had been made in the purchases ledger but not in the general ledger**

The contra entry must be put into the purchases ledger control account as a debit of £70

| Adjustment | Amount | Debit | Credit |
|---|---|---|---|
| | £ | (✓) | (✓) |
| Purchases ledger control | 70 | ✓ | |

Step 2    Adjust the control account balance for the errors that affect it.

**Purchases ledger control account**

|  | £ |  | £ |
|---|---|---|---|
|  |  | Balance b/d | 9,240 |
| (c) Discounts | 320 | (a) Purchases day book | 100 |
| (e) Contra | 70 |  |  |
| Balance c/d | 8,950 |  |  |
|  | 9,340 |  | 9,340 |
|  |  | Balance b/d | 8,950 |

Step 3    Adjust the total of the list of balances for any errors that affect the individual balances or their total.

|  | £ |
|---|---|
| Original total | 9,040 |
| Less:   (b) invoice misposting (863 – 683) | (180) |
| Add:   (e) balance misstated | 90 |
|  | 8,950 |

Now the amended balance on the purchases ledger control account of £8,950 agrees with the amended list of balances in the purchases ledger. This figure of £8,950 can now be used as the payables figure in the trial balance.

## Task 4

An invoice for £350 was entered into the individual supplier's account in the purchases ledger on the wrong side of the account. How should this be adjusted for in the purchases ledger control account reconciliation?

| Adjustment | Amount £ | Debit (✓) | Credit (✓) |
|---|---|---|---|
|  |  |  |  |

## Task 5

Which of the following items will appear as an item posted to the purchases ledger control account?

A    Irrecoverable debts written off

B    Returns inwards of the period

C    Discounts allowed in total in the period

D    Discounts received in total in the period

## Task 6

A business maintains a sales ledger control account. A debt of £1,500 is to be written off. Which of the following entries is correct (ignore VAT)?

A    Debit personal account of the customer, credit irrecoverable debts expense

B    Debit irrecoverable debts expense, credit sales ledger control

C    Debit sales ledger control, credit irrecoverable debt expense

D    Debit irrecoverable debts expense, credit personal account of the customer

## CHAPTER OVERVIEW

- The sales ledger control account is debited with the sales invoices from the sales day book and credited with cash receipts and discounts from the cash receipts book

- The individual accounts for each customer in the sales ledger are also debited with each invoice total and credited with the cash and discounts

- If all of the entries are correctly carried out then the total of the closing balances on the individual accounts from the sales ledger should agree to the balance on the sales ledger control account

- The same system applies to accounting for credit suppliers although the entries are all on the opposite sides

- The sales ledger control account will potentially have entries for sales returns, dishonoured cheques, irrecoverable debts written off and contra entries as well as the basic entries for invoices, cash and discounts

- The purchases ledger control account will potentially have entries for purchases returns and a contra entry as well as the basic entries for invoices, cash and discounts

- A contra entry is caused by netting off a sales ledger and a purchases ledger balance with the same party – in the general ledger this is done by debiting the purchases ledger control account and crediting the sales ledger control account – in the memorandum ledgers the customer's account will be credited and the supplier's account debited

- If all of the entries in the general ledger and memorandum ledger have not been properly performed then the ledger balances total will not agree to the balance on the control account – in which case the errors that cause the difference must be discovered and adjusted

- When a control account reconciliation has been completed and adjustments have been made, the control account balance and the total of the list of balances should agree

## Keywords

**Contra entry** – an amount owed by a customer which is set off against an amount owed to them as a supplier

**Sales ledger control account reconciliation** – an exercise which agrees the balance on the sales ledger control account to the total of the list of balances in the sales ledger

**Purchases ledger control account reconciliation** – an exercise which agrees the balance on the purchases ledger control account to the total of the list of balances in the purchases ledger

## TEST YOUR LEARNING

### Test 1

The balance on a business's sales ledger control account at the end of June was £41,774 and the total of the list of balances from the sales ledger came to £41,586.

The following errors were discovered:

(a) The sales day book was undercast by £100 on one page

(b) A page from the sales returns day book with a total of £450 had not been posted to the control account although the individual returns had been recorded in the memorandum ledger

(c) An invoice from the sales day book had been posted to the individual account of the customer as £769 instead of the correct figure of £679

(d) A discount allowed to one customer of £16 had been posted to the wrong side of the customer's account in the sales ledger

(e) An irrecoverable debt of £210 had been written off in the account in the sales ledger but not in the general ledger

(f) A credit balance in the memorandum ledger of £125 had been included in the list of balances as a debit balance

Use the following table to show the THREE adjustments you need to make to the sales ledger control account.

| Adjustment | Amount £ | Debit (✓) | Credit (✓) |
|---|---|---|---|
|  |  |  |  |
|  |  |  |  |
|  |  |  |  |

**Test 2**

The balance on a business's purchases ledger control account at the end of June is £38,694 and the total of the list of balances in the memorandum purchases ledger came to £39,741.

The following errors were noted for the month:

(a) A page in the purchases returns day book was overcast by £300

(b) A total from the cash payments book of £3,145 was posted in the general ledger as £3,415

(c) Settlement discounts received from suppliers of £267 were omitted from both the general ledger and the purchases ledger

(d) A credit note from a supplier for £210 was entered into the supplier's account in the purchases ledger as £120

(e) A debit balance on an account in the purchases ledger of £187 was omitted from the list of balances

(f) A credit balance in the purchases ledger should have been included in the list as £570 but instead was recorded as £770

Use the following table to show the THREE adjustments you need to make to the purchases ledger control account.

| Adjustment | Amount £ | Debit (✓) | Credit (✓) |
|---|---|---|---|
|  |  |  |  |
|  |  |  |  |
|  |  |  |  |

# chapter 11:
# THE TRIAL BALANCE, ERRORS AND THE SUSPENSE ACCOUNT

## chapter coverage 📖

So far in this Text we have seen how to account for non-current assets and adjustments such as depreciation, accruals and prepayments, irrecoverable and doubtful debts and inventory. We have also looked at various reconciliations that are prepared at the end of an accounting period and how the errors that these identify can be adjusted. In Basic Accounting we saw how to extract an initial trial balance and also how to redraft it if necessary. We now move on to look at how to complete a trial balance when taking into account the various adjustments that we have encountered.

In this chapter we first briefly revise the types of error that are found in ledger accounts, and whether they cause a suspense account on the trial balance or not. We then work through an example showing how to go from the year end balances for a sole trader to the completed trial balance via an initial trial balance and various accounting adjustments. In doing so we cover accounting for errors using the suspense account. The topics covered are:

- ✍ Revision of errors and the trial balance
- ✍ Preparing the initial trial balance
- ✍ Setting up a suspense account
- ✍ Clearing the suspense account
- ✍ Journal entries for adjustments
- ✍ Preparing an amended trial balance

# TYPES OF ERROR

In any accounting system there are several types of error that can be made when making entries to the ledger accounts. Some of these will be identified when reconciliations are prepared, as we saw in Chapters 9 and 10, and some will come to light when a trial balance is extracted. There are also, however, a number of types of error that do not affect the balancing of the trial balance – despite the error, the trial balance will still balance.

## Errors leading to an imbalance on the trial balance

The following types of error will mean that the debit balances on the trial balance do not equal the credit balances, so a suspense account must be opened and cleared.

| Type of error | Description | Correction | Example |
|---|---|---|---|
| **One-sided entry** | Only one side of the double entry has been made in the ledger accounts, eg the debit and not the credit | Make the missing entry and post the other side to the suspense account | *Error* £10 cash purchase only credited to cash<br><br>*Correction* Debit Purchases £10<br><br>Credit Suspense £10 |
| **Entry duplicated on one side, nothing on the other** | Instead of posting a transaction as a debit in one account and a credit in another, both accounts are posted with debit entries, or both with credit entries. One account is correct but the other is out of balance by twice the amount of the posting | Post the account that was posted on the wrong side with twice the amount, and post the other side to suspense | *Error* £10 cash purchase credited to both cash and purchases<br><br>*Correction* Debit Purchases £20<br><br>Credit Suspense £20 |

| Type of error | Description | Correction | Example |
|---|---|---|---|
| **Unequal entries, normally caused by a transposition error** | The correct amount is entered on one side, but there is an error in writing in the other side of the entry. Often this is caused by a transposition error in the incorrect entry, where the digits in a number are transposed (swapped round). If this is the only error in the accounts then the difference between the debits and the credits will be divisible by 9 | In the account with the wrong posting, post an amount to bring the entry to the right amount, and post the other side to suspense | *Error*<br>£10 cash purchase debited to purchases as £100 (correct credit to cash)<br><br>*Correction*<br>Debit Suspense £90<br><br>Credit Purchases £90 |
| **Account balance incorrectly transferred to the trial balance** | This may be because of a calculation error when calculating the balance on a ledger account, or it may be that a balance which has been calculated correctly in the ledger is entered incorrectly to the trial balance | In the account with the wrong balance, post an amount to bring the balance to the right amount, and post the other side to suspense | *Error*<br>£1,000 debit balance on purchases account written into trial balance as a £100 debit balance<br><br>*Correction*<br>Debit Purchases £900<br><br>Credit Suspense £900 |

| Type of error | Description | Correction | Example |
|---|---|---|---|
| **Balance omission** | A balance on a general ledger account is omitted from the trial balance completely | Enter the missing balance on the correct side and enter the suspense account with the same amount on the other side | *Error* £1,000 debit balance on purchases account omitted<br><br>*Correction* Debit Purchases on trial balance £1,000<br><br>Credit Suspense on trial balance £1,000 |

## Errors not revealed by an imbalance on the trial balance

Unfortunately there are also some types of error that do not cause a difference on the trial balance and therefore cannot be revealed through the trial balance process – though they must still be found of course!

| Type of error | Description | Correction | Example |
|---|---|---|---|
| **Error of principle** | The double entry is arithmetically correct but the wrong type of account has been used eg a non-current asset account is debited with expenses | Remove the incorrect entry and post it to the correct account | *Error* Motor expenses of £100 have been debited to the motor vehicles cost account<br><br>*Correction* Debit Motor expenses £100<br><br>Credit Motor vehicles cost £100 |

| Type of error | Description | Correction | Example |
|---|---|---|---|
| **Error of original entry** | Both the debit and the credit entries have been made using the wrong amount because:<br><br>– the transaction was recorded in the book of prime entry at the incorrect amount, or<br><br>– the wrong figure was picked up from the primary record (eg a transposition error was made), this incorrect figure was used to write up the book of prime entry and so to make both the debit and the credit entry | In both accounts, post an amount to bring the entry to the right amount | *Error*<br>Motor expenses of £100 have been recorded as £10 in the purchases day book<br><br>*Correction*<br>Debit Motor expenses £90<br><br>Credit Purchases ledger control £90 |
| **Error of omission** | A transaction is completely omitted from the ledger accounts | Make the appropriate posting | *Error*<br>Cash purchases of £10 have not been recorded<br><br>*Correction*<br>Debit Purchases £10<br><br>Credit Cash £10 |

| Type of error | Description | Correction | Example |
|---|---|---|---|
| **Reversal of entries** | The correct figure has been used and a debit and a credit entry made but the debit and the credit are on the wrong side of the respective accounts | Remove the incorrect entries and make the correct ones by posting the accounts correctly but with double the amount | *Error*<br>Cash purchases of £10 have been debited to cash and credited to purchases<br><br>*Correction*<br>Debit Purchases £20<br><br>Credit Cash £20 |
| **Error of commission** | The double entry is arithmetically correct but a wrong account of the same type has been used, eg a phone expense is debited to the electricity account rather than the phone account | Remove the incorrect entry and post it to the correct account | *Error*<br>Motor expenses of £100 have been debited to the office expenses account<br><br>*Correction*<br>Debit Motor expenses £100<br><br>Credit Office expenses £100 |

## COMPLETING THE TRIAL BALANCE

We will now work through a comprehensive example which will take you from ledger account balances through to a completed trial balance via adjustments and a suspense account.

# HOW IT WORKS

Given below are the brought down balances on the ledger accounts at the end of the day on 31 March 20X4, the year end, for John Thompson, who is not registered for VAT.

**Building at cost**

| | | £ | | | £ |
|---|---|---|---|---|---|
| 31 Mar | Balance b/d | 100,000 | | | |

**Furniture and fittings at cost**

| | | £ | | | £ |
|---|---|---|---|---|---|
| 31 Mar | Balance b/d | 4,800 | | | |

**Motor vehicles at cost**

| | | £ | | | £ |
|---|---|---|---|---|---|
| 31 Mar | Balance b/d | 32,700 | | | |

**Computer at cost**

| | | £ | | | £ |
|---|---|---|---|---|---|
| 31 Mar | Balance b/d | 2,850 | | | |

**Accumulated depreciation – building**

| | £ | | | £ |
|---|---|---|---|---|
| | | 31 Mar | Balance b/d | 4,000 |

**Accumulated depreciation – furniture and fittings**

| | £ | | | £ |
|---|---|---|---|---|
| | | 31 Mar | Balance b/d | 1,920 |

**Accumulated depreciation – motor vehicles**

| | £ | | | £ |
|---|---|---|---|---|
| | | 31 Mar | Balance b/d | 7,850 |

**Accumulated depreciation – computer**

| | £ | | | £ |
|---|---|---|---|---|
| | | 31 Mar | Balance b/d | 950 |

**Inventory**

| | | £ | | | £ |
|---|---|---|---|---|---|
| 31 Mar | Balance b/d | 4,400 | | | |

**Bank/cash**

| | | £ | | | £ |
|---|---|---|---|---|---|
| 31 Mar | Balance b/d | 3,960 | | | |

**Petty cash**

| | | £ | | | £ |
|---|---|---|---|---|---|
| 31 Mar | Balance b/d | 100 | | | |

### Sales ledger control

| | | £ | | | £ |
|---|---|---|---|---|---|
| 31 Mar | Balance b/d | 15,240 | | | |

### Purchases ledger control

| | | £ | | | £ |
|---|---|---|---|---|---|
| | | | 31 Mar | Balance b/d | 5,010 |

### Capital

| | | £ | | | £ |
|---|---|---|---|---|---|
| | | | 31 Mar | Balance b/d | 130,000 |

### Sales

| | | £ | | | £ |
|---|---|---|---|---|---|
| | | | 31 Mar | Balance b/d | 155,020 |

### Sales returns

| | | £ | | | £ |
|---|---|---|---|---|---|
| 31 Mar | Balance b/d | 2,100 | | | |

### Purchases

| | | £ | | | £ |
|---|---|---|---|---|---|
| 31 Mar | Balance b/d | 80,200 | | | |

### Purchases returns

| | | £ | | | £ |
|---|---|---|---|---|---|
| | | | 31 Mar | Balance b/d | 1,400 |

### Bank charges

| | | £ | | | £ |
|---|---|---|---|---|---|
| 31 Mar | Balance b/d | 200 | | | |

### Discounts allowed

| | | £ | | | £ |
|---|---|---|---|---|---|
| 31 Mar | Balance b/d | 890 | | | |

### Discounts received

| | | £ | | | £ |
|---|---|---|---|---|---|
| | | | 31 Mar | Balance b/d | 1,260 |

### Wages

| | | £ | | | £ |
|---|---|---|---|---|---|
| 31 Mar | Balance b/d | 32,780 | | | |

### Rates

| | | £ | | | £ |
|---|---|---|---|---|---|
| 31 Mar | Balance b/d | 5,500 | | | |

### Telephone

| | | £ | | | £ |
|---|---|---|---|---|---|
| 31 Mar | Balance b/d | 1,140 | | | |

### Electricity

| | | £ | | | £ |
|---|---|---|---|---|---|
| 31 Mar | Balance b/d | 1,480 | | | |

### Insurance

| | | £ | | | £ |
|---|---|---|---|---|---|
| 31 Mar | Balance b/d | 1,500 | | | |

### Motor expenses

| | | £ | | | £ |
|---|---|---|---|---|---|
| 31 Mar | Balance b/d | 1,580 | | | |

### Office expenses

| | | £ | | | £ |
|---|---|---|---|---|---|
| 31 Mar | Balance b/d | 960 | | | |

### Allowance for doubtful debts

| | £ | | | £ |
|---|---|---|---|---|
| | | 31 Mar | Balance b/d | 220 |

### Loan

| | £ | | | £ |
|---|---|---|---|---|
| | | 31 Mar | Balance b/d | 820 |

### Drawings

| | | £ | | | £ |
|---|---|---|---|---|---|
| 31 Mar | Balance b/d | 15,800 | | | |

The first stage is to transfer all of the closing balances on the ledger accounts to the trial balance, add it up and check that it balances. If it does not balance, first check your additions and if this doesn't clear it, then open up a suspense account to make the debits and credits equal.

## Draft trial balance as at 31 March 20X4

| | Debit £ | Credit £ |
|---|---|---|
| Buildings at cost | 100,000 | |
| Furniture and fittings at cost | 4,800 | |
| Motor vehicles at cost | 32,700 | |
| Computer at cost | 2,850 | |
| Accumulated depreciation – buildings | | 4,000 |
| Accumulated depreciation – furniture and fittings | | 1,920 |
| Accumulated depreciation – motor vehicles | | 7,850 |
| Accumulated depreciation – computer | | 950 |
| Inventory | 4,400 | |
| Bank/cash | 3,960 | |
| Petty cash | 100 | |
| Sales ledger control | 15,240 | |
| Purchases ledger control | | 5,010 |
| Capital | | 130,000 |
| Sales | | 155,020 |
| Sales returns | 2,100 | |
| Purchases | 80,200 | |
| Purchases returns | | 1,400 |
| Bank charges | 200 | |
| Discounts allowed | 890 | |
| Discounts received | | 1,260 |
| Wages | 32,780 | |
| Rates | 5,500 | |
| Telephone | 1,140 | |
| Electricity | 1,480 | |
| Insurance | 1,500 | |
| Motor expenses | 1,580 | |
| Office expenses | 960 | |
| Allowance for doubtful debts | | 220 |
| Loan | | 820 |
| Drawings | 15,800 | |
| Suspense | 270 | |
| | 308,450 | 308,450 |

## Suspense account

In this case the credit total was £270 larger than the debit total and so a suspense account was opened for the difference. The suspense account must of course be cleared and the errors that were discovered are given below:

(a) The purchases returns account was overcast by £100

(b) £200 of office expenses has been charged to the motor expenses account

(c) Discounts allowed of £170 have been correctly accounted for in the sales ledger control account but omitted from the discounts allowed account

We must now prepare journal entries to correct these errors and to clear the suspense account.

## Journal entries

(a) As purchase returns are a credit balance if the account has been overstated then the purchases returns account must be debited and the suspense account credited.

| Account name | Amount £ | Debit (✓) | Credit (✓) |
|---|---|---|---|
| Purchases returns | 100 | ✓ | |
| Suspense | 100 | | ✓ |

(b) The motor expenses account has been wrongly debited with office expenses so the motor expenses account must be credited and office expenses debited.

| Account name | Amount £ | Debit (✓) | Credit (✓) |
|---|---|---|---|
| Office expenses | 200 | ✓ | |
| Motor expenses | 200 | | ✓ |

(c) The correct double entry for discounts allowed is a debit to the discounts allowed account and a credit to sales ledger control. The credit has been done but the debit is missing. Therefore we must debit discounts allowed and credit the suspense account.

| Account name | Amount £ | Debit (✓) | Credit (✓) |
|---|---|---|---|
| Discounts allowed | 170 | ✓ | |
| Suspense | 170 | | ✓ |

BPP LEARNING MEDIA

## Year end adjustments

You are also given information about the following year end adjustments that must be made:

(a) Depreciation is to be charged for the year using the following depreciation policy:

- Building – 2% straight line
- Furniture and fittings – 20% straight line
- Motor vehicles – 30% reducing balance
- Computer – $33\frac{1}{3}$ % straight line

(b) Rates of £500 are to be accrued

(c) The insurance account includes an amount of £300 that relates to the year ended 31 March 20X5

(d) An irrecoverable debt of £240 is to be written off

(e) An allowance for 2% of the remaining debts is required

We must now prepare the journal entries that will complete these adjustments and close off the accounts for the period.

## Journal entries

(a) The accumulated depreciation accounts in the trial balance are as at the beginning of the year since the annual depreciation charge has yet to be accounted for. In each case the double entry is to debit a depreciation charge account and to credit the relevant accumulated depreciation account.

|  | Debit £ | Credit £ |
|---|---|---|
| Depreciation charge – building (100,000 × 2%) | 2,000 | |
| Accumulated depreciation – building | | 2,000 |
| | | |
| Depreciation charge – furniture and fittings (4,800 × 20%) | 960 | |
| Accumulated depreciation – furniture and fittings | | 960 |
| | | |
| Depreciation charge – motor vehicles ((32,700 – 7,850) × 30%) | 7,455 | |
| Accumulated depreciation – motor vehicles | | 7,455 |
| | | |
| Depreciation charge – computer (2,850 × $33\frac{1}{3}$) | 950 | |
| Accumulated depreciation – computer | | 950 |

(b) Rates of £500 are to be accrued.

|  | Debit £ | Credit £ |
|---|---|---|
| Rates | 500 | |
| Accruals | | 500 |

(c) Insurance has been prepaid by £300

|  | Debit £ | Credit £ |
|---|---|---|
| Prepayments | 300 | |
| Insurance | | 300 |

(d) An irrecoverable debt of £240 is to be written off

|  | Debit £ | Credit £ |
|---|---|---|
| Irrecoverable debts expense | 240 | |
| Sales ledger control | | 240 |

(e) An allowance for doubtful debts of 2% of the remaining debts is required.

|  | £ |
|---|---|
| Allowance required = (15,240 – 240) × 2% | 300 |
| Current level of allowance | 220 |
| Increase in allowance | 80 |

|  | Debit £ | Credit £ |
|---|---|---|
| Allowance for doubtful debts adjustment | 80 | |
| Allowance for doubtful debts | | 80 |

## Closing inventory

The closing inventory has been counted and valued at £5,200.

The inventory figure in the draft trial balance is the opening inventory which will eventually be debited to the income statement as part of cost of sales. The closing inventory must now be entered into the accounts with a journal entry.

|  | Debit £ | Credit £ |
|---|---|---|
| Inventory – statement of financial position | 5,200 | |
| Inventory – income statement | | 5,200 |

## Updating ledger accounts

All the journal entries have now been made for the correction of errors, adjustments and closing inventory. These journals must now be entered into the ledger accounts and the ledger accounts balanced to give their amended closing balances. This means that a number of new ledger accounts have to be opened.

## Errors

(a)

### Purchases returns

| | | £ | | | £ |
|---|---|---|---|---|---|
| 31 March | Journal | 100 | 31 March | Balance b/d | 1,400 |
| 31 March | Balance c/d | 1,300 | | | |
| | | 1,400 | | | 1,400 |
| | | | 31 March | Balance b/d | 1,300 |

### Suspense account

| | | £ | | | £ |
|---|---|---|---|---|---|
| 31 March | Balance b/d | 270 | 31 March | Journal | 100 |

(b)

### Office expenses

| | | £ | | | £ |
|---|---|---|---|---|---|
| 31 March | Balance b/d | 960 | | | |
| 31 March | Journal | 200 | 31 March | Balance c/d | 1,160 |
| | | 1,160 | | | 1,160 |
| 31 March | Balance b/d | 1,160 | | | |

### Motor expenses

| | | £ | | | £ |
|---|---|---|---|---|---|
| 31 March | Balance b/d | 1,580 | 31 March | Journal | 200 |
| | | | 31 March | Balance c/d | 1,380 |
| | | 1,580 | | | 1,580 |
| 31 March | Balance b/d | 1,380 | | | |

(c)

### Discounts allowed

| | | £ | | | £ |
|---|---|---|---|---|---|
| 31 March | Balance b/d | 890 | | | |
| 31 March | Journal | 170 | 31 March | Balance c/d | 1,060 |
| | | 1,060 | | | 1,060 |
| 31 March | Balance b/d | 1,060 | | | |

## Suspense account

| | | £ | | | £ |
|---|---|---|---|---|---|
| 31 March | Balance b/d | 270 | 31 March | Journal | 100 |
| | | | 31 March | Journal | 170 |
| | | 270 | | | 270 |

## Year end adjustments

(a) Depreciation charges for the year

### Depreciation charge – building

| | | £ | | £ |
|---|---|---|---|---|
| 31 March | Journal | 2,000 | | |

### Accumulated depreciation – building

| | | £ | | | £ |
|---|---|---|---|---|---|
| | | | 31 March | Balance b/d | 4,000 |
| 31 March | Balance c/d | 6,000 | 31 March | Journal | 2,000 |
| | | 6,000 | | | 6,000 |
| | | | 31 March | Balance b/d | 6,000 |

### Depreciation charge – furniture and fittings

| | | £ | | £ |
|---|---|---|---|---|
| 31 March | Journal | 960 | | |

### Accumulated depreciation – furniture and fittings

| | | £ | | | £ |
|---|---|---|---|---|---|
| | | | 31 March | Balance b/d | 1,920 |
| 31 March | Balance c/d | 2,880 | 31 March | Journal | 960 |
| | | 2,880 | | | 2,880 |
| | | | 31 March | Balance b/d | 2,880 |

### Depreciation charge – motor vehicles

| | | £ | | £ |
|---|---|---|---|---|
| 31 March | Journal | 7,455 | | |

### Accumulated depreciation – motor vehicles

| | | £ | | | £ |
|---|---|---|---|---|---|
| | | | 31 March | Balance b/d | 7,850 |
| 31 March | Balance c/d | 15,305 | 31 March | Journal | 7,455 |
| | | 15,305 | | | 15,305 |
| | | | 31 March | Balance b/d | 15,305 |

### Depreciation charge – computer

| | | £ | | £ |
|---|---|---|---|---|
| 31 March | Journal | 950 | | |

### Accumulated depreciation – computer

| | | £ | | | £ |
|---|---|---|---|---|---|
| | | | 31 March | Balance b/d | 950 |
| 31 March | Balance c/d | 1,900 | 31 March | Journal | 950 |
| | | 1,900 | | | 1,900 |
| | | | 31 March | Balance b/d | 1,900 |

(b)  Rates accrual

### Rates

| | | £ | | | £ |
|---|---|---|---|---|---|
| 31 March | Balance b/d | 5,500 | | | |
| 31 March | Journal | 500 | 31 March | Balance c/d | 6,000 |
| | | 6,000 | | | 6,000 |
| 31 March | Balance b/d | 6,000 | | | |

### Accruals

| | | £ | | | £ |
|---|---|---|---|---|---|
| | | | 31 March | Journal | 500 |

(c)  Insurance prepaid

### Insurance

| | | £ | | | £ |
|---|---|---|---|---|---|
| 31 March | Balance b/d | 1,500 | 31 March | Journal | 300 |
| | | | 31 March | Balance c/d | 1,200 |
| | | 1,500 | | | 1,500 |
| 31 March | Balance b/d | 1,200 | | | |

### Prepayments

| | | £ | | £ |
|---|---|---|---|---|
| 31 March | Journal | 300 | | |

(d)  Irrecoverable debt write off

### Irrecoverable debts expense

| | | £ | | £ |
|---|---|---|---|---|
| 31 March | Journal | 240 | | |

### Sales ledger control

| | | £ | | | £ |
|---|---|---|---|---|---|
| 31 March | Balance b/d | 15,240 | 31 March | Journal | 240 |
| | | | 31 March | Balance c/d | 15,000 |
| | | 15,240 | | | 15,240 |
| 31 March | Balance b/d | 15,000 | | | |

(e)   Allowance for doubtful debts

### Allowance for doubtful debts adjustment

| | | £ | | | £ |
|---|---|---|---|---|---|
| 31 March | Journal | 80 | | | |

### Allowance for doubtful debts

| | | £ | | | £ |
|---|---|---|---|---|---|
| | | | 31 March | Balance b/d | 220 |
| 31 March | Balance c/d | 300 | 31 March | Journal | 80 |
| | | 300 | | | 300 |
| | | | 31 March | Balance b/d | 300 |

## Closing inventory

### Inventory– statement of financial position

| | £ | | | £ |
|---|---|---|---|---|
| 31 March Journal | 5,200 | | | |

### Inventory – income statement

| | £ | | | £ |
|---|---|---|---|---|
| | | 31 March | Journal | 5,200 |

Once all the ledger accounts have been updated for the journal entries a new final trial balance is drawn up which reflects all of the error corrections and adjustments.

Note that we now have three inventory account balances. Do not worry about this at the moment as it will be explained in Chapter 12.

## Final trial balance as at 31 March 20X4

|  | Debit £ | Credit £ |
|---|---:|---:|
| Buildings at cost | 100,000 | |
| Furniture and fittings at cost | 4,800 | |
| Motor vehicles at cost | 32,700 | |
| Computer at cost | 2,850 | |
| Accumulated depreciation – buildings | | 6,000 |
| Accumulated depreciation – furniture and fittings | | 2,880 |
| Accumulated depreciation – motor vehicles | | 15,305 |
| Accumulated depreciation – computer | | 1,900 |
| Inventory at 1 April 20X3 | 4,400 | |
| Bank/cash | 3,960 | |
| Petty cash | 100 | |
| Sales ledger control | 15,000 | |
| Purchases ledger control | | 5,010 |
| Capital | | 130,000 |
| Sales | | 155,020 |
| Sales returns | 2,100 | |
| Purchases | 80,200 | |
| Purchases returns | | 1,300 |
| Bank charges | 200 | |
| Discounts allowed | 1,060 | |
| Discounts received | | 1,260 |
| Wages | 32,780 | |
| Rates | 6,000 | |
| Telephone | 1,140 | |
| Electricity | 1,480 | |
| Insurance | 1,200 | |
| Motor expenses | 1,380 | |
| Office expenses | 1,160 | |
| Allowance for doubtful debts | | 300 |
| Loan | | 820 |
| Drawings | 15,800 | |
| Suspense | – | |
| Depreciation charge – building | 2,000 | |
| Depreciation charge – furniture and fittings | 960 | |
| Depreciation charge – motor vehicles | 7,455 | |
| Depreciation charge – computer | 950 | |
| Accruals | | 500 |
| Prepayments | 300 | |
| Irrecoverable debts expense | 240 | |
| Allowance for doubtful debts adjustment | 80 | |
| Inventory – statement of financial position | 5,200 | |
| Inventory – income statement | | 5,200 |
| | 325,495 | 325,495 |

## Final ledger account adjustments

Once the balances on the trial balance have been taken to the income statement and statement of financial position there is one final set of adjustments that must be done to some of the ledger accounts.

The income and expense ledger accounts must be closed off as the balances are no longer required in the ledger. This is done by taking the balances on each individual income and expense ledger account to a new ledger account known as the INCOME STATEMENT LEDGER ACCOUNT.

## HOW IT WORKS

The final balances on the sales account, purchases account and wages account are shown below.

### Sales

| | £ | | £ |
|---|---|---|---|
| | | Balance b/d | 155,020 |

### Purchases

| | £ | | £ |
|---|---|---|---|
| Balance b/d | 80,200 | | |

### Wages

| | £ | | £ |
|---|---|---|---|
| Balance b/d | 32,780 | | |

These accounts must be closed off ready to start with a clean sheet at the beginning of the next accounting period. This is done by transferring the balances remaining to the income statement ledger account.

### Sales

| | £ | | £ |
|---|---|---|---|
| Income statement | 155,020 | Balance b/d | 155,020 |

### Purchases

| | £ | | £ |
|---|---|---|---|
| Balance b/d | 80,200 | Income statement | 80,200 |

## Wages

| | £ | | £ |
|---|---|---|---|
| Balance b/d | 32,780 | Income statement | 32,780 |

## Income statement

| | £ | | £ |
|---|---|---|---|
| Purchases | 80,200 | Sales | 155,020 |
| Wages | 32,780 | | |

This will be done for all income statement balances and there will need to be journal entries for each of these final adjustments. Therefore the final set of journal entries in full will be as follows:

### Journal entries

| | Debit | Credit |
|---|---|---|
| **Opening inventory** | £ | £ |
| Income statement | 4,400 | |
| Inventory | | 4,400 |
| **Sales** | | |
| Sales | 155,020 | |
| Income statement | | 155,020 |
| **Sales returns** | | |
| Income statement | 2,100 | |
| Sales returns | | 2,100 |
| **Purchases** | | |
| Income statement | 80,200 | |
| Purchases | | 80,200 |
| **Purchases returns** | | |
| Purchases returns | 1,300 | |
| Income statement | | 1,300 |
| **Bank charges** | | |
| Income statement | 200 | |
| Bank charges | | 200 |
| **Discounts allowed** | | |
| Income statement | 1,060 | |
| Discounts allowed | | 1,060 |
| **Discounts received** | | |
| Discounts received | 1,260 | |
| Income statement | | 1,260 |
| **Wages** | | |
| Income statement | 32,780 | |
| Wages | | 32,780 |
| **Rates** | | |
| Income statement | 6,000 | |
| Rates | | 6,000 |

|  | Debit £ | Credit £ |
|---|---|---|
| **Telephone** | | |
| Income statement | 1,140 | |
| Telephone | | 1,140 |
| **Electricity** | | |
| Income statement | 1,480 | |
| Electricity | | 1,480 |
| **Insurance** | | |
| Income statement | 1,200 | |
| Insurance | | 1,200 |
| **Motor expenses** | | |
| Income statement | 1,380 | |
| Motor expenses | | 1,380 |
| **Office expenses** | | |
| Income statement | 1,160 | |
| Office expenses | | 1,160 |
| **Depreciation charge – buildings** | | |
| Income statement | 2,000 | |
| Depr'n charge – buildings | | 2,000 |
| **Depreciation charge – furniture and** | | |
| Income statement | 960 | |
| Depr'n charge – furniture and fittings | | 960 |
| **Depreciation charge – motor vehicles** | | |
| Income statement | 7,455 | |
| Depr'n charge – motor vehicles | | 7,455 |
| **Depreciation charge – computer** | | |
| Income statement | 950 | |
| Depr'n charge – computer | | 950 |
| **Irrecoverable debt expense** | | |
| Income statement | 240 | |
| Irrecoverable debts expense | | 240 |
| **Allowance for doubtful debts** | | |
| Income statement | 80 | |
| Allowance for doubtful debts | | 80 |
| **Inventory – income statement** | | |
| Inventory – income statement | 5,200 | |
| Income statement | | 5,200 |

## Statement of financial position ledger account balances

There is no need to do any similar adjustments to statement of financial position ledger accounts ie assets and liabilities. This is because they remain as opening balances for the following accounting period in the ledger account. For example, the closing balance on the Buildings at cost account is £100,000 and this is the balance brought down or opening balance for the buildings at the start of the next accounting period.

## Task 1

What are the year-end journal entries required to clear the following accounts:

(a)    Purchases returns account

| Account name | Debit (✓) | Credit (✓) |
|---|---|---|
|  |  |  |
|  |  |  |

(b)    Insurance account

| Account name | Debit (✓) | Credit (✓) |
|---|---|---|
|  |  |  |
|  |  |  |

(c)    Sales ledger control account

| Account name | Debit (✓) | Credit (✓) |
|---|---|---|
|  |  |  |
|  |  |  |

## Task 2

Which of the following is an example of an error of commission where no control account is kept?

A    A receipt of £25 from J Gee entered in G Jay's account as a credit and debited to cash

B    A purchase of cleaning materials recorded as DR cash £50, CR cleaning materials £50

C    An invoice for £1,300 is lost and not recorded at all

D    An invoice for £2,500 sales is posted as £2,050

## Task 3

Which of the following errors would be a possible reason for the trial balance not balancing?

A    Sales of £500 entered correctly but entered as £1,500 in the sales ledger control account

B    A purchase of £550 on credit not being recorded

C    Cash wages being recorded as DR cash £250, CR wages £250

D    A non-current asset purchase of £750 being recorded ad DR machinery repairs £750, CR cash £750

## CHAPTER OVERVIEW

- Start by preparing an initial trial balance from the closing ledger account balances – you may need to set up a suspense account balance if the trial balance does not initially balance

- The suspense account must be cleared by journal entries to correct any errors identified

- Make journal entries for the period end adjustments for depreciation, accruals, prepayments, irrecoverable and doubtful debts and closing inventory

- Update the ledger account balances for the adjustments and corrections and prepare a final trial balance

- As a final year end adjustment all income and expense balances must be cleared out to the income statement ledger account

BPP
LEARNING MEDIA

# TEST YOUR LEARNING

### Test 1

The phone expense and insurance expense accounts of a sole trader have balances of £3,400 and £1,600 respectively at 30 September. However £300 of phone expense is to be accrued and £200 of insurance has been prepaid. What are the final expense figures that will appear in the income statement for the year to 30 September?

Phone expense          £ [        ]

Insurance expense      £ [        ]

# chapter 12:
# THE EXTENDED TRIAL BALANCE

———— **chapter coverage** 📖 ————

Accounts Preparation I requires you to use the extended trial balance in order to help prepare the financial statements. This technique builds on the trial balance and the preparation of adjustments in order to let us see whether balances are going into the income statement or the statement of financial position. It also helps in the calculation of the period's profit or loss. The topics covered in this chapter are:

✍ The layout of an extended trial balance (ETB)

✍ Correcting errors on the ETB

✍ Making year end adjustments

✍ Extending the ETB

# EXTENDED TRIAL BALANCE

In this chapter we introduce the EXTENDED TRIAL BALANCE. The extended trial balance (ETB) is a technique that allows the initial trial balance to be adjusted for the necessary year end adjustments, to be corrected for any errors that are found and eventually to form the basis for the preparation of the financial statements.

An extended trial balance will normally have a column for the account name followed by eight further working columns:

## Extended trial balance

| Account name | Ledger balances | | Adjustments | | Income statement | | Statement of financial position | |
|---|---|---|---|---|---|---|---|---|
| | DR | CR | DR | CR | DR | CR | DR | CR |

## HOW TO PREPARE THE EXTENDED TRIAL BALANCE

We will start with a summary of the procedure for preparing an extended trial balance (ETB) and then work through it on a step by step basis.

**Step 1** Enter each ledger account balance as either a debit or a credit in the ledger balance column. This is the initial trial balance and it should balance – however if there is a difference between the debits and the credits a suspense account balance should be added to make the trial balance add up. Leave a number of empty lines at the bottom of this trial balance before totalling it as these will be necessary for adjustments and corrections.

**Step 2** If there is a suspense account, deal with the errors that have caused this by entering the debits and credits to correct the errors in the adjustments column.

**Step 3** Enter any year end adjustments as directed in the adjustments column such as: the depreciation charge for the year, closing inventory, accruals and prepayments, irrecoverable debts written off and adjustments for allowance for doubtful debts. When doing this you may need to open up some new account lines in the ETB in the blank lines that you have left at the bottom of the ETB.

**Step 4** Total and extend each line of the ETB into the income statement or statement of financial position columns as appropriate.

**Step 5** Total the income statement columns. The difference is the profit or loss for the year. Enter this amount twice:

- in the appropriate column to make the income statement columns balance and

- in the opposite statement of financial position column then

- total the statement of financial position columns – they should be equal.

# HOW IT WORKS

We will use the example of John Thompson used in Chapter 11.

Given below is the list of ledger balances for John Thompson, a wholesaler of small electrical items, at his year end of 31 March 20X4.

|  | £ |
|---|---|
| Buildings at cost | 100,000 |
| Furniture and fittings at cost | 4,800 |
| Motor vehicles at cost | 32,700 |
| Computer at cost | 2,850 |
| Accumulated depreciation at 1 April 20X3 | |
| – buildings | 4,000 |
| – furniture and fittings | 1,920 |
| – motor vehicles | 7,850 |
| – computer | 950 |
| Inventory at 1 April 20X3 | 4,400 |
| Bank/cash (debit balance) | 3,960 |
| Petty cash | 100 |
| Sales ledger control | 15,240 |
| Purchases ledger control | 5,010 |
| Capital | 130,000 |
| Sales | 155,020 |
| Sales returns | 2,100 |
| Purchases | 80,200 |
| Purchases returns | 1,400 |
| Bank charges | 200 |
| Discounts allowed | 890 |
| Discounts received | 1,260 |
| Wages | 32,780 |
| Rates | 5,500 |
| Telephone | 1,140 |
| Electricity | 1,480 |
| Insurance | 1,500 |
| Motor expenses | 1,580 |
| Office expenses | 960 |
| Allowance for doubtful debts at 1 April 20X3 | 220 |
| Loan | 820 |
| Drawings | 15,800 |

Step 1   Enter these balances onto the ETB in the debit and credit columns of the ledger balance columns. Total the trial balance and check your totals carefully. Enter a suspense account balance if necessary.

## Extended trial balance

| Account name | Ledger balances | | Adjustments | | Income statement | | SFP | |
|---|---|---|---|---|---|---|---|---|
| | DR | CR | DR | CR | DR | CR | DR | CR |
| | £ | £ | £ | £ | £ | £ | £ | £ |
| Buildings at cost | 100,000 | | | | | | | |
| Furniture and fittings at cost | 4,800 | | | | | | | |
| Motor vehicles at cost | 32,700 | | | | | | | |
| Computer at cost | 2,850 | | | | | | | |
| Accumulated depreciation at 1 April 20X3: | | | | | | | | |
| – buildings | | 4,000 | | | | | | |
| – furniture and fittings | | 1,920 | | | | | | |
| – motor vehicles | | 7,850 | | | | | | |
| – computer | | 950 | | | | | | |
| Inventory at 1 April 20X3 | 4,400 | | | | | | | |
| Bank/cash | 3,960 | | | | | | | |
| Petty cash | 100 | | | | | | | |
| Sales ledger control | 15,240 | | | | | | | |
| Purchases ledger control | | 5,010 | | | | | | |
| Capital | | 130,000 | | | | | | |
| Sales | | 155,020 | | | | | | |
| Sales returns | 2,100 | | | | | | | |
| Purchases | 80,200 | | | | | | | |
| Purchases returns | | 1,400 | | | | | | |
| Bank charges | 200 | | | | | | | |
| Discounts allowed | 890 | | | | | | | |
| Discounts received | | 1,260 | | | | | | |
| Wages | 32,780 | | | | | | | |
| Rates | 5,500 | | | | | | | |
| Telephone | 1,140 | | | | | | | |
| Electricity | 1,480 | | | | | | | |
| Insurance | 1,500 | | | | | | | |
| Motor expenses | 1,580 | | | | | | | |
| Office expenses | 960 | | | | | | | |
| Allowance for doubtful debts at 1 April 20X3 | | 220 | | | | | | |
| Loan | | 820 | | | | | | |
| Drawings | 15,800 | | | | | | | |
| Suspense account | 270 | | | | | | | |
| | 308,450 | 308,450 | | | | | | |

In this case the trial balance does not balance. The total of the debit column is £308,180 and the total of the credit column is £308,450, so a suspense account balance of £270 is entered into the debit column in order to make the trial balance add up.

Take note of some of the entries in the trial balance. The accumulated depreciation and allowance for doubtful debts are as at 1 April 20X3. This means that the depreciation charge for the year has not yet been accounted for, nor has there been any adjustment to the allowance for receivables for the year.

The inventory figure in the trial balance is also as at 1 April 20X3, as it is the opening inventory. The inventory figure in the trial balance is always the opening inventory figure as the closing inventory is not entered into the accounts until the year end when it is counted and valued (see Chapter 7).

Step 2 Deal with the errors that have caused the balance on the suspense account. The errors that have been found are given below:

- The purchases returns account was overcast by £100

| Debit | Purchases returns | £100 |
| Credit | Suspense | £100 |

- £200 of office expenses has been charged to the motor expenses account

| Debit | Office expenses | £200 |
| Credit | Motor expenses | £200 |

- Discounts allowed of £170 had been correctly accounted for in the sales ledger control account but omitted from the discounts allowed account

| Debit | Discounts allowed | £170 |
| Credit | Suspense | £170 |

These three double entries will now be entered into the ETB.

| Account name | Ledger balances | | Adjustments | | Income statement | | SFP | |
|---|---|---|---|---|---|---|---|---|
| | DR £ | CR £ | DR £ | CR £ | DR £ | CR £ | DR £ | CR £ |
| Buildings at cost | 100,000 | | | | | | | |
| Furniture and fittings at cost | 4,800 | | | | | | | |
| Motor vehicles at cost | 32,700 | | | | | | | |
| Computer at cost | 2,850 | | | | | | | |
| Accumulated depreciation at 1 April 20X3: | | | | | | | | |
| – buildings | | 4,000 | | | | | | |
| – furniture and fittings | | 1,920 | | | | | | |
| – motor vehicles | | 7,850 | | | | | | |
| – computer | | 950 | | | | | | |
| Inventory at 1 April 20X3 | 4,400 | | | | | | | |
| Bank/cash | 3,960 | | | | | | | |
| Petty cash | 100 | | | | | | | |
| Sales ledger control | 15,240 | | | | | | | |
| Purchases ledger control | | 5,010 | | | | | | |
| Capital | | 130,000 | | | | | | |
| Sales | | 155,020 | | | | | | |
| Sales returns | 2,100 | | | | | | | |
| Purchases | 80,200 | | | | | | | |
| Purchases returns | | 1,400 | 100 | | | | | |
| Bank charges | 200 | | | | | | | |
| Discounts allowed | 890 | | 170 | | | | | |
| Discounts received | | 1,260 | | | | | | |
| Wages | 32,780 | | | | | | | |
| Rates | 5,500 | | | | | | | |
| Telephone | 1,140 | | | | | | | |
| Electricity | 1,480 | | | | | | | |
| Insurance | 1,500 | | | | | | | |
| Motor expenses | 1,580 | | | 200 | | | | |
| Office expenses | 960 | | 200 | | | | | |
| Allowance for doubtful debts at 1 April 20X3 | | 220 | | | | | | |
| Loan | | 820 | | | | | | |
| Drawings | 15,800 | | | | | | | |
| Suspense account | 270 | | | 100 + 170 | | | | |
| | 308,450 | 308,450 | | | | | | |

**Step 3**   Enter the year end adjustments in the adjustments columns:

(a)   Depreciation

    (i)   Buildings – 2% straight line

        £100,000 × 2% = £2,000

| | | |
|---|---|---:|
| Debit | Buildings depreciation charge | £2,000 |
| Credit | Buildings accumulated depreciation | £2,000 |

    (ii)   Furniture and fittings – 20% straight line

        £4,800 × 20% = £960

| | | |
|---|---|---:|
| Debit | Furniture depreciation charge | £960 |
| Credit | Furniture accumulated depreciation | £960 |

    (iii)   Motor vehicles – 30% reducing balance

        (£32,700 – 7,850) × 30% = £7,455

| | | |
|---|---|---:|
| Debit | Vehicles depreciation charge | £7,455 |
| Credit | Vehicles accumulated depreciation | £7,455 |

    (iv)   Computer – $33\frac{1}{3}$% straight line

        £2,850 × $33\frac{1}{3}$% = £950

| | | |
|---|---|---:|
| Debit | Computer depreciation charge | £950 |
| Credit | Computer accumulated depreciation | £950 |

(b)   Rates of £500 are to be accrued

| | | |
|---|---|---:|
| Debit | Rates | £500 |
| Credit | Accruals | £500 |

(c)   The insurance account includes an amount of £300 prepaid

| | | |
|---|---|---:|
| Debit | Prepayments | £300 |
| Credit | Insurance | £300 |

(d)   An irrecoverable debt of £240 is to be written off

| | | |
|---|---|---:|
| Debit | Irrecoverable debts expense | £240 |
| Credit | Sales ledger control | £240 |

(e) An allowance for 2% of the remaining receivables (debtors) is to be made

| | |
|---|---|
| Allowance required 2% × (£15,240 – 240) | = £300 |
| Balance on allowance account at start of the year | = £220 |
| Increase in allowance required £300 – 220 | = £80 |

| | | |
|---|---|---|
| Debit | Allowance for doubtful debts adjustment | £80 |
| Credit | Allowance for doubtful debts | £80 |

(f) Closing inventory at 31 March 20X4 has been valued at £5,200.

| | | |
|---|---|---|
| Debit | Inventory account – statement of financial position | £5,200 |
| Credit | Inventory account – income statement | £5,200 |

In the adjustment column of the ETB the entries to make are both a debit and a credit entry against the opening inventory line with the value of the closing inventory.

At this stage you have completed the adjustments. Therefore to check that all of the adjustments have consisted of complete double entry you should total the debit and credit adjustment columns – they should be equal.

| Account name | Ledger balances | | Adjustments | | Income statement | | SFP | |
| --- | --- | --- | --- | --- | --- | --- | --- | --- |
| | DR £ | CR £ | DR £ | CR £ | DR £ | CR £ | DR £ | CR £ |
| Buildings at cost | 100,000 | | | | | | | |
| Furniture and fittings at cost | 4,800 | | | | | | | |
| Motor vehicles at cost | 32,700 | | | | | | | |
| Computer at cost | 2,850 | | | | | | | |
| Accumulated depreciation at 1 April 20X3: | | | | | | | | |
| – buildings | | 4,000 | | 2,000 | | | | |
| – furniture and fittings | | 1,920 | | 960 | | | | |
| – motor vehicles | | 7,850 | | 7,455 | | | | |
| – computer | | 950 | | 950 | | | | |
| Inventory at 1 April 20X3 | 4,400 | | 5,200 | 5,200 | | | | |
| Bank | 3,960 | | | | | | | |
| Petty cash | 100 | | | | | | | |
| Sales ledger control | 15,240 | | | 240 | | | | |
| Purchases ledger control | | 5,010 | | | | | | |
| Capital | | 130,000 | | | | | | |
| Sales | | 155,020 | | | | | | |
| Sales returns | 2,100 | | | | | | | |
| Purchases | 80,200 | | | | | | | |
| Purchases returns | | 1,400 | 100 | | | | | |
| Bank charges | 200 | | | | | | | |
| Discounts allowed | 890 | | 170 | | | | | |
| Discounts received | | 1,260 | | | | | | |
| Wages | 32,780 | | | | | | | |
| Rates | 5,500 | | 500 | | | | | |
| Telephone | 1,140 | | | | | | | |
| Electricity | 1,480 | | | | | | | |
| Insurance | 1,500 | | | 300 | | | | |
| Motor expenses | 1,580 | | | 200 | | | | |
| Office expenses | 960 | | 200 | | | | | |
| Allowance for doubtful debts at 1 April 20X3 | | 220 | | 80 | | | | |
| Loan | | 820 | | | | | | |
| Drawings | 15,800 | | | | | | | |
| Suspense account | 270 | | | 100 + 170 | | | | |
| Buildings depreciation charge | | | 2,000 | | | | | |
| Furniture depreciation charge | | | 960 | | | | | |
| Motor vehicles depreciation charge | | | 7,455 | | | | | |

| Account name | Ledger balances | | Adjustments | | Income statement | | SFP | |
|---|---|---|---|---|---|---|---|---|
| | DR £ | CR £ | DR £ | CR £ | DR £ | CR £ | DR £ | CR £ |
| Computer depreciation charge | | | 950 | | | | | |
| Accruals | | | | 500 | | | | |
| Prepayments | | | 300 | | | | | |
| Irrecoverable debts expense | | | 240 | | | | | |
| Allowance for doubtful debts adjustment | | | 80 | | | | | |
| | 308,450 | 308,450 | 18,155 | 18,155 | | | | |

**Step 4**  Total and extend each line of the ETB into the income statement or statement of financial position columns as appropriate.

The approach here is to take each line in turn and firstly add it across, then decide whether this is an income statement balance or a statement of financial position balance. As examples:

- The buildings at cost account has a debit balance of £100,000 in the ledger balances column – there are no entries in the adjustment column so the only decision to make is whether this £100,000 is a debit in the income statement or the statement of financial position – it is of course a non-current asset that will appear in the debit column in the statement of financial position

- The accumulated depreciation for buildings has a credit of £4,000 in the ledger balance column and a further credit of £2,000 in the adjustment column – this totals to a credit of £6,000. This is the accumulated depreciation and therefore it is a statement of financial position figure – this £6,000 is therefore taken across to the credit column of the statement of financial position

- Inventory is a complicated one – there are three figures that need to be extended across:

  - Opening inventory of £4,400 (the debit balance in the ledger balances column) is taken to the debit of the income statement

  - The debit in the adjustment column is taken as a debit to the statement of financial position, being the closing inventory current asset

- – The credit in the adjustment column is taken as a credit in the income statement, being the reduction in purchases cost in the cost of sales

- The sales ledger control account has a debit balance in the ledger balances column of £15,240 and a credit of £240 in the adjustment column – therefore the credit of £240 is deducted from the debit of £15,240 to give a debit total of £15,000 which is taken to the debit column of the statement of financial position

- The suspense account has a debit of £270 in the ledger balances column – there are two credit entries in the adjustment column which total to £270 therefore meaning that there is no balance to be extended across

- The credit entry for accruals and the debit entry for prepayments are both taken across to the statement of financial position

Now work carefully through the fully extended ETB ensuring that you are happy with each total and that you understand why the balances appear in the income statement columns or the statement of financial position columns.

Remember:

| Income statement | – | income |
| | – | expenses |
| | | |
| Statement of financial position | – | assets |
| | – | liabilities |
| | – | capital |

| Account name | Ledger balances | | Adjustments | | Income statement | | SFP | |
|---|---|---|---|---|---|---|---|---|
| | DR £ | CR £ | DR £ | CR £ | DR £ | CR £ | DR £ | CR £ |
| Buildings at cost | 100,000 | | | | | | 100,000 | |
| Furniture and fittings at cost | 4,800 | | | | | | 4,800 | |
| Motor vehicles at cost | 32,700 | | | | | | 32,700 | |
| Computer at cost | 2,850 | | | | | | 2,850 | |
| Accumulated depreciation at 1 April 20X3: | | | | | | | | |
| – buildings | | 4,000 | | 2,000 | | | | 6,000 |
| – furniture and fittings | | 1,920 | | 960 | | | | 2,880 |
| – motor vehicles | | 7,850 | | 7,455 | | | | 15,305 |
| – computer | | 950 | | 950 | | | | 1,900 |
| Inventory at 1 April 20X3 | 4,400 | | 5,200 | 5,200 | 4,400 | 5,200 | 5,200 | |
| Bank/cash | 3,960 | | | | | | 3,960 | |
| Petty cash | 100 | | | | | | 100 | |
| Sales ledger control | 15,240 | | | 240 | | | 15,000 | |
| Purchases ledger control | | 5,010 | | | | | | 5,010 |
| Capital | | 130,000 | | | | | | 130,000 |
| Sales | | 155,020 | | | | 155,020 | | |
| Sales returns | 2,100 | | | | 2,100 | | | |
| Purchases | 80,200 | | | | 80,200 | | | |
| Purchases returns | | 1,400 | 100 | | | 1,300 | | |
| Bank charges | 200 | | | | 200 | | | |
| Discounts allowed | 890 | | 170 | | 1,060 | | | |
| Discounts received | | 1,260 | | | | 1,260 | | |
| Wages | 32,780 | | | | 32,780 | | | |
| Rates | 5,500 | | 500 | | 6,000 | | | |
| Telephone | 1,140 | | | | 1,140 | | | |
| Electricity | 1,480 | | | | 1,480 | | | |
| Insurance | 1,500 | | | 300 | 1,200 | | | |
| Motor expenses | 1,580 | | | 200 | 1,380 | | | |
| Office expenses | 960 | | 200 | | 1,160 | | | |
| Allowance for doubtful debts at 1 April 20X3 | | 220 | | 80 | | | | 300 |
| Loan | | 820 | | | | | | 820 |
| Drawings | 15,800 | | | | | | 15,800 | |
| Suspense account | 270 | | | 100 + 170 | | | | |
| Buildings depreciation charge | | | 2,000 | | 2,000 | | | |
| Furniture depreciation charge | | | 960 | | 960 | | | |
| Motor vehicles depreciation charge | | | 7,455 | | 7,455 | | | |
| Computer depreciation charge | | | 950 | | 950 | | | |
| Accruals | | | | 500 | | | | 500 |
| Prepayments | | | 300 | | | | 300 | |
| Irrecoverable debts expense | | | 240 | | 240 | | | |
| Allowance for doubtful debts adjustment | | | 80 | | 80 | | | |
| | 308,450 | 308,450 | 18,155 | 18,155 | | | | |

Step 5    Total the income statement columns to find the profit or loss for the year:

- If the credits in the income statement exceed the debits then there is more income than expense, so a profit has been made. This is the balancing debit in the income statement and it requires a new account line of profit/loss. This same figure is also a credit in the statement of financial position columns (because it is adding to the owner's capital, which is always a credit balance).

- If the debits in the income statement exceed the credits then there are more expenses than income and a loss has been made. This is the balancing credit in the income statement (again this uses the new account line of profit/loss). This same figure is entered as a debit in the statement of financial position columns (because it is reducing the owner's capital).

Total the statement of financial position columns – they should be equal.

| Account name | Ledger balance DR £ | Ledger balance CR £ | Adjustments DR £ | Adjustments CR £ | Income statement DR £ | Income statement CR £ | Statement of financial position DR £ | Statement of financial position CR £ |
|---|---|---|---|---|---|---|---|---|
| Buildings at cost | 100,000 | | | | | | 100,000 | |
| Furniture and fittings at cost | 4,800 | | | | | | 4,800 | |
| Motor vehicles at cost | 32,700 | | | | | | 32,700 | |
| Computer at cost | 2,850 | | | | | | 2,850 | |
| Accumulated depreciation at 1 April 20X3: | | | | | | | | |
| – buildings | | 4,000 | | 2,000 | | | | 6,000 |
| – furniture and fittings | | 1,920 | | 960 | | | | 2,880 |
| – motor vehicles | | 7,850 | | 7,455 | | | | 15,305 |
| – computer | | 950 | | 950 | | | | 1,900 |
| Stock (inventory) at 1 April 20X3 | 4,400 | | 5,200 | 5,200 | 4,400 | 5,200 | 5,200 | |
| Bank | 3,960 | | | | | | 3,960 | |
| Petty cash | 100 | | | | | | 100 | |
| Sales ledger control | 15,240 | | | 240 | | | 15,000 | |
| Purchases ledger control | | 5,010 | | | | | | 5,010 |
| Capital | | 130,000 | | | | | | 130,000 |
| Sales | | 155,020 | | | | 155,020 | | |
| Sales returns | 2,100 | | | | 2,100 | | | |
| Purchases | 80,200 | | | | 80,200 | | | |
| Purchases returns | | 1,400 | 100 | | | 1,300 | | |
| Bank charges | 200 | | | | 200 | | | |

| Account name | Ledger balance DR £ | Ledger balance CR £ | Adjustments DR £ | Adjustments CR £ | Income statement DR £ | Income statement CR £ | Statement of financial position DR £ | Statement of financial position CR £ |
|---|---|---|---|---|---|---|---|---|
| Discounts allowed | 890 | | 170 | | 1,060 | | | |
| Discounts received | | 1,260 | | | | 1,260 | | |
| Wages | 32,780 | | | | 32,780 | | | |
| Rates | 5,500 | | 500 | | 6,000 | | | |
| Telephone | 1,140 | | | | 1,140 | | | |
| Electricity | 1,480 | | | | 1,480 | | | |
| Insurance | 1,500 | | | 300 | 1,200 | | | |
| Motor expenses | 1,580 | | | 200 | 1,380 | | | |
| Office expenses | 960 | | 200 | | 1,160 | | | |
| Allowance for doubtful debts at 1 April 20X3 | | 220 | | 80 | | | | 300 |
| Loan | | 820 | | | | | | 820 |
| Drawings | 15,800 | | | | | | 15,800 | |
| Suspense account | 270 | | | 100 + 170 | | | | |
| Buildings depreciation charge | | | 2,000 | | 2,000 | | | |
| Furniture depreciation charge | | | 960 | | 960 | | | |
| Motor vehicles depreciation charge | | | 7,455 | | 7,455 | | | |
| Computer depreciation charge | | | 950 | | 950 | | | |
| Accruals | | | | 500 | | | | 500 |
| Prepayments | | | 300 | | | | 300 | |
| Irrecoverable debts expense | | | 240 | | 240 | | | |
| Allowance for doubtful debts adjustment | | | 80 | | 80 | | | |
| Profit/loss | | | | | 17,995 | | | 17,995 |
| | 308,450 | 308,450 | 18,155 | 18,155 | 162,780 | 162,780 | 180,710 | 180,710 |

In this case a profit of £17,995 was made. This is the balancing figure in the income statement columns and is shown as a credit in the statement of financial position, to be added to the capital for the period.

Once it is entered into the credit column in the statement of financial position the statement of financial position columns should be totalled and the two column totals should be equal.

## Task 1

If the credit balances exceed the debit balances in the income statement (profit and loss) columns this means the business has made a profit/loss for the period. The other entry to be made with this balancing amount is in the debit column/credit column of the statement of financial position (balance sheet).

## DISPOSALS AND THE ETB

When a business disposes of a non-current asset and a profit or loss on disposal arises, the ETB can be used to process the journals necessary for this, calculate the profit or loss on disposal and allocate it correctly in the income statement columns.

## HOW IT WORKS

Adam Singleton operates a very simple business and his trial balance as at 31 December is as follows:

| Ledger account | Dr £ | Cr £ |
| --- | --- | --- |
| Capital | | 5,000 |
| Sales | | 15,000 |
| Purchases | 7,000 | |
| Sales ledger control | 6,000 | |
| Purchases ledger control | | 2,000 |
| Bank/cash | 5,000 | |
| Machine at cost | 10,000 | |
| Machine accumulated depreciation | | 6,000 |
| | 28,000 | 28,000 |

After the extraction of the trial balance on 31 December Adam disposed of the machine in return for a cheque for £3,500.

We need to adjust for this transaction and extend the ETB to arrive at Adam's profit for the period.

243

**Step 1** Prepare journal entries for the disposal:

| Account name | Amount £ | Debit (✓) | Credit (✓) |
|---|---|---|---|
| Disposals | 10,000 | ✓ | |
| Machine at cost | 10,000 | | ✓ |
| Machine accumulated depreciation | 6,000 | ✓ | |
| Disposals | 6,000 | | ✓ |
| Bank/cash | 3,500 | ✓ | |
| Disposals | 3,500 | | ✓ |

**Step 2** Next we process these adjustments on the ETB:

## Extended trial balance as at 31 December

| | Ledger balances | | Adjustments | | Income statement | | SFP | |
|---|---|---|---|---|---|---|---|---|
| | DR £ | CR £ | DR £ | CR £ | DR £ | CR £ | DR £ | CR £ |
| Capital | | 5,000 | | | | | | |
| Sales | | 15,000 | | | | | | |
| Purchases | 7,000 | | | | | | | |
| Sales ledger control | 6,000 | | | | | | | |
| Purchases ledger control | | 2,000 | | | | | | |
| Bank/cash | 5,000 | | 3,500 | | | | | |
| Machine at cost | 10,000 | | | 10,000 | | | | |
| Machine acc depreciation | | 6,000 | 6,000 | | | | | |
| Disposals | | | 10,000 | 6,000 | | | | |
| | | | | 3,500 | | | | |
| | 28,000 | 28,000 | 19,500 | 19,500 | | | | |

**Step 3** Debits exceed credits by £500 on the disposal line of the ETB, so we know that the disposal has been at a £500 loss. This amount is entered in the debit column of the income statement, so the disposals line now cross casts.

## Extended trial balance as at 31 December

|  | Ledger balances | | Adjustments | | Income statement | | SFP | |
|---|---|---|---|---|---|---|---|---|
|  | DR £ | CR £ | DR £ | CR £ | DR £ | CR £ | DR £ | CR £ |
| Capital |  | 5,000 |  |  |  |  |  |  |
| Sales |  | 15,000 |  |  |  |  |  |  |
| Purchases | 7,000 |  |  |  |  |  |  |  |
| Sales ledger control | 6,000 |  |  |  |  |  |  |  |
| Purchases ledger control |  | 2,000 |  |  |  |  |  |  |
| Bank/cash | 5,000 |  | 3,500 |  |  |  |  |  |
| Machine at cost | 10,000 |  |  | 10,000 |  |  |  |  |
| Machine acc depreciation |  | 6,000 | 6,000 |  |  |  |  |  |
| Disposals |  |  | 10,000 | 6,000 | 500 |  |  |  |
|  |  |  |  | 3,500 |  |  |  |  |
| Profit |  |  |  |  |  |  |  |  |
|  | 28,000 | 28,000 | 19,500 | 19,500 | 500 |  |  |  |

**Step 4** The remainder of the balances are also extended, and the income statement columns are totalled:

## Extended trial balance as at 31 December

| Ledger account | Ledger balances | | Adjustments | | Income statement | | SFP | |
|---|---|---|---|---|---|---|---|---|
|  | DR £ | CR £ | DR £ | CR £ | DR £ | CR £ | DR £ | CR £ |
| Capital |  | 5,000 |  |  |  |  |  | 5,000 |
| Sales |  | 15,000 |  |  |  | 15,000 |  |  |
| Purchases | 7,000 |  |  |  | 7,000 |  |  |  |
| Sales ledger control | 6,000 |  |  |  |  |  | 6,000 |  |
| Purchases ledger control |  | 2,000 |  |  |  |  |  | 2,000 |
| Bank/cash | 5,000 |  | 3,500 |  |  |  | 8,500 |  |
| Machine at cost | 10,000 |  |  | 10,000 |  |  |  |  |
| Machine acc depreciation |  | 6,000 | 6,000 |  |  |  |  |  |
| Disposals |  |  | 10,000 | 6,000 | 500 |  |  |  |
|  |  |  |  | 3,500 |  |  |  |  |
| Profit |  |  |  |  |  |  |  |  |
|  | 28,000 | 8,000 | 19,500 | 19,500 | 7,500 | 15,000 |  |  |

Step 5    The profit for the year of £7,500 is entered on the debit side of the income statement, to make it balance, and on the credit side of the statement of financial position, again to make it balance. The income statement and statement of financial position columns are then totalled, and should balance.

**Extended trial balance as at 31 December**

|  | Ledger balances | | Adjustments | | Income statement | | SFP | |
| --- | --- | --- | --- | --- | --- | --- | --- | --- |
|  | DR £ | CR £ | DR £ | CR £ | DR £ | CR £ | DR £ | CR £ |
| Capital |  | 5,000 |  |  |  |  |  | 5,000 |
| Sales |  | 15,000 |  |  |  | 15,000 |  |  |
| Purchases | 7,000 |  |  |  | 7,000 |  |  |  |
| Sales ledger control | 6,000 |  |  |  |  |  | 6,000 |  |
| Purchases ledger control |  | 2,000 |  |  |  |  |  | 2,000 |
| Bank/cash | 5,000 |  | 3,500 |  |  |  | 8,500 |  |
| Machine at cost | 10,000 |  |  | 10,000 |  |  |  |  |
| Machine acc dep |  | 6,000 | 6,000 |  |  |  |  |  |
| Disposals |  |  | 10,000 | 6,000 | 500 |  |  |  |
|  |  |  |  | 3,500 |  |  |  |  |
| Profit |  |  |  |  | 7,500 |  |  | 7,500 |
|  | 28,000 | 28,000 | 19,500 | 19,500 | 15,000 | 15,000 | 14,500 | 14,500 |

---

# Task 2

The following balances have been taken from the trial balance of XYZ. Rent paid £1,800, capital £15,000, purchases £10,000, sales £12,000, wages £5,000, sundry expenses £1,000, cash £9,200. What is the trial balance total on the debit side?

A    £26,000

B    £29,000

C    £42,000

D    £27,000

## Task 3

A suspense account shows a credit balance of £130. This could be due to:

A   Omitting a sale of £130 from the sales ledger.

B   Recording a purchase of £130 twice in the purchases account.

C   Failing to write off an irrecoverable debt of £130.

D   Recording an electricity bill paid of £65 by debiting the bank account and crediting the electricity account.

# CHAPTER OVERVIEW

- Once the initial trial balance has been prepared any errors that have caused a suspense account and any year end adjustments are put through the accounts in order to arrive at the figures for the final accounts – this can all be done in the extended trial balance

- The first stage is to enter all of the ledger account balances into the ETB and to check that it balances – if it does not balance then a suspense account is entered in order to create a balanced trial balance

- The suspense account is then cleared by entering the correcting entries in the adjustments columns of the ETB

- Any year end adjustments are then also entered in the adjustment columns for depreciation, irrecoverable and doubtful debts and accruals and prepayments

- The closing inventory figure is entered as a debit and a credit entry in the adjustment columns on the inventory line

- Each line of the ETB is then totalled and extended into either the income statement columns or the statement of financial position columns as a debit or a credit – in the income statement there are income and expenses – in the statement of financial position there are assets, liabilities and capital

- The income statement columns are then totalled and the balancing figure is inserted as a new account line, the profit/loss, which is also inserted in the statement of financial position columns – a debit in the income statement column is a credit in the statement of financial position column and *vice versa*

- The final stage is to total the statement of financial position columns and these should now agree

## Keyword

**Extended trial balance** – an accounting technique of moving from the trial balance, through the year end adjustments to the figures for the final accounts

# TEST YOUR LEARNING

### Test 1

When preparing an extended trial balance what do you do if you discover that the initial trial balance does not balance?

### Test 2

What entries if any are made in the adjustments column for the closing inventory?

Both a debit and a credit

A debit

A credit

No entry

### Test 3

The closing inventory figure is a debit entry/credit entry in the income statement columns and a debit entry/credit entry in the statement of financial position columns of the ETB.

# ANSWERS TO CHAPTER TASKS

CHAPTER 1  **Accounting principles**

**1**  a receivable
**2**  a credit note
**3**  the purchases day book
**4**  the purchases ledger

**5**

### Sales ledger control account

| Date | Details | Amount £ | Date | Details | Amount £ |
|------|---------|----------|------|---------|----------|
| 4 Mar | Sales | 2,400 | | | |
| | | | | | |

### Sales

| Date | Details | Amount £ | Date | Details | Amount £ |
|------|---------|----------|------|---------|----------|
| | | | 4 Mar | Receivables | 2,400 |
| | | | | | |

### Purchases

| Date | Details | Amount £ | Date | Details | Amount £ |
|------|---------|----------|------|---------|----------|
| 4 Mar | Payables | 1,800 | | | |
| | | | | | |

### Purchases ledger control account

| Date | Details | Amount £ | Date | Details | Amount £ |
|------|---------|----------|------|---------|----------|
| | | | 4 Mar | Purchases | 1,800 |
| | | | | | |

## Phone

| Date | Details | Amount £ | Date | Details | Amount £ |
|------|---------|----------|------|---------|----------|
| 4 Mar | Bank/cash | 140 | | | |
| | | | | | |

## Bank/cash

| Date | Details | Cash £ | Bank £ | Date | Details | Cash £ | Bank £ |
|------|---------|--------|--------|------|---------|--------|--------|
| | | | | 4 Mar | Phone | | 140 |
| | | | | 4 Mar | Drawings | | 500 |

## Drawings

| Date | Details | Amount £ | Date | Details | Amount £ |
|------|---------|----------|------|---------|----------|
| 4 Mar | Bank/cash | 500 | | | |
| | | | | | |

6

## Sales ledger control account

| Date | Details | Amount £ | Date | Details | Amount £ |
|------|---------|----------|------|---------|----------|
| 17 Feb | Sales | 900 | 25 Feb | Bank/cash | 700 |
| | | | 28 Feb | Bal c/d | 200 |
| | Total | 900 | | Total | 900 |
| 1 Mar | Bal b/d | 200 | | | |

7    The correct answer is **B**

If the bookkeeping has been accurate, the total of the debits will equal the total of the credits in the trial balance.

# CHAPTER 2 Accounting concepts

**1**

| | £ | Description |
|---|---|---|
| Rent | 480 | Expense |
| Motor van | 7,400 | Asset |
| Payables | 1,900 | Liability |
| Heat and light | 210 | Expense |
| Discounts received | 50 | Income |
| Motor expenses | 310 | Expense |
| Sales | 40,800 | Income |
| Opening inventory | 2,100 | Asset |
| Loan | 2,000 | Liability |
| Stationery | 330 | Expense |
| Capital | 7,980 | Capital |
| Phone | 640 | Expense |
| Discount allowed | 60 | Expense |
| Purchases | 22,600 | Expense |
| Receivables | 3,400 | Asset |
| Wages | 9,700 | Expense |
| Drawings | 4,000 | Reduction of capital |
| Office cleaning | 220 | Expense |
| Travel and accommodation | 660 | Expense |
| Bank | 483 | Asset |
| Cash | 137 | Asset |

**2**

| | £ | £ |
|---|---|---|
| Sales | | 136,700 |
| Less: cost of sales | | |
| Opening inventory | 11,300 | |
| Purchases | 97,500 | |
| | 108,800 | |
| Less: closing inventory | (10,600) | |
| | | 98,200 |
| Gross profit | | 38,500 |

**3**

| | Debit | Credit | Income statement | SFP |
|---|---|---|---|---|
| | £ | £ | | |
| Rent | 480 | | ✓ | |
| Motor van | 7,400 | | | ✓ |
| Payables | | 1,900 | | ✓ |
| Heat and light | 210 | | ✓ | |
| Discounts received | | 50 | ✓ | |
| Motor expenses | 310 | | ✓ | |
| Sales | | 40,800 | ✓ | |
| Opening inventory | 2,100 | | ✓ | |
| Loan | | 2,000 | | ✓ |
| Stationery | 330 | | ✓ | |
| Capital | | 7,980 | | ✓ |
| Phone | 640 | | ✓ | |
| Discount allowed | 60 | | ✓ | |
| Purchases | 22,600 | | ✓ | |
| Receivables | 3,400 | | | ✓ |
| Wages | 9,700 | | ✓ | |
| Drawings | 4,000 | | | ✓ |
| Office cleaning | 220 | | ✓ | |
| Travel and accommodation | 660 | | ✓ | |
| Bank | 483 | | | ✓ |
| Cash | 137 | | | ✓ |
| | 52,730 | 52,730 | | |

**4** Accruals

## CHAPTER 3  **Purchase of non-current assets**

**1**   Capital expenditure £15,000

Revenue expenditure £4,000

Expenditure on Machine A is capital expenditure as it is a major improvement of the asset. The £4,000 repair costs of Machine B is revenue expenditure as this is just the running costs of the machine.

**2**

### Machinery account

| | £ | | £ |
|---|---|---|---|
| Purchases ledger control | 17,000 | | |
| Wages | 1,400 | | |

### Purchases ledger control account

| | £ | | £ |
|---|---|---|---|
| | | Machinery | 17,000 |

### Wages account

| | £ | | £ |
|---|---|---|---|
| | | Machinery | 1,400 |

**3**

| Account | Amount | Debit | Credit |
|---|---|---|---|
| | £ | | |
| Motor vehicles | 78,800 | ✓ | |
| Motor expenses | 800 | ✓ | |
| Bank account | 79,600 | | ✓ |

**4**

| Account name | Amount | Debit | Credit |
|---|---|---|---|
| | £ | | |
| Motor vehicles | 25,000 | ✓ | |
| Bank / cash | 15,000 | | ✓ |
| Disposals | 10,000 | | ✓ |
| Being the purchase of a new car for cash / part exchange. | | | |

## CHAPTER 4 Depreciation of non-current assets

1 Carrying amount = Cost – depreciation to date

Carrying amount = £8,000 – £3,000 = £5,000

2 Depreciation charge $= \dfrac{£22,000 - 9,000}{4}$

= £3,250 per annum

Carrying amount = £22,000 – (2 × 3,250) = £15,500

3

|  | £ |
|---|---|
| Original cost | 22,000 |
| Year 1 depreciation 22,000 × 20% | (4,400) |
| Carrying amount at end of year 1 | 17,600 |
| Year 2 depreciation 17,600 × 20% | (3,520) |
| Carrying amount at end of year 2 | 14,080 |
| Year 3 depreciation 14,080 × 20% | (2,816) |
| Carrying amount at end of year 3 | 11,264 |
| Year 4 depreciation 11,264 × 20% | (2,253) |
| Carrying amount | 9,011 |

4

**Depreciation charge**

| | £ | | £ |
|---|---|---|---|
| Accumulated depreciation | 24,000 | | |

**Accumulated depreciation**

| | £ | | £ |
|---|---|---|---|
| | | Depreciation charge | 24,000 |

**Income statement**

Expenses:

| | £ |
|---|---|
| Depreciation charge | 24,000 |

**SFP**

Non-current assets:

| | Cost | Depreciation | Carrying amount |
|---|---|---|---|
| | £ | £ | £ |
| Machinery | 120,000 | 24,000 | 96,000 |

5 False

The reducing balance method results in larger amounts being charged in earlier years and smaller amounts in subsequent years.

CHAPTER 5   **Disposal of non-current assets**

**1**

(a)

|  | £ |
|---|---|
| Original cost | 11,200 |
| 20X7 depreciation 11,200 × 30% | 3,360 |
| Carrying amount 31 Dec 20X7 | 7,840 |
| 20X8 depreciation 7,840 × 30% | 2,352 |
| Carrying amount 31 Dec 20X8 | 5,488 |

(b)

|  | £ |
|---|---|
| Carrying amount at 31 December 20X8 | 5,488 |
| Disposal proceeds | 5,000 |
| Loss on disposal | 488 |

(c)

**Motor car at cost account**

|  | £ |  | £ |
|---|---|---|---|
| 1 Jan 20X7 Bank | 11,200 | 31 Dec 20X8 Disposal | 11,200 |

**Accumulated depreciation on the motor car account**

|  | £ |  | £ |
|---|---|---|---|
| 31 Dec 20X7 Balance c/d | 3,360 | 31 Dec 20X7 Depreciation | 3,360 |
| 31 Dec 20X8 Disposal | 5,712 | 1 Jan 20X8 Balance b/d | 3,360 |
|  |  | 31 Dec 20X8 Depreciation | 2,352 |
|  | 5,712 |  | 5,712 |

**Disposals account**

|  | £ |  | £ |
|---|---|---|---|
| 31 Dec 20X8 Motor car at cost | 11,200 | 31 Dec 20X8 Motor car accumulated depreciation | 5,712 |
|  |  | 31 Dec 20X8 Proceeds | 5,000 |
|  |  | 31 Dec 20X8 IS – loss | 488 |
|  | 11,200 |  | 11,200 |

**2**

### Car at cost account

| | £ | | £ |
|---|---|---|---|
| 1 Mar 20X6 Bank/cash | 10,000 | 31 May 20X8 Disposals | 10,000 |
| 31 May 20X8 Bank/cash | 6,200 | 31 May 20X8 Balance c/d | 11,000 |
| 31 May 20X8 Disposals | 4,800 | | |
| | 21,000 | | 21,000 |
| 1 June 20X8 Balance b/d | 11,000 | | |

### Car accumulated depreciation account

| | £ | | £ |
|---|---|---|---|
| 31 May 20X8 Disposals | 5,500 | 31 May 20X8 Balance b/d | 5,500 |

### Disposals account

| | £ | | £ |
|---|---|---|---|
| 31 May 20X8 Car at cost | 10,000 | 31 May 20X8 Car accumulated depreciation | 5,500 |
| 31 May 20X8 IS – profit on disposal | | 31 May 20X8 Car at cost | |
| | 300 | | 4,800 |
| | 10,300 | | 10,300 |

**3**

**Non-Current Asset Register**

| Non-current asset number | 24116 |
| Description | Fork lift truck XC355 |
| Location | Warehouse |
| Supplier | Leyland Machinery |

| Date | Cost £ | Expected life (years) | Estimated residual value £ | Depreciation method | Depreciation rate | Depreciation charge for the year £ | Acc dep at end of the year £ | Carrying amount at end of year £ | Disposal proceeds £ | Profit or loss on disposal £ |
|---|---|---|---|---|---|---|---|---|---|---|
| **20X5** | | | | | | | | | | |
| 1 May | 34,000 | 4 | 6,250 | Reducing balance | 30% | | | | | |
| 31 Dec | | | | | | 10,200 | 10,200 | 23,800 | | |
| **20X6** | | | | | | | | | | |
| 31 Dec | | | | | | 7,140 | 17,340 | 16,660 | | |
| **20X7** | | | | | | | | | | |
| 31 Dec | | | | | | 4,998 | 22,338 | 11,662 | | |
| **20X8** | | | | | | | | | | |
| 20 Mar | | | | | | | | | 10,500 | (1,162) |

**4**    The correct answer is **D**

## CHAPTER 6   Accruals and prepayments

**1**   This will ⌞increase⌟ phone expenses in the old accounting year, and it will be shown as ⌞a liability⌟ on the statement of financial position at the year end.

**2**

### Phone account

|  | £ |  |  | £ |
|---|---|---|---|---|
| 31 Dec Balance b/d | 2,600 |  |  |  |
| 31 Dec Accrual c/d | 480 | 31 Dec Income statement | | 3,080 |
|  | 3,080 |  |  | 3,080 |
|  |  | 1 Jan Accrual b/d | | 480 |

**3**

### Rent account

|  | £ |  |  | £ |
|---|---|---|---|---|
| 31 Dec Balance b/d | 3,200 | 31 Dec Income statement | | 2,900 |
|  |  | 31 Dec Prepayment c/d | | 300 |
|  |  | (£900 x 1/3) | | |
|  | 3,200 |  |  | 3,200 |
| 1 Jan Prepayment b/d | 300 |  |  |  |

**4**   Asset

**Accrued income is due but has not been received, therefore it is a form of asset.**

CHAPTER 7 **Inventory**

1   Cost      =      £13.80

   Net realisable value      =      £14.00 – 0.50

                               =      £13.50

   Each unit should be valued at £13.50, the lower of cost and net realisable value

2   12 May – sale –70 units @ £3.50

   30 May – sale – 80 units        30 units @ £3.50

                                     50 units @ £4.00

   Closing inventory  – 50 units @ £4.00 = £200.00

3   The purchases account.

   The cost of goods purchased should **never** be debited to the inventory account. The inventory account is adjusted at the end of the accounting period only.

## CHAPTER 8   Irrecoverable debts and doubtful debts

**1**

| Account name | Debit £ | Credit £ |
|---|---|---|
| Irrecoverable debts expense | 976 | |
| Sales ledger control | | 976 |
| Being the write-off of a specific receivable | | |

**2**

| Account name | Debit £ | Credit £ |
|---|---|---|
| Bank/cash account | 1,000 | |
| Irrecoverable debts expense account | | 1,000 |
| Being the recovery of a specific receivable previously written-off | | |

**3**

| Account name | Debit £ | Credit £ |
|---|---|---|
| Irrecoverable debts expense | 680 | |
| Sales ledger control | | 680 |
| Allowance for doubtful debts adjustment | 630 | |
| Allowance for doubtful debts | | 630 |
| Being the write-off of one debt and the set-up of a new general allowance for doubtful debts | | |

**4**

| Account name | Debit £ | Credit £ |
|---|---|---|
| Irrecoverable debts expense | 2,400 | |
| Sales ledger control | | 2,400 |
| Allowance for doubtful debts | 924 | |
| Allowance for doubtful debts adjustment | | 924 |
| Being write-off of irrecoverable debt and reduction of allowance for doubtful debts from £1,500 to ((£60,000 − £2,400) × 1%) = £576 | | |

**5**

| Account name | Debit £ | Credit £ |
|---|---|---|
| Allowance for doubtful debts (SFP) | √ | |
| Allowance for doubtful debts adj (IS) | | √ |

**6**   Prudence.

## CHAPTER 9 Bank reconciliations

**1** £12,255

| Workings | Debit £ | Credit £ |
|---|---|---|
| Balance per cash book | 12,450 | |
| Standing order for rent | | 400 |
| BGC receipt from customer | 230 | |
| Bank charges | | 25 |
| Adjusted cash book balance c/d | | 12,255 |
| | 12,680 | 12,680 |

**2**

| Account name | Amount £ | Debit (✓) | Credit (✓) |
|---|---|---|---|
| Sales ledger control account | 500 | √ | |
| Cash book | 500 | | √ |

**3** The correct answer is **C**

## CHAPTER 10 Control account reconciliations

**1**

| Account name | Debit £ | Credit £ |
|---|---|---|
| Purchases ledger control | 500 | |
| Sales ledger control | | 500 |
| Being the setting off of sales ledger and purchases ledger balances | | |

**2** The sales ledger control account but not the individual balances in the sales ledger.

**3**

| Adjustment | Amount £ | Debit (✓) | Credit (✓) |
|---|---|---|---|
| Sales ledger control | 120 | | ✓ |

The other side of the entry would be a debit to the discounts allowed account.

**4**

| Adjustment | Amount £ | Debit (✓) | Credit (✓) |
|---|---|---|---|
| Purchases ledger balances | 700 | | ✓ |

**5** The correct answer is **D**

**6** The correct answer is **B**

CHAPTER 11  **The trial balance, errors and the suspense account**

1  (a)  Debit      Purchases returns
        Credit     Income statement

    (b)  Debit      Income statement
        Credit     Insurance

    (c)  No adjustment required as this is a statement of financial position item.

2   The correct answer is **A**

3   The correct answer is **A**

CHAPTER 12 **The extended trial balance**

1 This means that the business has made a **profit** for the period and the other entry is in the **credit column** of the statement of financial position.

2 The correct answer is **D**

Workings:

| | DR £ | CR £ |
|---|---|---|
| Rent | 1,800 | |
| Capital | | 15,000 |
| Purchases | 10,000 | |
| Sales | | 12,000 |
| Wages | 5,000 | |
| Sundry expenses | 1,000 | |
| Cash | 9,200 | |
| | 27,000 | 27,000 |

3 The correct answer is **B**

£130 will be debited twice to purchases, giving rise to a credit balance in the suspense account.

# TEST YOUR LEARNING – ANSWERS

## CHAPTER 1    Accounting principles

**1**

### Bank account

| Date | Details | £ | Date | Details | £ |
|------|---------|---|------|---------|---|
| 1/3 | Capital | 20,000 | 1/3 | Furn & fit | 3,200 |
| 10/3 | Sales | 1,800 | 4/3 | Purchases | 4,400 |
| 24/3 | Receivables | 3,500 | 6/3 | Rent | 600 |
| | | | 28/3 | Drawings | 1,000 |
| | | | 30/3 | Payables | 1,800 |
| | | | 31/3 | Wages | 900 |
| | | | 31/3 | Balance c/d | 13,400 |
| | | 25,300 | | | 25,300 |
| 1/4 | Balance b/d | 13,400 | | | |

### Capital account

| Date | Details | £ | Date | Details | £ |
|------|---------|---|------|---------|---|
| | | | 1/3 | Bank/cash | 20,000 |
| | | | | | |
| | | | | | |
| | | | | | |
| | | | | | |

### Furniture and fittings account

| Date | Details | £ | Date | Details | £ |
|------|---------|---|------|---------|---|
| 1/3 | Bank/cash | 3,200 | | | |
| | | | | | |
| | | | | | |
| | | | | | |
| | | | | | |

### Purchases account

| Date | Details | £ | Date | Details | £ |
|---|---|---|---|---|---|
| 4/3 | Bank/cash | 4,400 | 31/3 | Balance c/d | 7,100 |
| 20/3 | Payables | 2,700 | | | |
| | | | | | |
| | | | | | |
| | | | | | |
| | | 7,100 | | | 7,100 |
| 1/4 | Balance b/d | 7,100 | | | |

### Rent account

| Date | Details | £ | Date | Details | £ |
|---|---|---|---|---|---|
| 6/3 | Bank/cash | 600 | | | |
| | | | | | |
| | | | | | |
| | | | | | |
| | | | | | |

### Sales account

| Date | Details | £ | Date | Details | £ |
|---|---|---|---|---|---|
| 31/3 | Balance c/d | 8,300 | 10/3 | Bank/cash | 1,800 |
| | | | 15/3 | Receivables | 4,900 |
| | | | 29/3 | Receivables | 1,600 |
| | | 8,300 | | | 8,300 |
| | | | 1/4 | Balance b/d | 8,300 |

### Sales ledger control account

| Date | Details | £ | Date | Details | £ |
|---|---|---|---|---|---|
| 15/3 | Sales | 4,900 | 24/3 | Bank/cash | 3,500 |
| 29/3 | Sales | 1,600 | 31/3 | Balance c/d | 3,000 |
| | | 6,500 | | | 6,500 |
| 1/4 | Balance b/d | 3,000 | | | |

### Purchases ledger control account

| Date | Details | £ | Date | Details | £ |
|---|---|---|---|---|---|
| 30/3 | Bank/cash | 1,800 | 20/3 | Purchases | 2,700 |
| 31/3 | Balance c/d | 900 | | | |
| | | 2,700 | | | 2,700 |
| | | | 1/4 | Balance b/d | 900 |

## Drawings account

| Date | Details | £ | Date | Details | £ |
|------|---------|-----|------|---------|-----|
| 28/3 | Bank/cash | 1,000 | | | |
| | | | | | |
| | | | | | |
| | | | | | |
| | | | | | |
| | | | | | |

## Wages account

| Date | Details | £ | Date | Details | £ |
|------|---------|-----|------|---------|-----|
| 31/3 | Bank/cash | 900 | | | |
| | | | | | |
| | | | | | |
| | | | | | |
| | | | | | |

## Trial balance as at 31 March

| | Debits £ | Credits £ |
|------|--------|---------|
| Bank | 13,400 | |
| Capital | | 20,000 |
| Furniture and fittings | 3,200 | |
| Purchases | 7,100 | |
| Rent | 600 | |
| Sales | | 8,300 |
| Receivables | 3,000 | |
| Payables | | 900 |
| Drawings | 1,000 | |
| Wages | 900 | |
| | 29,200 | 29,200 |

## 2 General ledger

### Sales ledger control account

| Date | Details | £ | Date | Details | £ |
|------|---------|---|------|---------|---|
| 31 Mar | SDB | 1,390 | 31 Mar | SRDB | 60 |
| | | | 31 Mar | CRB | 720 |
| | | | 31 Mar | CRB - discounts | 10 |
| | | | 31 Mar | Balance c/d | 600 |
| | | 1,390 | | | 1,390 |
| 1 Apr | Balance b/d | 600 | | | |

### Sales account

| Date | Details | £ | Date | Details | £ |
|------|---------|---|------|---------|---|
| | | | 31 Mar | SDB | 1,390 |
| 31 Mar | Balance c/d | 3,060 | 31 Mar | CRB | 1,670 |
| | | 3,060 | | | 3,060 |
| | | | 1 Apr | Balance b/d | 3,060 |

### Sales returns account

| Date | Details | £ | Date | Details | £ |
|------|---------|---|------|---------|---|
| 31 Mar | SRDB | 60 | | | |
| | | | | | |
| | | | | | |
| | | | | | |

### Purchases ledger control account

| Date | Details | £ | Date | Details | £ |
|------|---------|---|------|---------|---|
| 31 Mar | PRDB | 80 | 31 Mar | PDB | 1,400 |
| 31 Mar | CPB | 870 | | | |
| 31 Mar | CPB – discounts | 40 | | | |
| 31 Mar | Balance c/d | 410 | | | |
| | | 1,400 | | | 1,400 |
| | | | 1 Apr | Balance b/d | 410 |

### Purchases account

| Date | Details | £ | Date | Details | £ |
|------|---------|---|------|---------|---|
| 31 Mar | PDB | 1,400 | | | |
| 31 Mar | CPB | 2,250 | 31 Mar | Balance c/d | 3,650 |
| | | 3,650 | | | 3,650 |
| 1 Apr | Balance b/d | 3,650 | | | |

## Purchases returns account

| Date | Details | £ | Date | Details | £ |
|------|---------|---|------|---------|---|
| | | | 31 Mar | PRDB | 80 |
| | | | | | |
| | | | | | |
| | | | | | |

## Capital account

| Date | Details | £ | Date | Details | £ |
|------|---------|---|------|---------|---|
| | | | 31 Mar | CRB | 15,000 |
| | | | | | |
| | | | | | |
| | | | | | |

## Discounts allowed account

| Date | Details | £ | Date | Details | £ |
|------|---------|---|------|---------|---|
| 31 Mar | CRB | 10 | | | |
| | | | | | |
| | | | | | |
| | | | | | |

## Wages account

| Date | Details | £ | Date | Details | £ |
|------|---------|---|------|---------|---|
| 31 Mar | CPB | 2,200 | | | |
| | | | | | |
| | | | | | |
| | | | | | |

## Shop fittings account

| Date | Details | £ | Date | Details | £ |
|------|---------|---|------|---------|---|
| 31 Mar | CPB | 1,100 | | | |
| | | | | | |
| | | | | | |
| | | | | | |

## Discounts received account

| Date | Details | £ | Date | Details | £ |
|------|---------|---|------|---------|---|
| | | | 31 Mar | CPB | 40 |
| | | | | | |
| | | | | | |
| | | | | | |

BPP
LEARNING MEDIA

271

**Bank/cash**

| Date | Details | £ | Date | Details | £ |
|---|---|---|---|---|---|
| 31 Mar | CRB | 17,390 | 31 Mar | CPB | 6,420 |
| | | | 31 Mar | Balance c/d | 10,970 |
| | | 17,390 | | | 17,390 |
| 1 Apr | Balance b/d | 10,970 | | | |

## Sales ledger

**J Simpson**

| Date | Details | £ | Date | Details | £ |
|---|---|---|---|---|---|
| 4 Mar | SDB 0001 | 420 | 20 Mar | CRB | 420 |
| | | | | | |
| | | | | | |
| | | | | | |

**F Barnet**

| Date | Details | £ | Date | Details | £ |
|---|---|---|---|---|---|
| 12 Mar | SDB 0002 | 350 | 19 Mar | SRDB CN 001 | 40 |
| | | | 31 Mar | CRB | 300 |
| | | | 31 Mar | CRB – discount | 10 |
| | | 350 | | | 350 |

**H Jerry**

| Date | Details | £ | Date | Details | £ |
|---|---|---|---|---|---|
| 18 Mar | SDB 0003 | 180 | 25 Mar | SRDB CN 002 | 20 |
| | | | 31 Mar | Balance c/d | 160 |
| | | 180 | | | 180 |
| 1 Apr | Balance b/d | 160 | | | |

**D Dawson**

| Date | Details | £ | Date | Details | £ |
|---|---|---|---|---|---|
| 28 Mar | SDB 0004 | 440 | | | |
| | | | | | |
| | | | | | |

## Purchases ledger

**L Lilley**

| Date | Details | £ | Date | Details | £ |
|---|---|---|---|---|---|
| 12 Mar | CPB 0003 | 560 | 1 Mar | PDB 89432 | 590 |
| 12 Mar | CPD – discounts | 30 | | | |
| | | 590 | | | 590 |

**O Rools**

| Date | Details | £ | Date | Details | £ |
|---|---|---|---|---|---|
| 10 Mar | PRDB C357 | 80 | 7 Mar | PDB 12332 | 400 |
| 20 Mar | CPB | 310 | | | |
| 20 Mar | CPB – discounts | 10 | | | —— |
| | | 400 | | | 400 |

**R Terry**

| Date | Details | £ | Date | Details | £ |
|---|---|---|---|---|---|
| | | | 24 Mar | PDB 0532 | 410 |
| | | | | | |
| | | | | | |
| | | | | | |

**Trial balance as at 31 March**

| | Debits £ | Credits £ |
|---|---|---|
| Receivables | 600 | |
| Sales | | 3,060 |
| Sales returns | 60 | |
| Payables | | 410 |
| Purchases | 3,650 | |
| Purchases returns | | 80 |
| Capital | | 15,000 |
| Discounts allowed | 10 | |
| Wages | 2,200 | |
| Shop fittings | 1,100 | |
| Discounts received | | 40 |
| Bank/cash | 10,970 | |
| | 18,590 | 18,590 |

## CHAPTER 2   Accounting concepts

**1**

|  | Debit £ | Credit £ | Type of balance | IS or SFP |
|---|---|---|---|---|
| Sales |  | 41,200 | Income | IS |
| Loan |  | 1,500 | Liability | SFP |
| Wages | 7,000 |  | Expense | IS |
| Non-current assets | 7,100 |  | Asset | SFP |
| Opening inventory | 1,800 |  | Expense (see note) | IS |
| Receivables | 3,400 |  | Asset | SFP |
| Discounts received |  | 40 | Income | IS |
| Postage | 100 |  | Expense | IS |
| Bank | 300 |  | Asset | SFP |
| Capital |  | 9,530 | Capital | SFP |
| Rent | 500 |  | Expense | IS |
| Purchases | 30,100 |  | Expense | IS |
| Payables |  | 2,500 | Liability | SFP |
| Discounts allowed | 70 |  | Expense | IS |
| Drawings | 3,000 |  | Reduction of capital | SFP |
| Electricity | 800 |  | Expense | IS |
| Telephone | 600 |  | Expense | IS |
|  | 54,770 | 54,770 |  |  |

**Note**   Opening inventory is included in the income statement as part of the calculation of cost of sales. It is the closing inventory balance, which is an asset at the end of the accounting period, that is included in the statement of financial position.

**2**   (a)   The gross profit of a business is the profit from the **trading activities**.

(b)   The total of the current assets minus the current liabilities is known as **net current assets**.

**3**   (a)   Accruals concept

(b)   Going concern concept

(c)   Materiality concept

## CHAPTER 3 **Purchase of non-current assets**

**1** (a) Capital expenditure   £15,700
     Revenue expenditure    £100

   (b) Capital expenditure   £61,100

   (c) Capital expenditure   £68,600
     Revenue expenditure    £800

**2**

| | Account | Amount | Debit | Credit |
|---|---|---|---|---|
| | | £ | | |
| (a) | Furniture and fittings | 4,200 | ✓ | |
| | Bank/cash | 4,200 | | ✓ |
| | Being purchase of desks and chairs for head office | | | |
| | | | | |
| (b) | Computers | 2,300 | ✓ | |
| | Computer expenses | 100 | ✓ | |
| | Purchases ledger control | 2,400 | | ✓ |
| | Being purchase of computer and rewritable CDs | | | |
| | | | | |
| (c) | Machinery | 10,600 | ✓ | |
| | Purchases | 200 | | ✓ |
| | Wages | 800 | | ✓ |
| | Bank/cash | 9,600 | | ✓ |
| | Being purchase and installation of machine | | | |

**3** On the date of payment of the deposit

CHAPTER 4   **Depreciation of non-current assets**

1   The main accounting concept underlying the depreciation of non-current assets is the accruals concept.

2   Depreciation charge $= \dfrac{£11,500 - 2,500}{5 \text{ years}} = £1,800$ per annum

**Carrying amount at 31 December 20X8 = £11,500 – (2 × £1,800) = £7,900**

3                                                                                            £

Original cost                                                                    16,400

Depreciation to 31 Dec 20X7 (16,400 × 35%)                      5,740

Carrying amount at 31 Dec 20X7                                     10,660

Depreciation to 31 Dec 20X8 (10,660 × 35%)                    3,731

Carrying amount at 31 Dec 20X8                                      6,929

4   Depreciation charge   =   (£240,000 – £135,000) × 30%

                                        =   £31,500

5   Depreciation charge   =   £24,000 × 20% × 7/12

                                        =   £2,800

## CHAPTER 5　Disposal of non-current assets

**1** (a)

| | £ |
|---|---:|
| Original cost | 2,200 |
| 20X5 depreciation 2,200 × 40% | 880 |
| 20X5 carrying amount | 1,320 |
| 20X6 depreciation 1,320 × 40% | 528 |
| 20X6 carrying amount | 792 |
| 20X7 depreciation 792 × 40% | 317 |
| 20X7 carrying amount | 475 |
| Disposal proceeds | 200 |
| Loss on disposal | 275 |

(b)

**Computer at cost account**

| Date | Details | £ | Date | Details | £ |
|---|---|---:|---|---|---:|
| 1 April 20X5 | Bank | 2,200 | 14 May 20X8 | Disposal | 2,200 |

**Computer accumulated depreciation account**

| Date | Details | £ | Date | Details | £ |
|---|---|---:|---|---|---:|
| 31 Dec 20X5 | Balance c/d | 880 | 31 Dec 20X5 | Expense | 880 |
| | | | 1 Jan 20X6 | Balance b/d | 880 |
| 31 Dec 20X6 | Balance c/d | 1,408 | 31 Dec 20X6 | Expense | 528 |
| | | 1,408 | | | 1,408 |
| | | | 1 Jan 20X7 | Balance b/d | 1,408 |
| 31 Dec 20X7 | Balance c/d | 1,725 | 31 Dec 20X7 | Expense | 317 |
| | | 1,725 | | | 1,725 |
| 14 May 20X8 | Disposal | 1,725 | 1 Jan 20X8 | Balance b/d | 1,725 |

**Disposals account**

| Date | Details | £ | Date | Details | £ |
|------|---------|---|------|---------|---|
| 14 May 20X8 | Cost | 2,200 | 14 May 20X8 | Depreciation | 1,725 |
| | | | 14 May 20X8 | Proceeds | 200 |
| | | | 14 May 20X8 | Income statement – loss | 275 |
| | | 2,200 | | | 2,200 |

**2  (a)**

| | £ |
|---|---|
| Original cost | 7,200 |
| 20X6 depreciation 7,200 × 25% × 2/12 | (300) |
| 20X7 depreciation 7,200 × 25% | (1,800) |
| 20X8 depreciation 7,200 × 25% × 8/12 | (1,200) |
| Carrying amount 31 July 20X8 | 3,900 |
| Proceeds | (3,800) |
| Loss on disposal | 100 |

**(b)**

**Machine at cost account**

| Date | Details | £ | Date | Details | £ |
|------|---------|---|------|---------|---|
| 1 Oct 20X6 | Bank | 7,200 | 31 July 20X8 | Disposal | 7,200 |

**Machine accumulated depreciation account**

| Date | Details | £ | Date | Details | £ |
|------|---------|---|------|---------|---|
| 30 Nov 20X6 | Balance c/d | 300 | 30 Nov 20X6 | Expense | 300 |
| | | | 1 Dec 20X6 | Balance b/d | 300 |
| 30 Nov 20X7 | Balance c/d | 2,100 | 30 Nov 20X7 | Expense | 1,800 |
| | | 2,100 | | | 2,100 |
| | | | 1 Dec 20X7 | Balance b/d | 2,100 |
| 30 July 20X8 | Disposal | 3,300 | 31 July 20X8 | Expense | 1,200 |
| | | 3,300 | | | 3,300 |

**Disposals account**

| Date | Details | £ | Date | Details | £ |
|---|---|---|---|---|---|
| 31 July 20X8 | Cost | 7,200 | 31 July 20X8 | Depreciation | 3,300 |
| | | | 31 July 20X8 | Proceeds | 3,800 |
| | | | 31 July 20X8 | IS – loss | 100 |
| | | 7,200 | | | 7,200 |

**3** (a) A loss on disposal can also be described as **under-depreciation**.

(b) A profit on disposal can also be described as **over-depreciation**.

**4**

**Van at cost account**

| Date | Details | £ | Date | Details | £ |
|---|---|---|---|---|---|
| 1 July 20X5 | Bank | 13,600 | 30 Apr 20X8 | Disposal | 13,600 |
| 30 Apr 20X8 | Bank | 12,200 | | | |
| 30 Apr 20X8 | Disposal | | | | |
| | (16,700 –12,200) | 4,500 | 30 Apr 20X8 | Balance c/d | 16,700 |
| | | 30,300 | | | 30,300 |

**Van accumulated depreciation account**

| Date | Details | £ | Date | Details | £ |
|---|---|---|---|---|---|
| 30 Apr 20X8 | Disposal | 9,000 | 30 Apr 20X8 | Balance b/d | 9,000 |

**Disposals account**

| Date | Details | £ | Date | Details | £ |
|---|---|---|---|---|---|
| 30 Apr 20X8 | Cost | 13,600 | 30 Apr 20X8 | Depreciation | 9,000 |
| | | | 30 Apr 20X8 | Cost | 4,500 |
| | | | 30 Apr 20X8 | IS – loss | 100 |
| | | 13,600 | | | 13,600 |

**5**

NON-CURRENT ASSET REGISTER
**Non-current asset number** 10435
**Description** Computer 1036525
**Location** Sales Department
**Supplier** **Timing Company Ltd**

| Date | Cost £ | Expected life (years) | Estimated residual value £ | Depreciation method | Depreciation rate | Depreciation charge for the year £ | Acc dep at end of the year £ | Carrying amount at end of year £ | Disposal proceeds £ | Profit or loss on disposal £ |
|---|---|---|---|---|---|---|---|---|---|---|
| **20X6** 1 Mar | 4,800 | 4 | 600 | Reducing balance | 40% | | | | | |
| 31 July | | | | | | 1,920 | 1,920 | 2,880 | | |
| **20X7** 31 July | | | | | | 1,152 | 3,072 | 1,728 | | |
| **20X8** 27 Jun | | | | | | | | | 700 | (1,028) |

## CHAPTER 6    Accruals and prepayments

1    (a)    Rent paid in advance for the following accounting period would appear as **a prepayment** in the statement of financial position.

(b)    Motor expenses owing to the local garage would appear as **an accrual** in the statement of financial position.

2    (a)    In the income statement the heat and light expense would be £**870**. In the statement of financial position there would be an **accrual** for £**200**.

(b)    In the income statement the rental income would be £**340**. In the statement of financial position there would be a **prepayment of income** of £**40**.

(c)    In the income statement the insurance expense would be £**1,100**. In the statement of financial position there would be a **prepayment** of £**300**.

(d)    In the income statement commissions income would be £**200**. In the statement of financial position there would be an **accrual of income** of £**20**.

3

**Motor expenses account**

| Date | Details | £ | Date | Details | £ |
|---|---|---|---|---|---|
| 30 June | Balance b/d | 845 | 30 June | Prepayments c/d (150 × 6/12) | 75 |
| | | | 30 June | Income statement | 770 |
| | | 845 | | | 845 |
| 1 July | Prepayments b/d | 75 | | | |

4

**Electricity account**

| Date | Details | £ | Date | Details | £ |
|---|---|---|---|---|---|
| 31 Mar | Balance b/d | 470 | 31 Mar | Income statement | 650 |
| 31 Mar | Accruals c/d | 180 | | | |
| | | 650 | | | 650 |
| | | | 1 Apr | Accruals b/d | 180 |

## CHAPTER 7  **Inventory**

**1**  (a)  Cost    =    £25.80 + 1.00 = £26.80

   NRV    =    £28.00 – 1.10 = £26.90

   (b)  120 × £26.80 = £3,216.00

## CHAPTER 8  Irrecoverable debts and doubtful debts

### 1    General ledger

#### Sales ledger control account

| | £ | | £ |
|---|---|---|---|
| Balance b/d | 25,673 | Irrecoverable debts expense (157 + 288) | 445 |
| | | Balance c/d | 25,228 |
| | 25,673 | | 25,673 |
| Balance b/d | 25,228 | | |

#### Irrecoverable debts expense account

| | £ | | £ |
|---|---|---|---|
| Sales ledger control | 445 | Income statement | 445 |

### Sales ledger

#### H Taylor

| | £ | | £ |
|---|---|---|---|
| Balance b/d | 157 | Irrecoverable debts expense | 157 |

#### C Phelps

| | £ | | £ |
|---|---|---|---|
| Balance b/d | 288 | Irrecoverable debts expense | 288 |

### 2

#### Bank account

| | £ | | £ |
|---|---|---|---|
| Irrecoverable debts expense account | 250 | | |

#### Irrecoverable debts expense account

| | £ | | £ |
|---|---|---|---|
| | | Bank account | 250 |

**3** (a)

| | £ |
|---|---|
| Sales ledger control account | 11,650 |
| Irrecoverable debt | (350) |
| | 11,300 |
| Specific allowance | (200) |
| Remaining receivables (debtors) | 11,100 |
| | |
| General allowance 2% × £11,100 | 222 |
| Specific allowance | 200 |
| Total allowance for doubtful debts | 422 |

(b)

**Irrecoverable debts expense account**

| | £ | | £ |
|---|---|---|---|
| Sales ledger control account | 350 | Income statement | 350 |

**Sales ledger control account**

| | £ | | £ |
|---|---|---|---|
| Balance b/d | 11,650 | Irrecoverable debts expense | 350 |
| | | Balance c/d | 11,300 |
| | 11,650 | | 11,650 |
| Balance b/d | 11,300 | | |

**Allowance for doubtful debts adjustment account**

| | £ | | £ |
|---|---|---|---|
| Allowance for doubtful debts | 422 | Income statement | 422 |

**Allowance for doubtful debts account**

| | £ | | £ |
|---|---|---|---|
| | | Allowance for doubtful debts adjustment account | 422 |

**4**

### Irrecoverable debts expense account

| | | £ | | | £ |
|---|---|---|---|---|---|
| 20X7 | | | 20X7 | | |
| 31 Dec | Sales ledger control | 370 | 31 Dec | Income statement | 370 |
| 20X8 | | | 20X8 | | |
| 31 Dec | Sales ledger control | 400 | 31 Dec | Income statement | 400 |

### Allowance for doubtful debts adjustment account

| | | £ | | | £ |
|---|---|---|---|---|---|
| 20X7 | | | 20X7 | | |
| 31 Dec | Allowance for doubtful debts | 228 | 31 Dec | Income statement | 228 |
| 20X8 | | | 20X8 | | |
| 31 Dec | Income statement | 168 | 31 Dec | Allowance for doubtful debts | 168 |

### Allowance for doubtful debts account

| | | £ | | | £ |
|---|---|---|---|---|---|
| 20X7 | | | 20X7 | | |
| | | | 1 Jan | Balance b/d | 1,460 |
| 31 Dec | Balance c/d | 1,688 | 31 Dec | Allowance for doubtful debts adjustment | 228 |
| | | 1,688 | | | 1,688 |
| 20X8 | | | 20X8 | | |
| 31 Dec | Allowance for doubtful debts adjustment | 168 | 1 Jan | Balance b/d | 1,688 |
| 31 Dec | Balance c/d | 1,520 | | | |
| | | 1,688 | | | 1,688 |
| | | | 20X9 | | |
| | | | 1 Jan | Balance b/d | 1,520 |

## CHAPTER 9    Bank reconciliations

**1**    (a)    General ledger accounts:

| | | £ | £ |
|---|---|---|---|
| Debit | Sales ledger control account | 9.00 | |
| Credit | Bank account | | 9.00 |

(b)    General ledger accounts:

| | | £ | £ |
|---|---|---|---|
| Debit | Bank charges account | 15.80 | |
| Credit | Bank account | | 15.80 |

(c)    Bank reconciliation:

Unpresented cheque 10462

(d)    General ledger accounts:

| | | £ | £ |
|---|---|---|---|
| Debit | Gas expense account | 300.00 | |
| Credit | Bank account | | 300.00 |

(**Note** that if an analysed cash book is used and the postings are made to the general ledger from the totals of the analysis columns at the period end, the above amounts would be included in the totals and posted via the totals.)

**2**

### Cash Receipts Book

| Date | Details | £ |
|---|---|---|
| 4 March | J Killick | 365.37 ✓ |
| | D Francis | 105.48 ✓ |
| 5 March | I Oliver | 216.57 ✓ |
| 6 March | L Canter | 104.78 |
| 7 March | R Trent | 268.59 |
| 8 March | P Otter | 441.78 |
| | | 1,502.57 |

### Cash Payments Book

| Date | Details | Cheque number | £ |
|---|---|---|---|
| 4 March | L L Partners | 002536 | 186.90 ✓ |
| | P J Parler | 002537 | 210.55 ✓ |
| 5 March | J K Properties | 002538 | 500.00 ✓ |
| | Harmer & Co | 002539 | 104.78 ✓ |
| | Plenith Ltd | 002540 | 60.80 |
| 7 March | Wessex & Co | 002541 | 389.40 |
| 8 March | Filmer Partners | 002542 | 104.67 |
| | | | 1,557.10 |

**Bank reconciliation statement at 1 March**

|  | £ | £ |
|---|---|---|
| Balance per bank statement | | 835.68 |
| Less: unpresented cheques | | |
| 002530 | 110.46 ✓ | |
| 002534 | 230.56 ✓ | |
| 002535 | 88.90 ✓ | |
| | | (429.92) |
| | | 405.76 |
| Add: outstanding lodgement | | 102.45 ✓ |
| Amended cash book balance | | 508.21 |

# STATEMENT

**first national**
30 High Street
Benham
DR4 8TT

**SOUTHFIELD ELECTRICAL LTD**     **Account number:** 20-26-33 3126897

CHEQUE ACCOUNT     **Sheet 023**

| Date | | Paid out | Paid in | Balance |
|---|---|---|---|---|
| 1 Mar | Balance b/f | | | 835.68 |
| 4 Mar | Cheque No 002534 | 230.56✓ | | |
| | Credit | | 102.45✓ | 707.57 |
| 5 Mar | DD – National Telephones | 145.00 | | |
| | Bank charges | 7.80 | | 554.77 |
| 6 Mar | Cheque No 002530 | 110.46✓ | | |
| | BACS JT Turner | | 486.20 | 930.51 |
| 7 Mar | Credit | | 470.85✓ | |
| | Cheque No 002537 | 210.55✓ | | |
| | Cheque No 002536 | 186.90✓ | | |
| | Cheque No 002538 | 500.00✓ | | 503.91 |
| 8 Mar | Cheque No 002535 | 88.90✓ | | |
| | Credit | | 216.57 ✓ | |
| | Cheque No 002539 | 104.78✓ | | 526.80 |
| 8 Mar | Balance c/f | | | 526.80 |

## Bank account

| | £ | | £ |
|---|---|---|---|
| Balance b/d (from previous rec) | 508.21 | Payments | 1,557.10 |
| Receipts | 1,502.57 | Direct debit | 145.00 |
| BACS | 486.20 | Bank charges | 7.80 |
| | | Balance c/d | 787.08 |
| | 2,496.98 | | 2,496.98 |
| Balance b/d | 787.08 | | |

## Bank reconciliation as at 8 March

| | £ |
|---|---|
| Balance per bank statement | 526.80 |
| Add Outstanding lodgements: | |
| L Canter | 104.78 |
| R Trent | 268.59 |
| P Otter | 441.78 |
| Total to add: | 815.15 |
| Less Unpresented cheques: | |
| 002540 | 60.80 |
| 002541 | 389.40 |
| 002542 | 104.67 |
| Total to subtract: | 554.87 |
| Balance as per cash book | 787.08 |

CHAPTER 10   **Control account reconciliations**

**1**

| Adjustment | Amount £ | Debit (✓) | Credit (✓) |
|---|---|---|---|
| Undercast SDB | 100 | ✓ | |
| Sales returns | 450 | | ✓ |
| Irrecoverable debt | 210 | | ✓ |

**2**

| Adjustment | Amount £ | Debit (✓) | Credit (✓) |
|---|---|---|---|
| PRDB overcast | 300 | | ✓ |
| CPB overstated | 270 | | ✓ |
| Discount | 267 | ✓ | |

CHAPTER 11 **The trial balance, errors and the suspense account**

**1**

$$\text{Phone} = £3,400 + 300 \qquad = £3,700$$
$$\text{Insurance} = £1,600 - 200 \qquad = £1,400$$

## CHAPTER 12   **The extended trial balance**

1   Open up a suspense account to record this difference

2   Both a debit and a credit

3   The closing inventory figure is a credit entry in the income statement columns and a debit entry in the statement of financial position columns of the ETB.

# INDEX

**A**ccounting concepts, 45
Accounting equation, 8
Accruals, 123
Accruals and Prepayments, 121
Accruals concept, 45, 122
Accruals of income, 126
Accumulated depreciation, 90
Acquisition application, 70
Allowance for doubtful debts, 150
Automated payments, 3
Average cost (AVCO), 139

**B**ank reconciliation statement, 172
Books of prime entry, 6

**C**apital expenditure, 3, 56
Carrying amount, 83
Cash payments book, 6
Cash purchases, 3
Cash receipts book, 6
Cash sales, 3
Cheque book stub, 4
Concepts, 35
Contra entry, 186
Cost, 137
Credit note, 4
Credit purchases, 3
Credit sales, 3
Current asset, 42
Current liabilities, 42

**D**epreciation, 82
Depreciation charge, 90
Depreciation policies, 83
Dishonoured cheques, 166
Disposals account, 102
Doubtful, 147
Doubtful debts, 150

**E**xtended traial balance, 228

**F**IFO, 139
Finance lease, 72
Financial Reporting Standards, 45
First in first out, 139
FRS 15, 57
FRSs, 45

**G**eneral allowance, 151
General ledger, 7
Going concern concept, 45
Gross profit, 40

**H**ire purchase agreement, 72

**I**AS 16, 57
IAS 2, 137
IASs, 45
IFRSs, 45
Income statement, 38
International Accounting Standards,
   45
International Financial Reporting
   Standards, 45
Inventory count, 135
Inventory reconciliation, 135
Irrecoverable debt, 148
Irrecoverable debts expense
   account, 148

**J**ournal, 6

**L**ast in first out, 139
LIFO, 139
Loan, 72
Loss on disposal, 102

**M**ateriality, 47
Mortgage, 72

**N**et current assets, 42
Net realisable value, 137
Non-current asset register, 74
Non-current assets, 3, 56
Non-current liabilities, 42

**O**utstanding lodgements, 171
Overdraft, 166

**P**art exchange, 73, 107
Part exchange allowance, 107
Payables, 3
Petty cash book, 6
Petty cash box, 5
Petty cash voucher, 5
Prepayment, 124
Prepayment of income, 127
Primary record, 4
Principles, 1
Profit for the year, 40
Profit on disposal, 102
Provision for depreciation, 90
Purchase invoice, 5
Purchase ledger, 7
Purchases, 3
Purchases day book, 6
Purchases ledger, 183
Purchases ledger control account, 183

Purchases ledger control account reconciliation, 188, 193
Purchases returns, 3
Purchases returns day book, 6

**R**eceivables, 3
Reconciliations, 165
Reducing balance method, 86
Remittance advance note, 4
Residual value, 83
Revenue expenditure, 4, 56

**S**ales day book, 6
Sales invoice, 4
Sales ledger, 7, 180
Sales ledger control account, 180
Sales ledger control account reconciliation, 188, 189
Sales returns, 3
Specific allowance, 151
SSAP 9, 137
SSAPs, 45
Statement of financial position total, 42
Statements of Standard Accounting Practice, 45
Straight line method, 83

**T**iming differences, 171
Trial balance, 17

**U**K GAAP, 45
UK Generally Accepted Accounting Practice, 45
Unpresented cheques, 171
Useful life, 83

**W**eighted average cost, 139

NOTES